CLARITY

CRYSTAL LEONARDI

First published in Far North Queensland, 2025 by Bowerbird Publishing

@ 2025 Crystal Leonardi

The moral rights of the author have been asserted. All rights reserved. Except as permitted under the Australian Copyright Act 1968 (for example, fair dealing for the purposes of study, research, criticism or review), no part of this book may be reproduced, stored in a retrieval system, communicated or transmitted in any form or by any means without prior written permission. All enquiries should be made to the author.

ISBN 978 1 7636148 9 5 (print)
ISBN 978 1 7637660 0 6 (ebook)

Clarity
By Crystal Leonardi

Edited by: Crystal Leonardi & Georgie Montague
Front Cover & Interior Design: Bowerbird Publishing
Cover Photographs: Nakia Morrison Photography

Distributed by Bowerbird Publishing
Available in National Library of Australia

Disclaimer: The material in this publication is of the nature of general comment only and does not represent professional advice. It is not intended to provide specific guidance for particular circumstances. It should not be relied on as the basis of any decision to take action or not take action on any matter it covers. Readers should obtain professional advice, where appropriate, before making any such decision. To the maximum extent permitted by law, the author and publisher disclaim all responsibility and liability to any person, arising directly or indirectly from any person taking or not taking action based on the information in this publication.

Bowerbird Publishing
Julatten, Queensland, Australia
www.crystalleonardi.com

'Clarity' by Rob the Poet

What you think is what you get.
Best to think positive to avoid the fret.
Throw out all those negative thoughts
That create your negative rorts.
It takes practice to remain positive,
To master it is the way to live.
Keeping your mind open and clear,
Reducing the garbage in the ear.
Tell yourself you are okay.
Do it often, every single day.
By staying away from those negative jolts,
Your positive vibes give positive results.

Book 1
Boy of Steel: Little Sebastian's Little Miracle
Pages 1-188

Book 2
An Unexpected Privilege: Celebrating Five Years
Pages 189-250

Book 3
Daring to Dream: From Farm to Fergie
Pages 251- 313

BOOK 1

Boy of Steel
- Little Sebastian's Big Miracle -

To every child, every parent, every sibling.
For every fight, every survivor, every loss.
With all my heart, my admiration, my love.
I affectionately dedicate this book to you.

To my son, Sebastian, I will always stand beside you in this fight against brain cancer. Thank you for sharing your life and choosing us as your parents. You bring so much joy and love to our family.

To Nate, who taught us strength, your suffering was not in vain as we honour your life by finding the courage to continue raising awareness and providing support and empowerment to those touched by a childhood cancer diagnosis.

Nate Moule: 12.6.2016 - 15.12.2020

Disclaimer: This book addresses sensitive topics, including cancer, mental health, and death. The content may evoke strong emotional responses and is only intended for informational and educational purposes. It is not a substitute for professional medical advice, diagnosis, or treatment. Readers are encouraged to seek guidance from qualified health professionals for personal concerns or issues related to these topics. The stories and experiences shared in this book are not exhaustive and may not reflect every individual's experience.

CONTENTS

	Foreword by Bec Dent	Page I
	Preface	Page V
	Introduction	Page VI

Part 1

1	Little Sebastian	Page 1
2	Queensland Children's Hospital: Our New Home Away from Home	Page 11
3	Surgery	Page 18
4	The Aftermath	Page 23
5	"It's Cancer"	Page 29
6	Our Girls: The Calm Amongst the Storm	Page 34
7	Unstable	Page 40
8	Meningitis	Page 44
9	10 More Days	Page 52
10	Finally, Freedom	Page 54
	Timeline of Events – January	Page 57
	Messages of Love	Page 59

Part 2

11	Leaps & Bounds	Page 62
12	Preparing for Battle	Page 69
13	The Battle Begins	Page 76
14	All of a Sudden, Pure Joy	Page 80
	Timeline of Events – February	Page 84
	Messages of Love	Page 85

Part 3

		Page 87
		Page 94
15	Inside Out & Upside Down	Page 101
16	The Wuhan Effect	Page 105
17	Choosing to Fight, not Fly	Page 107
	Timeline of Events – March	
	Messages of Love	

CONTENTS

Part 4

18	Trust the Wait	Page 108
19	"There's no Place Like Home"	Page 113
20	Twenty-Eight Days	Page 121
	Timeline of Events – April & May	Page 125
	Messages of Love	Page 128

Part 5

21	Dreaming of Sleep	Page 129
22	No Stone Left Unturned	Page 133
23	Watch & Wait	Page 136
	Timeline of Events – June, July & August	Page 140
	Messages of Love	Page 143

Part 6

24	Matters of the Heart	Page 146
25	Anaphylaxis	Page 150
26	More Love than Fear	Page 159
	Timeline of Events – September, October, November & December	Page 166
	Messages of Love	Page 168

Part 7

27	One Year On	Page 171
28	In the Beginning	Page 176
	Acknowledgements	Page 180
	Sebastian's Medical Team	Page 181
	Charities & Volunteers	Page 183
	Glossary	Page 184

PRAISE FOR BOY OF STEEL

"This incredible memoir recounting such a delicate and traumatic experience has been written with such grace. It is a story of true love and survival, filled with hope. Sebastian certainly is one courageous 'boy of steel' and you can understand why with parents like Crystal and Sam always by his side."
Marlies Hobbs, Lawyer and Author F.L.Y. Financially Literate Youth

"All I can say is - WOW!"
Danielle Bellero, President of KIND Inc. Kids in Need of Donations

"My heart-strings were pulled as the writing drew on my imagination to look beyond the words—and to picture the difficult and poignant moments with Sebastian as he endured his treatments and you held emotions at bay. How brave you and your husband were, especially how you maintained your family cohesion..."
Fay McGrath, Former Principal and Author

"Reading this book is an essential read for all. One cannot fathom how an ordinary, everyday life can completely transform in the blink of an eye, be turned upside down, and where everything comes to a screaming halt, because a child has been diagnosed with cancer. And all that family yearns for, is that ordinary, everyday life again. What shone through this book, is the love of family, a terrific health team, and the invaluable support by a community, who had this family's back the entire time. I wouldn't wish this on any family, but if you do find yourself in this situation, a book such as this might give you comfort, where there might be little to be found."
Frances Dall'alba, Author of several books including Little Blue Box

"Engaging, relatable, inspiring."
Chantal Munro, Eco-warrior and Author of 3 books including TickleTouch, An Environmental FairyTale

FOREWORD

Written by Bec Dent
Radio and Television Presenter, Producer, Magazine Editor, Emcee
and most importantly – A friend of Crystal's.

> "We all have battles to fight.
> And it's often in those battles that we are most alive:
> it's on the frontlines of our lives that we earn wisdom,
> create joy, forge friendships, discover happiness, find love,
> and do purposeful work."
>
> -Eric Greitens, Resilience-

I am blessed to know Crystal Leonardi. If you don't already know her, you're about to discover what an incredible human and mother she is.

The 8th of January 2020 changed her family's life forever when her two-year-old son Sebastian was diagnosed with brain cancer. In the haze of this news and all that swiftly followed, travelling 1800km from their Far North Queensland home in Julatten to Brisbane for treatment, this book started as a record for Sebastian and herself—making notes to process all that the doctors had to say, all Sebastian went through, and how they, their family, and their community of supporters responded at the most difficult of times.

These records quickly morphed into much more. Crystal shared the original memoir with a friend, who then encouraged her to share it with the world to help others or make it easier for those who come after and who will share a similar journey.

I am among many who are so grateful she did. It's a lesson no one wants or is prepared for. But by opening this intimate window into her world and sharing her and Sebastian's story, she has created something truly beautiful from the trauma. When someone is diagnosed with cancer, everyone who loves them is impacted.

If you have felt helpless after a loved one's diagnosis, Crystal's words will take your hand with honesty, compassion and strength to help guide you through an unimaginably difficult time.

I won't ruin the reading experience for you, but there is a favourite anecdote shared about chook poo making great fertiliser. Unfortunately, shit does happen. Like this book, I'm not going to sugarcoat it... life can be messy, brutal and heartbreaking. But, as this book shows, you still have the power of choice and action. In all the uncertainty, sometimes the only thing you can control is how you respond. The shit can either bury you... or use it to grow.

Sometimes, it takes going through the worst to know what you can endure and become. I am in awe of Crystal. It would have been very easy and understandable for her to have been broken by this experience, but she used it to develop her 'superpower.' Major life events like these shape you; Crystal calls them 'reset and restart' moments.

You will follow her journey as this experience frees her from fear, changes her, and catalyses a new beginning as an author, publisher, and speaker. She discovered her voice and ability to communicate what is often hard to put into words. More than a writer, her words will imprint on your soul. She has also used this steep learning curve to assist others in finding their own voice and writing their own stories through coaching and by becoming a publisher.

It wasn't easy, but fortunately, Crystal found ways to overcome her barriers and ensured she could make those lessons learned the hard way for both her and Sebastian easier for those who may follow in their footsteps.

The title of this book is accurate; Sebastian definitely is the Boy of Steel, made of the toughest stuff, but like steel, made stronger by being forged in the fire. This book details that fire. As his mother, Crystal's genetic right is to be called 'Super Mum,' which accurately describes who Sebastian and Crystal are as individuals. But they are not alone. This story is, unfortunately, one shared by many. As Crystal's incredible research details in this book, there are far too many people diagnosed with cancer. I do not know a single person who hasn't been impacted either through their own diagnosis or someone they love being diagnosed.

I was fortunate to lead a discussion on this book at the 2024 Cairns Tropical Writers Festival. Still, I initially met Crystal through my work at 'COUCH' (Cairns Organisation United for Cancer Health). COUCH provides services and support to Far North Queenslanders and their loved ones impacted by cancer. It was initially started as an action committee to fundraise and petition for better Oncology services in Far North Queensland. The passionate work of the committee and community paid off with the Liz Plummer Cancer Care Centre opening in 2011. Before this, there was limited local treatment in the Far North, and families were separated as patients were required to travel long distances to Brisbane or Townsville for extended periods of time. Being displaced from your support network when you need them the most is an unfortunate reality for those who are diagnosed with cancer and live regionally around Australia. This was the case for Sebastian and Crystal. Unable to receive treatment locally, they had to spend significant periods of time away from their loved ones. As you can imagine, this was extremely hard for their entire family, friends, and community.

Crystal shares the difficulties of this separation from her husband Sam and her girls – Antonia, Josie and Alyssa; the mum's guilt of not being there for her other children whilst watching her baby go through intense treatments, seeing his pain, detailing her feelings of loss and helplessness as she finds herself adapting to constant change, sleepless nights, non-stop-worry and experiencing mental health struggles. This is a real story. Told by an extremely real and authentic woman. Get ready to sob… big ol' salty tears (I know I did) as she moves from hopelessness to hope in this record of the first 12 months of Sebastian's treatment.

All I can say is thank you to Crystal and her family. You are truly inspiring. It would have been much easier to close the door on this chapter of their lives to push those BIG feelings down. Still, Crystal chose to expose herself at her most vulnerable, re-living the trauma with every word she wrote, motivated by the need to understand and to capture Sebastian's battle for him to read in the future and understand how much he overcame at such a young age. Later, this motivation grew to include reaching outward to help others navigate when it feels like there are no stars in the darkness to be guided by.

These words can be the firmament you can look to find your position and chart a course forward when you feel lost. Use them to buoy you when you feel like you are sinking and know you are not alone. Like Crystal, may you find your inner strength, and when you find it wavering, may this book and those you love carry you through. Boy of Steel: Little Sebastian's Big Miracle epitomises Ralph Waldo Emerson's famous quote: "What lies behind us, and what lies before us, are tiny matters compared to what lies within us."

Sebastian is powerful beyond measure, Crystal is powerful beyond measure, and so are you. I am so grateful to be a small part of this book. Thank you for your friendship, Crystal and for showing the world how truly remarkable you both are.

PREFACE

Keeping a diary throughout Sebastian's cancer journey was both therapeutic and essential for my husband, Sam, and me. When confronted with such tragic news, the need to act swiftly overwhelms one's ability to retain every detail: the days blur, times merge, names and faces become a jumbled mess. Sam and I found solace in debriefing at the end of each day, piecing together the fragments of conversations and events. It became a collaborative effort, transforming our notes into a vital reference guide as we navigated the unfamiliar realms of Neurology, Oncology, Endocrinology, and beyond. Each day felt like learning a new language without a single lesson.

Though revisiting these records remains emotionally arduous, they will undoubtedly serve as a poignant resource when the time comes to convey to Sebastian the magnitude of his battle against brain cancer at the tender age of two.

In sharing our story, my aim is not only to offer solace to others traversing similar paths but also to ignite hope in those grappling with a childhood cancer diagnosis. Even when it feels like we've lost the innate parental ability to "kiss it better," may our journey serve as a beacon of resilience and courage.

"One day you will tell your story of how you've overcome what you're going through now, and it will become part of someone else's survival guide."

-Christopher Ferry-

INTRODUCTION

My love story with Sam, a small-town country boy from Mt Molloy in Far North Queensland, began in 2001, when I was just 19. Six years of adventure, career pursuits, and the weaving of lifelong friendships culminated in our marriage in 2007. With the dawn of 2010, our lives changed forever with the arrival of our first child, Antonia. At just five weeks old, she became our reason for migrating from Ipswich, Queensland, to Sam's cherished hometown, nestled near my own roots in Cairns.

Bound by shared family values and a yearning to be close to our loved ones, Sam and I found ourselves swiftly immersed in the rhythm of life back in Far North Queensland. While Sam endeavoured to carve his niche in the regional office of his Brisbane-based employer, I grappled with the newfound role of a full-time mother in the quaint embrace of our small country town. Amidst the challenges, the sense of belonging was palpable, affirming our choice to return "home."

2013 heralded the arrival of our second daughter, Josephine, expanding our hearts once more. In 2016, we embarked on yet another chapter, relocating to Sam's ancestral family farm in Julatten. Here, against the backdrop of rolling hills and azure skies, we welcomed our third daughter, Alyssa. Each of our daughters, cherished treasures, epitomised joy, their early days marked by breastfeeding and peaceful, nightly slumber.

The desire for balance and completion spurred Sam and me to pursue one more addition to our family—our destiny realised with the unexpected early arrival of Sebastian on December 23rd, 2017. His birth, though ahead of schedule, unfolded seamlessly. Christmas of that year resonated with unparalleled joy as we welcomed Sebastian into the fold, a symbol of hope and renewal.

Yet, amidst the bliss of early parenthood, subtle signs hinted at an impending journey of challenges. At two days old, Sebastian's feeding difficulties unveiled a series of tongue, lip, and cheek ties, necessitating corrective procedures in Townsville. Though the initial hurdle was overcome, it was a prelude to a journey fraught with unexpected twists and turns, one that would test the resilience of our familial bonds.

At six months old, a sudden disruption in Sebastian's sleeping patterns marked the onset of a perplexing nighttime routine. Initially attributed to the notorious "6-month sleep regression," I sought solace in familiar experiences of other mothers. Transitioning Sebastian to formula and weaning him from breastfeeding seemed logical in addressing his sleep disturbances. However, the nights remained fraught with sweat-soaked awakenings, defying conventional remedies. As Sebastian revelled in nighttime playfulness, the conviction that he was simply a "hot-bodied" boy eased my concerns, attributing his nocturnal antics to gender variances.

As Sebastian blossomed, his vibrant personality illuminated our home, masking subtle clues to underlying health concerns. His cheeky demeanour, intertwined with mischievous antics, mirrored the typical behaviour of a thriving toddler. It wasn't until he took his first tentative steps at 11 months that his bowed legs and pigeon toes drew our attention. Despite reassurances from medical professionals regarding the potential for self-correction, lingering doubts nagged at our parental instincts.

In November 2019, Sebastian's left hand and arm suddenly exhibited uncharacteristic limitations. Observing this development with growing apprehension, I confided in Sam, who echoed my concerns. With my stepfather, Dr. Gary Litherland, away on holidays, we sought immediate medical attention.

Dr. Murugesampillai from Mountain View Medical in Mossman corroborated our observations, leading to a referral to paediatrician, Dr. Tim Warnock in Cairns.

The subsequent weeks tested our patience as we awaited our appointment with Dr. Warnock. His thorough assessment painted a picture of a vibrant, albeit medically complex, almost two-year-old boy. Noting Sebastian's diminished facial movement on the left side, Dr. Warnock broached the possibility of left-side hemiplegia, prompting discussions about cerebral palsy. The prospect of an MRI loomed large, offering the promise of clarity amidst the fog of uncertainty.

Despite the daunting array of potential diagnoses, Dr. Warnock's optimism buoyed our spirits, offering a glimmer of hope amidst the fear and trepidation. His reassurance that Sebastian did not fit the typical profile of a brain tumour patient provided a sense of comfort, grounding us in the present moment.

Leaving Dr. Warnock's office that day, we clutched onto a bundle of cerebral palsy pamphlets and research materials, a tangible reminder of the daunting journey ahead. Our hearts weighed heavy with sorrow and helplessness as we navigated the journey home, grappling with the enormity of Sebastian's diagnosis. Tearful calls to our parents echoed our shared anguish, yet amidst the despair, a flicker of determination ignited within us.

Swiftly, we shifted gears, channelling our grief into action. Research became our guiding light, illuminating the path forward as we vowed to provide Sebastian with the best possible care. Wiping away tears, we embraced a newfound resolve, united in our determination to confront any challenge head-on.

With the urgency of securing a definitive diagnosis pressing upon us, I embarked on a relentless pursuit, reaching out to the Cairns Hospital to inquire about Sebastian's MRI scheduling. Faced with daunting waiting lists, the prospect of months-long delays threatened to extinguish our hopes. Desperation fuelled my persistence as I dialled the Hospital's number daily, clinging to the faintest glimmer of possibility.

Simultaneously, Gary's unwavering advocacy echoed my efforts, as he too sought to expedite Sebastian's evaluation. Against the backdrop of a public holiday, a serendipitous turn of events unfolded on January 3rd, 2020. Amidst the holiday lull, a cancellation materialised, offering Sebastian an expedited MRI appointment on January 8th.

Reflecting on this pivotal moment, I remain steadfast in my belief that our persistence, coupled with Gary's unwavering support, undoubtedly saved Sebastian's life. It's a poignant reminder that in the face of adversity, relentlessness can pave the path to regaining a sense of control.

This journey, fraught with uncertainty and despair, serves as a testament to the unwavering power of parental love and advocacy. As we share our story, may it serve as a beacon of hope for others facing similar battles, inspiring them to never surrender in the pursuit of their loved ones' well-being.

Sebastian Michael Leonardi. Born December 23rd, 2017 weighing 3.94kg & 52cm long.

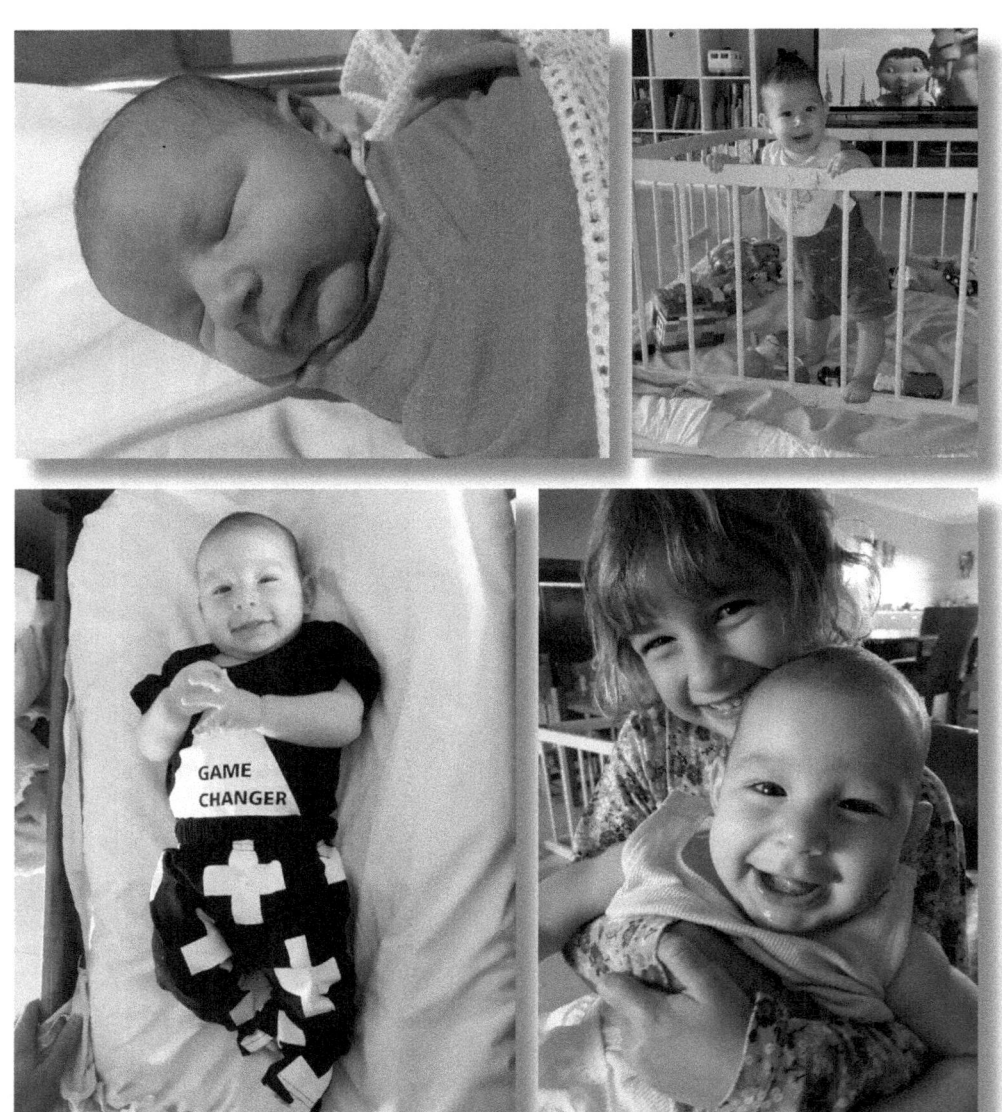

Sebastian's 1st year

Sebastian, 18 months old

Sebastian just before his 2nd birthday in December 2019

PART 1

Fact: As of 2023, it is estimated that approximately 1,000 children aged 0-14 years will be newly diagnosed with cancer in Australia, with a similar gender distribution observed. The number of new diagnoses is notably higher in the 0–4-year age group, with estimates of around 450 children, followed by 5–9-year-olds at approximately 250 children and 10–14-year-olds at about 300 children.[1]

1

LITTLE SEBASTIAN

As the clock struck 2:19 pm on that fateful Friday, January 3rd, the Cairns Hospital sealed Sebastian's fate with a booking for his MRI on Wednesday, January 8th. With instructions to arrive promptly at 6 am, we braced ourselves for what lay ahead, hopeful yet apprehensive about the impending procedure. Given the timing amidst the school holidays, we decided to entrust our girls with their grandparents in Mareeba, safe in familiar arms during the tumultuous day ahead.

The eve of Sebastian's MRI found us nestled in my mother's home in Cairns. Clad in his work uniform, Sam prepared to return to work following the procedure, while Sebastian and I would return to Mareeba to reunite with the girls.

At 9:10 am on January 8th, 2020, Sebastian made his way through the MRI machine, succumbing to the gentle embrace of anaesthesia as the clock struck 8:30 am. Despite the smooth administration of gas and anaesthesia, Sam and I

---

[1] Australian Institute of Health and Welfare (AIHW) Cancer Data.

found ourselves engulfed in overwhelming emotions, tears streaming down our cheeks as we awaited the nurse's call signalling Sebastian's awakening. With coffee cups in hand, we sought solace in fleeting moments of normalcy, desperately clinging to the facade of composure amidst the chaos.

An excerpt from Sam's Carer Impact Statement in 2024 further reflects our recollection of the day:

'Have you ever had to put one of your children under general anesthesia? Until the day of Sebby's first MRI, I had not. The doctors informed us that the experience could be quite upsetting, as a child may flail around and fight for a few seconds while going under. Crystal asked if I would take on that responsibility, as she understandably didn't want to go through it. Unfortunately, that is exactly what happened. I wept as he went under, telling myself it would all be over soon. Afterward, I stepped outside, called my father, and broke down on the phone while discussing the experience.'

In the days leading up to the MRI, I sought solace in conversations with Anne-Marie Boss, a renowned physiotherapist specialising in young children with Cerebral Palsy. Our anticipation mounted as we awaited our first appointment with her, scheduled for January 10th, hopeful for insights into Sebastian's condition.

As Sebastian stirred from his slumber, our hearts plummeted at the radiologist's insistance on immediate Hospital admission. Suddenly, Tim's foreboding words reverberated in our minds. "Stroke, blood clot, or brain tumour," he had said—an incantation of dread that haunted our every waking moment.

An excerpt from Sam's Carer Impact Statement in 2024 further reflects our recollection of the day:

'I went back inside to be greeted by a doctor who told us we were not to leave the Hospital. He showed us the scans of Sebby's brain and the tumor inside it. From that moment on, all I could think about was that my son was going to die. For the years since his diagnosis, that has been my constant thought. I honestly do not go two minutes at any point throughout the day without thinking about my son and how much time I have left with him.'

Up on the ward, we were guided by the compassionate presence of a Paediatric Cardiologist, our hearts now heavy with the weight of Sebastian's diagnosis. There, on the computer screen, was the haunting image of his brain, consumed by a shadowy mass. An image that seared itself into my memory forever.

I remember looking up at the ceiling, my eyes dry but my mind racing, and all I could think to say through my quivering voice was, "Is he going to die?"

We were instructed to await word from the Townsville Hospital as the hours ticked on. The leading Paediatric Neurologist from the Townsville Hospital was on a flight. Still, the images had been sent to him for review, and he would contact the Cairns Hospital as soon as possible to advise us on what happens next.

As we grappled with the harrowing reality of Sebastian's diagnosis, we found solace in the embrace of our newfound medical support group. Denise Petersen, a Clinical Oncology Nurse, along with a compassionate huddle of nurses, enveloped Sebastian in their care, their hearts charmed by his irrepressible spirit. It was surreal to witness Sebastian's playful interactions with the nurses, his mischievous charm undiminished by the shadow of his diagnosis looming over him. Yet, amidst his innocent antics, Sam and I bore the weight of his diagnosis, a burden that sparked conflicting emotions of relief and distress, emotions we learned to navigate with each passing day.

By mid-afternoon, the Paediatric Cardiologist delivered the news of his referral to the Queensland Children's Hospital Neurological team, as per the recommendation of the Paediatric Neurologist in Townsville. We were told that no-one in the North was willing to "touch Sebastian's tumour," sending shockwaves through our already fragile hearts. In that moment of despair, the notion that no one was willing to save our beloved son shattered our spirits, leaving us in a sea of hopelessness. All at once, our spirits, souls and hearts were broken.

Despite the devastating blow, arrangements were made for Sebastian's transfer to the Queensland Children's Hospital. Yet, even amidst the chaos, the Cairns Hospital's suggestion for us to return home in the face of such dire circumstances served as a stark reminder of the bleak outlook ahead. In a daze of shock and disbelief, Sam and I complied, returning to the familiar embrace of my mother's home to process the grim reality unfolding before us.

However, our respite was short-lived as the Hospital called us back, under the directive of the Queensland Children's Hospital. With heavy hearts, we returned to the Children's Ward, where Sebastian was meticulously monitored in anticipation of his impending transfer. As Sam departed for Julatten to make arrangements for our home and pets, the weight of uncertainty bore down upon me, a relentless tide of fear and anxiety threatening to overwhelm.

With Mareeba a distant memory and the girls left in limbo, I didn't have the strength to call them; I had no idea what to say. This was the beginning of a long period of shock that Sam and I endured. Our bodies ran on pure adrenalin, and we held on to each other tight as we tried to understand how this could happen to our little boy.

Sam left Cairns on a commercial flight the following day while I remained in the Cairns Hospital with Sebastian. We departed Cairns in the early hours of Thursday 9th January via Royal Flying Doctors. I was physically ill the entire flight to Brisbane. A mixture of anxiety, shock and exhaustion overwhelming my body.

Throughout the long, sleepless nights that followed, my thoughts raced, haunted by Sebastian's MRI images.

Sam and I shielded ourselves with a cloak of intense protection and privacy. Our beloved Sebastian, a lively and jubilant 2-year-old, deserved to be seen for the joyous soul he was, not through the lens of pity or sorrow. The mere thought of others treating him differently or casting sympathetic glances filled us with dread. Initially, when we entertained the possibility of a diagnosis like Cerebral Palsy, we hesitated to divulge the news to anyone beyond our immediate family circle. We clung to the hope that diligent physiotherapy and determination would pave the way for Sebastian to lead a life brimming with vitality, much like any other healthy child.

However, fate had a cruel twist in store for us. The diagnosis we received shattered our illusions and altered the course of our lives irreversibly. Our world was plunged into darkness as we grappled with the harsh reality of Sebastian's condition.

By Thursday evening, amidst the turmoil of emotions, Sam and I reached a pivotal decision. It was time to break the silence and share our burdens with those closest to us. Initiating a group message, we created a lifeline—a digital haven where we could share updates and draw strength from the unwavering support of our loved ones. This book serves as a poignant testament to that journey, encapsulating the raw emotions that engulfed Sam and me, while illuminating the indomitable spirit of our beloved Sebastian.

This is an excerpt from the very first update we sent out to our nearest and dearest…

9:58 pm, Thursday 9 January 2020

Unfortunately, Sebastian's MRI yesterday morning revealed our worst fears. Sebastian has a large tumour in the middle of his brain and was admitted to the Cairns Hospital for several tests to determine which areas of his body are affected (other than the obvious). This does rule out Cerebral Palsy (CP) as there was no evidence of scar tissue or stroke, which would typically be present if it was CP. Unfortunately, CP would have been a better outcome. The tumour is more prominent on the right side of the brain, which explains the limitations Sebastian has been experiencing on his left side.

Today, Sam, Sebastian and I arrived at the Queensland Children's Hospital in Brisbane. Sebastian and I came via the Royal Flying Doctors, and Sam arrived via patient travel on a commercial flight. We are now settled into Sebastian's very generous room, which has everything we need. It is on level 11a, room 11. Sebastian has been admitted, and Sam and I will share the sleepover duties at night so Sebastian isn't alone. Whichever parent isn't with Sebastian will stay at Ronald McDonald house across the road, which is lovely, comfortable and has everything we need.

We met in Triage at QCH earlier tonight with Neuro-Oncologist Dr Rick Walker. He began by explaining to us specifically where Sebastian's tumour is located in the brain, based on the MRI images. He reported that the tumour rests against the optic nerves and sits on top of the pituitary gland. Dr Walker also believes the tumour consists of different substances, including a watery-type liquid, an oily substance and a solid mass. Examining the contents of the tumour during surgery will also confirm a diagnosis – Dr Walker believes it is presenting like a Cranio-Pharyngioma; however, there is a slight, rare chance it could be an Optic Nerve Gliomas. It's also unknown whether the tumour is affecting Sebastian's eyesight or the function of his pituitary gland. Still, tests conducted yesterday in the Cairns Hospital should give us more clarity around that. Dr. Walker plans to operate ASAP, drain the fluid and scoop out as much of the solid mass as possible without damaging the brain. This will accomplish two things: 1. The size reduction of the tumour will release the pressure in Sebastian's brain and reverse or begin to correct the left-side hemiplegia he is experiencing; 2. Give the specialists something to test (solid mass) to determine whether the tumour is cancerous. Following the surgery, Sebastian may also need chemotherapy or radiation.

In addition to the tumour, Sebastian has two cysts behind each of his temporal lobes. The Surgical team believe the cysts contain a watery substance and may be drained after examination during surgery. Other than taking up room in Sebastian's already compromised brain due to the tumour, the cysts are of far less concern.

Dr Rick Walker was warm and relaxed and made us feel comfortable immediately. He could answer all of our questions without overwhelming or confusing us. When we expressed our concerns about giving Sebastian the best chance of survival, he got straight to the point by assuring us that we didn't need to call Dr Charlie Teo, arguably Australia's best brain surgeon. He said he was confident that the medical team at QCH could handle the task at hand and give Sebastian a great chance of survival and recovery—a stark contrast to how we felt after consulting with the staff in Cairns and Townsville Hospitals.

Despite his balding head and mature, professional attire, Rick had a youthful, almost brotherly disposition. He had a big smile that complemented his equally friendly, almond-shaped, kind eyes. He was honest and sensitive and made our meetings with him highly anticipated, encouraging and valuable to Sam and me. He never rushed through our meetings and was always open to questions, further explanation and conversation when we needed it. Rick had a quiet confidence about him, and like so many of Sebastian's medical team, we developed a deep respect for him. He respectfully addressed surgery and treatment like it was just another day at the office.

We now look forward to meeting some of the Neurological team tonight to get their opinion and further understanding of what's ahead of us. Sam and I feel we are taking an uncontrollable leap into the unknown. We quickly become patient and persistent childhood brain cancer researchers, finding comfort in knowledge and understanding.

Sebastian is a perfect example of how resilient children are. He is happy and seems entirely at ease in our new surroundings. He is becoming warier of the nursing staff as he undergoes 4-hourly obs, becoming quite distressed each time a nurse enters his room. As we try to keep him busy, walking the corridors of the 11th floor, he cheerfully giggles and flirts with each person he encounters, completely charming them, as he does in his everyday life. He is revelling in the uninterrupted attention he receives from Mum and Dad, something I'm sure a 4th child rarely experiences.

Antonia, Josie and Alyssa have remained in Mareeba with their grandparents. We haven't had much time to speak to them, and they are always at the forefront of my mind when we're not entirely engulfed in talk about brain tumours and surgery.

The outstanding Welfare and Patient Travel teams have booked Sam and me into Ronald McDonald House, conveniently located across the road. We are yet to head over there, but we've been booked in for 1-month by the recommendation of the QCH medical team.

If anyone is local to QCH, we are in a large private room to have visitors anytime during the day. Thank you, everyone, for your messages, love and support. The comfort it's bringing us is making this terrifying experience manageable.

Lots of love, Sam, Crystal & Sebastian xo

10:33 pm, Thursday 9 January 2020

We just finished meeting with Neurosurgeon Dr Sarah Mills. She had met with Rick after meeting with us earlier and agreed with his plan for Sebastian moving forward. She has requested Sebastian have a CT scan tomorrow, as this should give us more information about the content of the tumour. Sarah has also asked for an MRI of Sebastian's brain and spine post-surgery to assist further with diagnosis.

Sarah was helpful and, like Rick, exuded confidence, strengthening and comforting us. So far, it feels like the team is confident that they can give us a diagnosis and successfully improve Sebastian's condition. I hope it continues on this path in the days to come.

Tomorrow, we look forward to meeting Lead Surgeon Dr. Gert Tollesson. Night all xo

An excerpt from Sam's Carer Impact Statement in 2024 further reflects our recollection of the day:

'We left our daughters with dad and packed our things almost immediately, moving to Brisbane indefinitely. I abandoned all responsibilities I had as a man and a father so I could focus solely on my son. I left my family farm, which I have inherited as a third-generation owner, to fall into disrepair. I also left my job, telling my employer I would reach out when I knew more, effectively abandoning them as well. I had never done that in my life, but all I cared about was my son. I didn't think about putting food on the table or whether the animals were fed or the trees were sprayed. I began to feel bitter about all my responsibilities—perhaps in a vain effort to blame something or someone for what my son was going through. I saw the farm as a burden, questioning all the time I had spent on it instead of with my children. For what? Why was I working so hard?

After getting settled in QCH, we received a clearer plan and direction from the medical staff. We knew that Sebby's situation was critical, and this knowledge weighs heavily on me at all times.'

> "Nothing in life is to be feared,
> it is only to be understood."
> -Maria Sklodowska Curie-

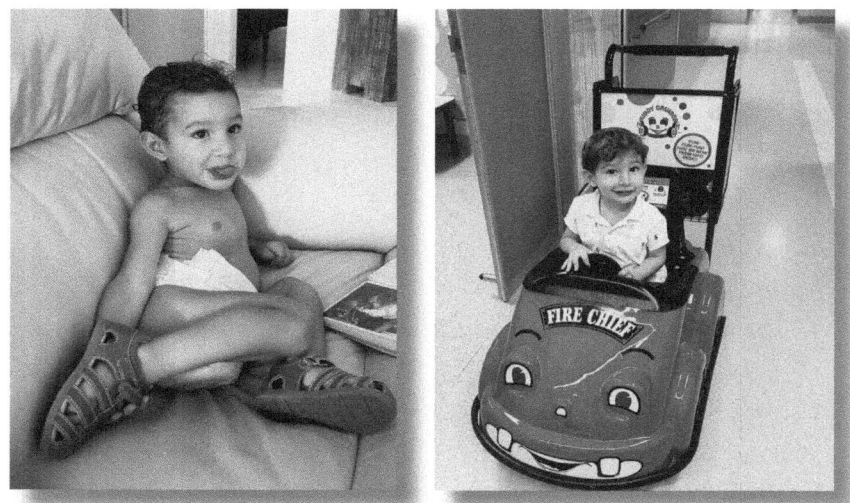
Sebastian, the day his brain tumour was discovered at Cairns Hospital on 8 January 2020

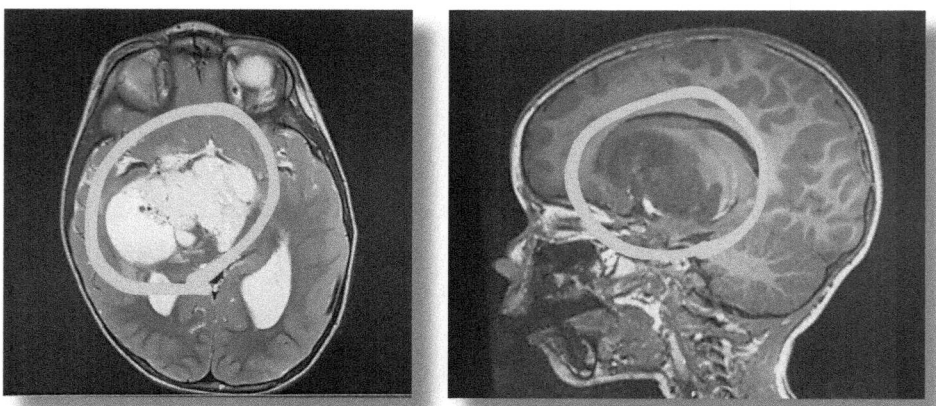
Sebastian's MRI from Cairns Hospital on 8 January 2020 (tumour circled)

QUEENSLAND CHILDREN'S HOSPITAL: OUR NEW HOME AWAY FROM HOME

Our initial night at QCH proved challenging. Following the end of all our meetings and consultations, Sebastian finally succumbed to sleep. Meanwhile, Sam and I remained awake, reflecting on the tumultuous events of the past 48 hours. Eventually, at around 1:00 am, Sam decided to head over to Ronald McDonald House to catch some sleep. I stayed with Sebastian, hoping to grab a few hours of rest myself. However, true to form, Sebastian woke and for much of the night, indulged in various activities like eating, playing, and watching TV, seemingly content with his nighttime routine. The next day, Friday, January 10th, was just as draining as the ones preceding it...

9:21 pm, Friday 10 January 2020

This morning, Neurosurgeon Sarah came in to meet Sebastian (he was asleep last night) and to do a brief neurological assessment of him.

Sam and I were truly impressed by Sarah. Despite her youthful appearance, she exuded ambition and confidence, dressed in designer trousers and stylish blouses, complemented by the latest eyewear trends. Her urban-chic appearance seamlessly matched her detailed and assured delivery when discussing Sebastian's diagnosis and the proposed plan of action from a neurological perspective. Sarah's ability to articulate her concerns in such a relatable manner had an unexpectedly calming effect on us. Even when broaching the topic of brain surgery, she maintained a poised demeanour that helped alleviate some of the fear associated with such a procedure.

Sarah's assistance and empathy toward our concerns were invaluable, and we always anticipated our meetings with her. As the first member of Sebastian's QCH Neurological team whom we encountered, she instilled in us a sense of hope that the rest of the team, particularly the lead surgeon, would be equally impressive.

Sarah has requested that Sebastian start taking steroids twice daily, which will relieve some pressure in the brain and give Sebastian a little more comfort. It will also make things easier when they operate, freeing up some space between the tumour and the brain, nerves, glands and artery.

Sam and I appreciated this plan, as it shed light on something we hadn't fully grasped before: Sebastian likely endured headaches and pressure pain his entire life because of the tumour. The medical team speculated that Sebastian was likely born with the tumour, but its growth didn't significantly affect his functioning until he began experiencing sleep disturbances. It was then that the pressure became too intense for him to bear.

Hearing this broke our hearts. The thought that our sweet baby had been silently suffering, unable to communicate his pain or discomfort, was incredibly difficult for us to accept. Coming to terms with this reality as parents was a heavy burden that we knew would weigh on us for a long time to come.

Sebastian had an additional catheter put in his arm so he now has one in his hand and a bigger one on the inside of his elbow. He doesn't like it but he is getting better at having his obs done, which is great for all of us. The additional cannula is for the dye that's added to his body during a CT scan, which Sarah has recommended he has before surgery.

The CT scan was completed tonight at roughly 8:30 pm after 2 other failed attempts today. It was very difficult to complete successfully as Sebastian was required to lay still whilst moving in and out of the CT machine for a few minutes, also whilst having a dye added to his body via the catheter. We finally got it done tonight, after he was asleep. In addition to confirming the contents of the tumour, the CT scan will also confirm whether there appears to be calcium present or not.

We also met with a Social Worker today, Katie Lindeberg, who was a great comfort to us. She is helping us to understand what's happening to Sebastian and how to manage the stresses, concerns and fears that come with this sort of diagnosis but also the fact that there are other things in our life to worry about; the girls, home, work, etc. Basically, how to balance everything to ensure we can remain focused on Sebastian. We will continue to see her throughout Sebastian's journey, especially on the day of his surgery and significantly difficult days for all of us.

Alex, the Ophthalmologist from the Oncology team came in to complete a full eye examination on Sebastian, including looking at the optic nerves, behind the eyeballs. This test was also completed at the Cairns Hospital on Wednesday and all results from today were in accordance with the Cairns Ophthalmologist's report. The findings were that Sebastian has less active ability in his left-side peripheral vision and may also have a slight turning in of the left eye ball. This is something that we hadn't noticed but should correct with the brain surgery, as it is directly impacted by the size and location of the tumour.

Overall, it's been a day of lots of waiting and persevering with the usual challenges of a 2-year-old suddenly locked in a Hospital room, having strangers examine him often. Sebastian is holding up well, we are going to try a video call with his sisters tomorrow as I think all of the children would love to 'see' each other.

We had a few visitors today also which was lovely, despite the circumstances. Sebastian is very social so loves the attention.

Tomorrow, we meet with Rick and Sarah again first thing in the morning to review the findings from today's CT scan.

Lots of love, Sam, Crystal & Sebastian xoxo

5:43pm, Saturday 11 January 2020

Today we have met with Rick and Sebastian's Lead Surgeon Dr Gert Tollesson. The CT scan has revealed that there is calcium inside the tumour. The team are all in full agreement that the tumour is life-threatening and needs to be controlled and removed as much as possible without damaging the brain and any of the glands, nerves or cells surrounding it.

The plan for surgery is to access the tumour through the top of the brain by cutting open the skull and going in between the left and right side of the brain. Gert explained that the brain can be safely separated down it's centre by 2-3cm, which is how he intends to access the tumour. He does not want to fully remove the tumour due to risk of brain damage but instead is opting to 'debulk' the hard mass and remove the fluid, resulting in a reduction in the tumours size by 50%. The priority during surgery is to relieve pressure on the brain and provide lots of tissue for testing. At this early stage, Gert believes the tumour is presenting like an Optic Nerve Gliomas.

Gert always commanded a formidable presence whenever he entered the room. It's hard to pinpoint whether it was because, for us, he held the key to Sebastian's health and survival, or if there was something inherently special about him. Personally, I'm inclined to believe it was the latter.

Tall and well-built, Gert was always impeccably dressed in a tailored suit and tie. Accompanied by no less than six understudies, whom Sam and I jokingly referred to as his protégé or minions, Gert would launch into his agenda with an almost overwhelming barrage of medical terminology. His visits felt like a whirlwind of information, leaving us feeling unprepared and inadequate to fully grasp everything he was conveying.

Gert's rapid-fire delivery, thick European accent, and sheer brilliance often left us struggling to keep pace. We hung onto his every word, hastily jotting down notes as he raced through his highly detailed explanations of Sebastian's upcoming surgery. After he left, Sam and I would piece together what we could understand, discussing any parts that eluded us. Despite his occasional arrogance or impersonal demeanour, Gert commanded respect through his undeniable intellect, clarity, and confidence. In our darkest moments, he provided us with reassurance and confidence that he was the one who could save our little boy.

Gert went on to explain that during surgery, an EVD (External Ventricular Drain) will also be inserted into Sebastian's brain via an additional opening to check for brain fluid release. The installation of the EVD will determine whether or not Sebastian will require a shunt post-surgery. A shunt is a permanent version of an EVD that would assist in releasing pressure on the brain and would remain in his body long term, possibly his whole life. At this point the surgeons would like to operate ASAP although due to multiple operations scheduled for the next day or so, it may not happen until Wednesday. There is a small chance the operation will be performed tomorrow, if the team can come together in time. We have signed all of the relevant consent forms so as soon as a theatre becomes available, we are all systems go.

There are obvious risks with this type of surgery but Gert is confident that he can get good results and improve Sebastian's condition.

After surgery Sebastian will spend some time in PICU (Paediatric Intensive Care Unit) on level 4 of QCH whilst they monitor the EVD, which will remain in his brain for up to a week. All going well, the EVD will then be removed, the brain and wound will heal and chemotherapy will begin 4 weeks post-surgery.

Following surgery there is also uncertainty around Sebastian's physical improvement (left-side hemiplegia). It may correct straight away or it may get worse before it improves slowly. There is also a risk of complications and/or additional damage to the brain but none of this will be evident until the surgery is complete and recovery begins.

As parents we must move forward and focus on long term results. Unfortunately, in this situation there are very few certainties but focusing on long term results means we must begin to remove the tumour and reduce the pressure from Sebastian's brain.

Sebastian is to continue on 4 hourly obs and his steroid dosage until surgery. This is all a lot of information to take in and is continuing to exceed our worst nightmare. We have our little boy though and we have each other. The love and support we are receiving from near and far is welcomed and cherished.

Despite the dismal circumstances, we've had a wonderful time catching up with friends and family so far, thank you to everyone who's been able to come in and spoil us and Sebastian.

Lots of love, Sam, Crystal & Sebastian xoxo

Medical Report produced following MRI at QCH on 10 January 2020:

MRI BRAIN CLINICAL: Left sided mild inattention and movement left arm. Mild fistula. Hypermobility of joints. Possible mild left hemiplegia. ? cause.

TECHNIQUE: Multiplanar multisequence pre and post contrast MRI of the head. Comparison: No prior imaging available for review.

FINDINGS: There is a large solid cystic mass arising from the suprasellar region. It is estimated to measure approximately 76 x 50mm on axial dimensions and approximately 60mm in craniocaudal extent. A fluid/fluid level seen within the dominant cystic component of the mass which tracks towards the right temporal and inferior right frontal lobe. The mass abuts the proximal middle cerebral arteries bilaterally. There is no evidence of stenosis or occlusion of the middle cerebral arteries. There is some vasogenic oedema noted in the white matter of the right frontal and temporal lobe. The mass displaces the ventricles superiorly and there is asymmetric dilation of the left lateral ventricle suggestive of some early/evolving hydrocephalus. There is no increased periventricular T2 signal to suggest trans ependymal migration of CSF. There are foci of susceptibility artefact within the suprasellar mass, however, there is no diffuse hemosiderin staining or evidence of large volume intracranial haematoma. Dual venous sinuses appear patent. Craniocervical junction and included upper cervical spine shows no gross abnormality.

COMMENT: Large solid cystic suprasellar mass, suspected craniopharyngioma. Mass effect on the adjacent cerebral cortexes with suspected early hydrocephalus of the left lateral ventricle. The duty Paediatric Registrar has been advised of the findings and has reviewed the patient with view to admission.

3

SURGERY

8:21pm, Saturday 11 January 2020

Things certainly change and move quickly in QCH. Sebastian has been moved to PICU (Paediatric Intensive Care Unit) and will undergo surgery in the morning. Sam and I are both allowed to stay with Sebastian in PICU tonight but there is only an armchair so Sam will return to Ronald McDonald House shortly and I will remain in PICU with Sebastian tonight. Sebastian has a bedside nurse 24/7 now until further notice so we are just keeping him company to make him feel safe and comfortable.

9:49pm, Saturday 11 January 2020

Sebastian has finally fallen asleep and Sam is making his way over to Ronald McDonald House. Fasting and IV Fluids start at 2am in preparation for surgery. Sebastian is 1st on the list for surgery so unless an emergency occurs, he will go in quite early. We will be in touch with any news as it comes in tomorrow.

Lots of love, Sam, Crystal & Sebastian xoxo

Reflecting back on January 12th, months later, I can still feel the overwhelming anxiety that gripped me throughout Sebastian's surgery. Each time the phone rang, my heart would leap into my throat, dreading the possibility of receiving the worst news. Sebastian, our little one, was undergoing an incredibly daunting procedure, and we had placed our trust entirely in the hands of a team of strangers. The emotional turmoil was surreal, akin to an out-of-body experience, where I felt paralysed by fear and helplessness, as if an unstoppable freight train was hurtling towards me.

The nearly nine-hour wait for Sebastian to emerge from surgery was agonising. In an attempt to pass the time, we gathered with family and friends; cousins Daniel, Tamlyn and Hannah, Caitlin and Dominic, Aunty Julie and Uncle Brendan, and friends Jayne, Andrew, Miranda and Hugo. We ventured to The Brewhouse Pub for lunch, accompanied by loved ones, hoping to distract ourselves from the looming uncertainty. However, the moment the Hospital called, we rushed back, congregating in the family waiting room on level 4 outside the PICU.

Entering the PICU around 6:00 pm, we were met with a jarring sight: Sebastian, reliant on breathing apparatus, tubes, and monitors, surrounded by a team of medical professionals. As we made our way through the unit, glimpses into other rooms revealed infants and young children in critical conditions, underscoring the gravity of our own son's situation.

Arriving at Sebastian's bedside, we felt dwarfed by the bustling activity of the medical team. We were introduced to the PICU staff, though our surgical team was noticeably absent. Our focus shifted to Sebastian's immediate need: to breathe independently.

Sending out an update to our family and friends that night brought a sense of relief. We could sense the collective exhale of worry as Sebastian weathered this critical phase. Our little fighter had overcome the first hurdle, and we hoped he had the strength to endure the journey ahead.

I firmly believe that the outpouring of love, thoughts, and prayers from our community sustained us through that challenging day. Even from afar, we felt the unwavering support and warm embrace of our loved ones, rallying behind Sebastian with every heartbeat.

7:00pm, Sunday 12 January 2020

Thank you everyone for being so patient today. Sebastian is now in PICU, and is intubated. After a huge 6 hrs in theatre the surgical team reported that everything went to plan and the post-surgery MRI showed no obvious evidence of additional damage to the brain or spine. An x-ray showed a small collapse to his lungs but apparently this is expected after this type of surgery.

He is being kept heavily sedated until about 9pm tonight when they plan to start waking him. If this is successful and he doesn't struggle with all the tubes and monitors on him, and also responds when his eyes are open, they will remove the breathing tube but keep him under mild sedation. If removal of the breathing tube doesn't work tonight, it will be attempted again in the morning. Tonight, Sam and I have been advised we should stay and talk to Sebastian and keep him calm. We are beyond relieved and eager to see what tomorrow brings. We meet with the Surgeons tomorrow morning so will update you with what's next then. For now, we just want to keep an eye on our brave little boy.

Thank you all for your thoughts and love today, it has got us through the hardest day of our lives so far.

Lots of love, Sam, Crystal & Sebastian xoxo

Sam and I observed with profound admiration as the nurses meticulously executed each directive from the Scientist. He exuded meticulousness, precision, and fluency in the language of medicine and science, a language we were still struggling to grasp. Despite his unassuming appearance, dressed in scrubs, he commanded the room with an air of authority, orchestrating the team around Sebastian as if he held divine power. It was evident that he was seasoned in his role, a master of his craft.

As the moment arrived to test Sebastian's lungs and coax him into breathing independently, the Scientist responded to Sam's inquiries with reassuring simplicity. He leaned in and explained, "He will take three breaths in the first minute, then six in the second minute, then twelve, and so on, until his breathing returns to normal in about four minutes." True to his words, Sebastian's breathing followed this pattern precisely. It was a moment of immense relief, reaffirming that we were indeed in the most capable hands within the confines of the PICU at QCH.

9:40am, Monday 13 January 2020

Good morning, everyone. Last night was good, Sebastian's breathing tube was removed and he is now breathing on his own. He is still on heavy pain medication though so isn't at all alert, but is responsive enough to keep the doctors happy. He makes subtle movements but doesn't open his eyes willingly. He did call 'Mumma' a few times last night and threw his right arm around my neck at an attempt at a cuddle, which soothed my heart.

Sam has met with the Surgeons this morning and have reported that his left side is weaker post op but that was a side effect we were ready for and is normal. The physiotherapist will start working with Sebastian today.

We remain by his bedside with all the nurses and doctors at his beck and call. He is a tough little guy, just not ready to wake up yet. It's tough watching him struggle between wanting to wake up and not having the strength to but all we want is for him to take as long as he needs so we can see his beautiful smile again.

Thank you for your continued love and kind words of hope and faith.

Lots of love, Sam, Crystal & Sebastian xoxo

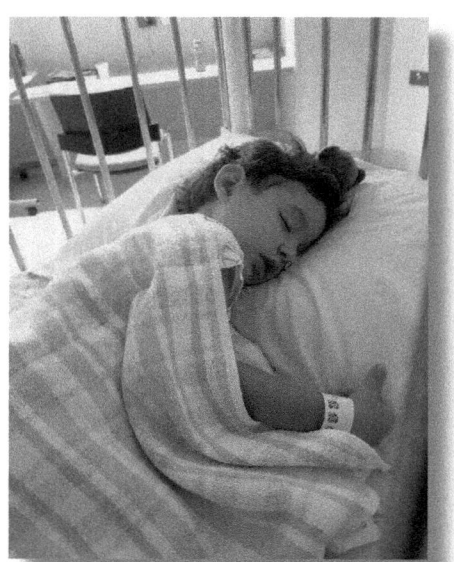
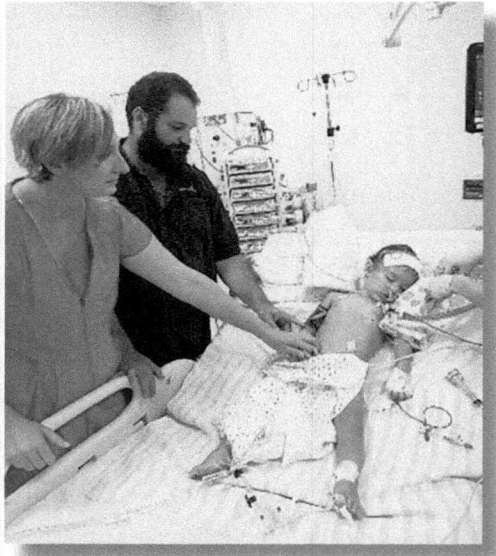

Sebastian, before and after surgery on 12 January 2020 at QLD Children's Hospital

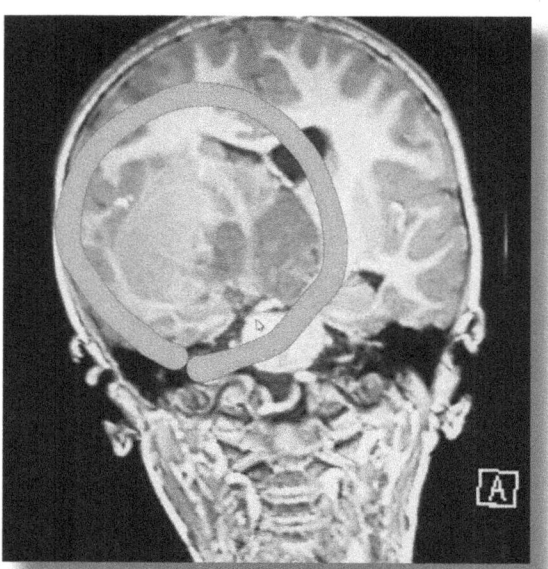

Sebastian's MRI from QLD Children's Hospital on 12 January 2020 & in recovery on 13 January 2020

THE AFTERMATH

By midday on the first day post-surgery, Sebastian had his initial session with a physiotherapist. Despite not witnessing much voluntary movement from Sebastian since surgery, the physiotherapist positioned him into a sitting posture to assess his strength. Surprisingly, albeit with some discomfort and tears, Sebastian managed to sit up independently for around 30 seconds, supporting his neck and head on his own. Despite the taxing nature of this evaluation, the medical team advised keeping Sebastian in a subdued environment to facilitate his gradual brain recovery. Physiotherapy would play a crucial role in his rehabilitation, promoting circulation and aiding healing. Hence, Sebastian would undergo daily bedside physiotherapy sessions during these initial weeks of recovery.

During surgery, an NG (Nasal Gastric) tube was inserted into Sebastian's stomach via his nose to facilitate feeding in the early stages. This method provided him with nutrition, fluids, and medication, ensuring he received the necessary calories. Sebastian displayed interest in drinking when offered water from a bottle, allowing him to consume small amounts happily. Nursing staff recommended trying ice-cream or custard next, which he consumed slowly but contentedly.

Observing Sebastian's gradual improvement throughout the day, it was time for him to transition from the PICU to the Acute Ward on level 11a. This ward housed four patients, each attended by two nurses. One nurse was solely dedicated to Sebastian, providing individualised care as Sam and I grappled with the emotional aftermath of surgery and Sebastian's slow recovery. Despite our lingering apprehension, Sebastian began exhibiting spontaneous movements by evening, offering a glimmer of optimism. The ensuing nights remained as restless as the previous ones, albeit finding solace in the televised coverage of the Australian Open, a small reprieve in our sleepless vigil by Sebastian's side.

5:12pm, Tuesday 14 January 2020

Today has been a huge day for us all. We've seen almost everyone on Sebastian's medical team which has been great but also overwhelming with the amount of new information we are receiving.

Unfortunately, Sebastian has a postoperative fever which can be a sign of an underlying problem. Sebastian's medical team have been working tirelessly to identify any sign of infection today, with no luck. He has had several blood and urine tests that haven't revealed any signs of infection. He has also had an x-ray of his lungs to check on the status of the small collapse after surgery. There has been no change there so that also is good news. To keep him safe and as a precaution, he will begin a 48hr course of antibiotics to cover for infection and hopefully help bring the fever down.

Sebastian is also showing early signs of a disfunction in his hormones, possibly caused by aggravation or damage to the pituitary gland during surgery. The concern has risen as Sebastian's body seems to lack the ability to control his fluid input and output; a pattern I had noticed last year when he seemed to drink and urinate more than I ever remember the girls doing. Hindsight is a wonderful thing; I believe this may have been one of the subtle clues Sebastian's body was giving me that something wasn't quite right. In response to this concern for his pituitary gland function, the team have given Sebastian one dose of a hormone replacement drug tonight and tests will be done to monitor the impact of the hormone drug tomorrow.

Despite all of this, Sebastian still managed to complete another Physiotherapy session today, which went really well. He was able to sit on my lap and also cuddle me whilst I stood up. During the 20-minute session he held his own neck and head and felt really strong on both sides. It was very therapeutic for both Sebastian and I to have a cuddle, and he was very reluctant to go back into his bed, which broke my heart. We are to continue exercises we've been shown to improve his muscle strength, tone and movement in his left calf muscle, until we see the Physiotherapist again tomorrow. We haven't begun work on his left arm or hand as it still has a catheter inserted and a splint dressing applied.

On another positive note, Sebastian is making slow but good progress. Although he is still quite groggy, he seems a little brighter today. The first time he saw Sam this morning he waved and said 'Dadda'. He also reached out with both arms for a hug from Sam, which has been so emotionally soothing for both of them, and certainly brought a tear to my eye. With the help of Cousin Caitlin, I've put together an album of photos from home for Sebastian to look at and stimulate him mentally and emotionally, in a very gentle way. Today, he recognised Roger (our pup) and Sarge (our calf) in photos from home and waved at my friend Nat when she visited today. All positive signs that Sebastian is 'still in there', something I'm desperately and incessantly looking for every waking minute.

This afternoon Sebastian managed a 10-minute nap. Very small steps I know but Sam and I haven't seen him sleep much at all without waking in pain or discomfort since surgery. We are also beginning to see signs of trauma, where he begins to cry and shake uncontrollably when any of the medical team approach him, especially the nurses. Unfortunately, we are told that this is quite normal, given the amount of contact he's had with strangers all of a sudden and in a very foreign environment. Sadly, we are still in the early stages of recovery where most if not all contact he has with the medical team is to perform blood tests, poke and prod him and just generally disrupt his comfort and impose on his personal space. It's beginning to become very traumatising for Sam and I also to witness Sebastian so upset so often but we remain with him at all times so that he calms quickly once the medical team leave his bedside.

We were advised today by QCH Welfare that our accommodation at Ronald McDonald House has been extended until the end of February. It's unreal to think we will still be here then but at least we don't have to worry about accommodation, and it certainly is a relief to be able to stay so close by in such an amazing facility. Sam and I have both agreed there'll be no more guilt around spending money at McDonalds, it truly is an amazing company that is doing such wonderful things for kids and families in need.

Antonia, Josie and Alyssa are now in Cairns with my Mum. They will also spend some time with my Dad this week which will be lovely for them all. My Father-in-law, Sebastian (Snr) is coming down to Brisbane tomorrow and my Mother-in-law, Pam will head down at the end of the week. If anyone wishes to visit from afar, please know that you can stay with us at Ronald McDonald house. We have a very generous room and Sam and I unfortunately don't use it much so there's plenty of room for guests.

We will keep in touch as always.

Lots of love, Sam, Crystal & Sebastian xo

The following day was far less strenuous on Sebastian with only one meeting with our Surgical team and our daily bedside appointments with Physiotherapy, Occupational Therapy (OT) and Katie, our Social Worker.

4:09pm, Wednesday 15 January 2020

Sebastian had an overall good night with the commencement of the 48hr course of antibiotics and hormone replacement medication, both improving his postoperative fevers and fluid input/output function. His fluid intake and urine output were still *being measured and weighed, as well as daily blood culture and urine tests, to keep the team updated on the status of the pituitary gland function. In this Hospital environment, the condition didn't cause Sebastian any discomfort, however it was still too soon to determine how it would affect his daily life once he was home.*

During our morning meeting with the team, Dr. Ahmad, a member of Sebastian's neurosurgical team, mentioned the likelihood of Sebastian needing a permanent shunt based on his brain's appearance during surgery. If the upcoming EVD challenge indicates failure in brain fluid function, Gert will implant a catheter and valve, known as a shunt, which will run from the brain, under the skin, behind the ear, and into the abdomen. However, the EVD challenge was postponed due to Sebastian's complications, including fever (indicative of a possible infection) and inconsistencies in urine/fluid output and intake. Until these issues are stabilized or managed, the team is satisfied with the EVD's fluid parameters and will postpone the challenge.

On Wednesday, Sebastian's left-hand cannula, urine catheter, and monitoring devices for temperature, heart rate, and blood pressure were removed, leaving him with only a cannula in his right elbow, the NG tube for medications and nightly feeds, and the EVD. This reduction in medical equipment provided him with greater comfort and freedom of movement. Another highlight of the day was being able to cuddle Sebastian during physiotherapy and hearing him greet his grandmother on the phone with a cheerful "Hi Baba."

We also met with a dietitian who advised us to feed Sebastian whatever he can eat during the day and rely on the NG tube for nighttime nutrition. With this guidance, Sebastian enjoyed his first piece of steak since leaving home, savouring every bite.

At that stage, our focus remained on allowing Sebastian's body to heal before challenging the EVD. Dr. Ahmad emphasized that Sebastian's skull fracture was incredibly painful, akin to a broken bone but intensified a hundredfold. Given the trauma he had endured, recovery would take time. Consistent physiotherapy and occupational therapy, along with keeping Sebastian medicated and calm, were crucial for expediting his recovery. We anticipated receiving more information about the type of brain tumour in the following week.

Sebastian's spirits improved each day, evident in his recognition of familiar voices during phone calls and his lively reactions to videos from home. This reassured us that Sebastian's memory remained intact, bringing immense relief and joy. His early progress, marked by his returning smiles and chuckles, filled us with pride and served as a therapeutic source for our tight-knit trio, solely focused on Sebastian's recovery. Each day of recovery offered us hope for the future.

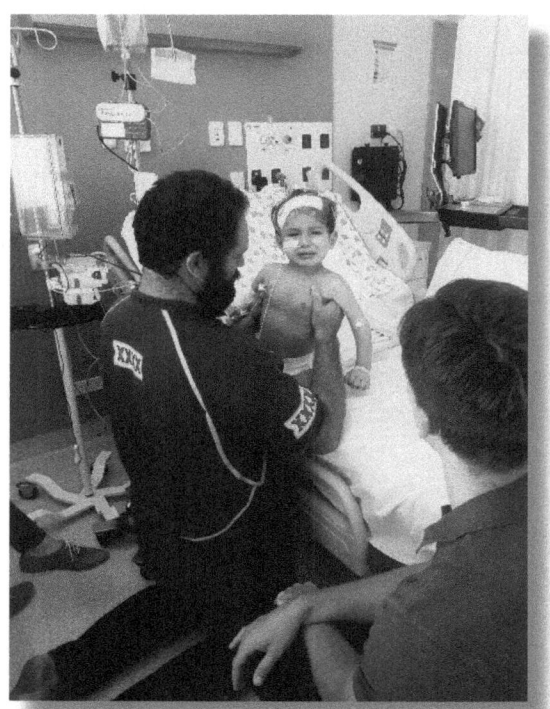

Physiotherapy begins, Bed 18, Acute Ward, level 11a,
QLD Children's Hospital, 14 January 2020

5

"IT'S CANCER"

On Thursday, January 16th, we received Sebastian's official diagnosis. In a consultation room on level 11a, we met with Rick and Brooke Spencer, Sebastian's Clinical Chemotherapy Nurse, while a nurse attended to Sebastian. The delivery of the diagnosis, though overwhelming, was handled with such delicacy, consideration, and compassion. Rick and Brooke, true medical paediatric gems, provided us with much-needed clarity and confidence in what seemed like an unimaginable situation.

The diagnosis revealed that Sebastian has a benign, slow-growing tumour known as a Juvenile Pilocytic Astrocytoma (JPA), a type of glioma. Sebastian's tumour is classified as Grade I, the least severe grade. Treatment involves two main components: chemotherapy followed by further surgery to remove more of the tumour. Chemotherapy aims to control the tumour's growth and eliminate any remaining reproducing or dividing cells, ultimately reducing its size.

Rick presented us with two treatment options tailored to Sebastian's condition. Option 1 involved weekly chemotherapy for six weeks in Cairns followed by monthly chemotherapy for 13 months in QCH, Brisbane. Option 2, a trial-based approach, required a 68-week course of chemotherapy administered at QCH. We had numerous questions, particularly regarding the feasibility of performing parts of both options at the Cairns Oncology Clinic.

The desired outcome of treatment was for Sebastian's tumour to stabilize or even shrink by up to 5%. Achieving either of these outcomes would be considered successful. Following chemotherapy, Sebastian would undergo quarterly MRI scans to monitor tumour growth. The hope was that chemotherapy would provide Sebastian's body with time to grow and better prepare for future brain surgery, essentially buying us more time.

After our meeting with Rick and Brooke, Sam and I gathered in the Family Room on level 11a to collect ourselves before reuniting with Sebastian. Holding back tears during the meeting, I found solace in releasing them once alone. The fear and anguish of Sebastian undergoing chemotherapy overwhelmed me, and I wished I could bear his pain. I remember sobbing and saying "he's just a baby, this is so unfair!" Sam, ever steadfast, reassured me that Sebastian could endure this and that it was necessary for his recovery. "Baby, he can do this, this is what he needs to get better". His words resonated deeply, though my heart still ached for our son.

As we prepared to return to Sebastian, visiting family members, Cousins Daniel and Tamlyn, Tony and Sarina and my father-in-law Sebastian (Snr) arrived, eager for an update on Sebastian's diagnosis. Despite feeling vulnerable, I strived to maintain composure, shielding my loved ones from my inner turmoil. My grandmother's wise words echoed in my mind. I would always hear her thick Croatian accent saying to me, "You must be strong for your family." She had endured poverty, hardship, heartbreak and more recently the death of her true love of over 50 years, my grandfather, yet always had the strength to get up each day and see the good in every situation and everyone. Her teachings and outlook on life motivated me in some of our darkest days.

Sam's explanation to the family provided me with renewed clarity and determination to focus on a positive outcome for Sebastian.

Later that day, we sent an update to family and friends, sharing Sebastian's diagnosis and other important progress as we embarked on the next chapter of his medical journey.

6:23pm Thursday 16 January 2020

Tonight, Sebastian will complete his 48hr course of antibiotics for infection. We hope Sebastian continues to improve tomorrow, without the antibiotics on board.

On Monday the Neurological team are planning on challenging Sebastian's EVD to monitor the function of his brain fluid drainage. If successful, the EVD will be removed. If not, either a replacement EVD or a shunt will be surgically inserted into Sebastian's brain.

Something else on the 'watch and wait' list is his sodium levels and the potential for a disfunction there. His urine and bloods are being tested twice daily to monitor any spikes or dips in his sodium levels. This could be a ripple on effect from pituitary gland damage during surgery.

Sebastian is still struggling to have a bowel movement, post operatively. Tonight will be his first night without the NG tube, which the Dietician agrees may be a bit of overkill, considering how well he is eating during the day now. Hopefully now that the antibiotics are also completed, his bowel will be able to relax.

Generally, Sebastian has shown lots of gradual improvements again today. He is happily sitting up in bed now for short periods and is really enjoying more interaction for longer periods of time. He sat up and listened to 2 stories in a row today, before lying back down on his own. He is still really tired and spends most of the day awake but drifting in and out of rest periods.

For now, our goal is to help Sebastian recover from surgery. If all goes smoothly, Sebastian will have a 'Port-a-cath' (Port) surgically implanted in his chest, where the chemotherapy will be infused into his body at each treatment session. Ideally, this will allow Chemotherapy to begin in 4 weeks-time.

Thank you to everyone who has spent time with our special boy but also to those who are keeping him in their thoughts, it all counts.

Lots of love, Sam, Crystal & Sebastian xo

On Sunday, January 19th, we had the opportunity to witness Sebastian's surgical wounds during a dressing change. The sight was incredibly confronting, serving as a stark reminder of the ordeal Sebastian had endured. Despite the gravity of the situation, both Sam and I were impressed by the cleanliness and size of the incision. It resembled a curving line across the top of his head, approximately 1cm back from his hairline. A loose patch replaced the previous bandaging, allowing for better airflow and enabling the nursing staff to monitor the wound without frequent removal of bandages. Sherie from Neurology expressed satisfaction with the progress of the wound healing.

We were also eagerly awaiting the EVD challenge scheduled for the following day. While we were prepared to wait for one to three days to determine its success, this step brought us closer to the next phase of treatment and was highly anticipated.

At this point, Sebastian was seven days post-surgery. Sam and I were still adjusting to the realisation of the lengthy recovery process. We found hope in the smallest signs of progress, clinging to every subtle movement or change Sebastian exhibited, desperately longing for each to signify another step toward recovery. Despite his grogginess and limited interest in our attempts to engage him, we took solace in his increasing time spent sitting up in bed and participating in physiotherapy sessions.

Although we were apprehensive about pushing Sebastian too hard too soon, Sam remained confident in his ability to embrace any challenge. Meanwhile, discussions continued regarding the logistics of bringing our girls to Brisbane. We desperately missed them and were deeply concerned for their well-being. Mum agreed to escort them on a plane to Brisbane, providing immense relief as we anticipated their arrival at Ronald McDonald House. We hoped their presence would bring courage to Sebastian and offer a comforting slice of home amidst the Hospital environment.

> *"When someone has cancer,
> the whole family and everyone
> who loves them does, too."*
> -Terry Clark-

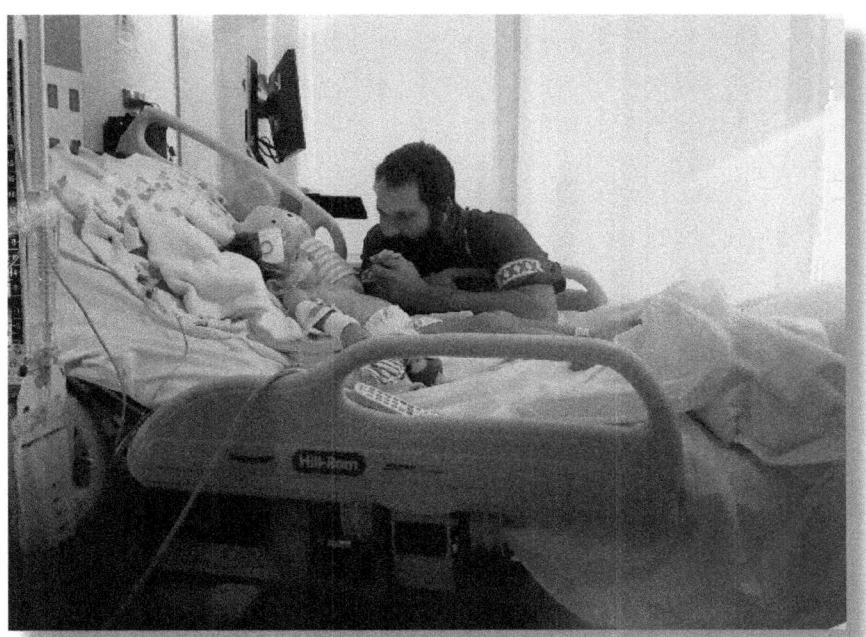

Many, many hours spent holding Sebastian's hand and talking quietly to him.
We watched every breath and didn't leave his side for months. 15 January 2020

6

OUR GIRLS: THE CALM AMONG THE STORM

On Monday, January 20th, when the girls arrived in Brisbane, their excitement and love filled the air as they jumped out of the cab to greet me. Tears flowed freely as we reunited, caught up in a beautiful moment of connection amidst the chaos of tragedy. The image of their little voices calling out "Mummy! Mummy!" from the cab window, desperate for it to stop so they could leap out and into my arms, remains etched in my heart forever.

During the brief journey up to level 11a, I briefed the girls and Mum on hand hygiene and approaching Sebastian quietly. Despite my initial concerns, they complied silently, demonstrating remarkable resilience and understanding. Spotting Sam first, they hurried toward him before redirecting their attention and affection to Sebastian upon seeing him. Sebastian's lack of interest in their presence concerned me initially, but in hindsight, I realised the extent of his discomfort and illness.

Sam and I took turns taking the girls on outings around South Bank, providing a much-needed break from the Hospital environment. While Sebastian's condition declined over the next few days, having the girls around filled our hearts with courage and strength. Their presence energised us for the challenges ahead, even if Sebastian's response to their visit was subdued.

Sebastian appeared to handle the EVD challenge relatively well on Monday night, but our focus shifted to addressing his discomfort due to constipation. It had been 11 days since he started taking steroids and 8 days since starting pain relief, hormone replacement drugs, a calorie rich diet via the NG tube and sedatives used during and after surgery. This had caused Sebastian's bowel immense discomfort and irritability. He was placed on laxatives twice daily and switched to a low carb, liquid diet where possible to give him some relief. Managing his symptoms became a significant challenge, exacerbated by the effects of steroids on his appetite and irritability.

The girls were booked on a flight home with Sam on Wednesday night, with Sam then returning to Brisbane on Saturday. He needed time to settle them back into home and get them ready to start school the following Tuesday. We really didn't know how it would work long term but for the first week of school, Mum had offered to live on the farm with the girls so they could start school on time and get back into some kind of normal routine. Sam was so hesitant to leave on Wednesday with the girls. He felt torn between needing to be with Sebastian and I and taking the girls home, but one of us had to do it. While it was difficult for Sam to step back from Sebastian, we found solace in the knowledge that the girls needed us too. It was a trying time, but we knew we had to remain strong for Sebastian and the girls.

We navigated through each day one step at a time, however, and the updates continued...

7:59pm, Monday 20 January 2020

Sebastian's EVD challenge is so far going well. We will know more in the coming days.

Our decision about which chemotherapy option Sebastian will undergo is still pending, as we await more information from the team about how much can be done in the Cairns Oncology Clinic, if any.

His sodium levels are still a little irregular (low) so this will continue to be monitored daily via urine and blood tests.

We had a visit from the Occupational Therapist today which was a good opportunity to discuss the lack of progress in Sebastian's left arm and hand post-surgery. We are told that there is a period of time where Sebastian's hand will have trouble with gripping and releasing objects. This is expected and very normal post brain surgery. I was shown how to assist Sebastian with exercises that will 'wake up' his muscles and remind them to grip and release when required. He has had a few moments where he grasps a toy and his hand freezes and won't release, even when he pulls the toy with his right hand. This is proving to be frustrating for Sebastian but now that we have strategies to assist him with it, we should see some improvement quickly.

I've had a few very kind friends ask if it's ok to start a GoFundMe account for Sebastian. Sam and I have discussed this but have decided that although it's a lovely offer, we wouldn't feel comfortable accepting. When the time comes, I would love for everyone to get behind fundraising for research into childhood brain cancer, as there is no known cause. I love fundraising so I'll make sure I let you all know when it happens. In the meantime, when Sebastian and I return to Julatten in the coming months, we will be in Cairns a couple of days a week and in Brisbane once a month for chemotherapy and other appointments. This is another time when your help would be welcomed! Babysitting or school drop off and pick-up help will be a constant for the girls, I'm sure. Our girls are going to need loads of support and the 'warm hug' of Julatten around them whilst we get Sebastian through the next 12-15 months of chemotherapy. So, thank you so much for the sentiment.

We have been inundated with gifts for Sebastian which has been just so absolutely humbling and appreciated. Family, friends, the Cancer Council, Brain Child, RedKite, the Starlight Foundation and this wonderful Hospital have showered our little boy in gifts, love and support and we want to say a big thank you to you all.

He has a long way to go but it's so important for his journey to know he is loved and that we all believe he can get through it.

Another thanks to everyone who has come to see Sebastian. He's not always up to visitors so Sam and I appreciate all of your patience.

Lots of love, Sam, Crystal & Sebastian xoxo

5:54pm, Wednesday 22 January 2020

Unfortunately, Sebastian's EVD challenge has failed today. He has been quite unwell this afternoon, due to the build-up of pressure in his brain and is being closely monitored. The Neurology team have been informed and we expect to see them soon. Being the 1st failed attempt at an EVD challenge, it probably means that Sebastian will either have a replacement EVD or a shunt implanted via surgery, possibly this weekend. The surgical team continue to wait for the results from Monday's tests to rule out infection (flagged by fevers). Once no infection is detected, surgery can occur.

Further surgery so soon concerns us greatly but the Neurosurgeons have compared his marathon brain surgery last week to a 50m sprint for the surgery he's about to have, and are confident Sebastian's body can handle it.

Sam and I have decided on Option 1 for Sebastian's chemotherapy treatment. There is still some uncertainty around time frames and how much of his chemotherapy can be completed in Cairns but we will find all of that out in the coming days. Once we are clear about these details we will know more about when we can come home.

Sebastian continues to make slow but positive progress with his Physiotherapy and Occupational Therapy. It is all about his body learning how to move again and build some strength in his weaker areas, predominantly on his left side. He stood aided for about 10 seconds today which is a great achievement!

It amazes us constantly how strong and determined Sebastian is, especially today when he's been feeling so unwell. We continue to keep a close eye on him until we get further direction from Neurology regarding his EVD.

In the following hours, Sebastian's condition deteriorated rapidly. A CT scan around 9:30 pm revealed a significant leak from his EVD site, accompanied by extreme lethargy and unequal pupil size, indicating a suspected brain infection leading to meningitis. Immediate antibiotic treatment was initiated, prompting a remarkable response from Sebastian within 20 minutes, as he opened his eyes and uttered "Mumma." Despite this improvement, his fever persisted, and his heart rate remained elevated (at 140-150, even during sleep), signalling ongoing concerns.

After a long couple of hours of blood tests, brain fluid samples and waiting, I was visited by Neurosurgeon Sherie. Sam phoned in just after midnight to have a conference call with us. The results from Sebastian's CT scan earlier in the night showed no concern regarding the performance of the EVD, extra pressure or fluid in or around his brain. It did, however, show signs of an infection around the EVD wound site. Sherie ordered that he be nil by mouth and treated with a large dose of antibiotics for the infection. Her plan was to take Sebastian into theatre at 8am the following morning to remove his current EVD and replace it with a new one. Once Sebastian was clear of infection, he would then undergo surgery to remove the new EVD and insert a shunt. The timeline for initiating chemotherapy depended on his response to antibiotics, a decision Sherie approached with cautious optimism, assuring us of the team's diligent management.

Later that night, a visit from a social worker provided both solace and added worry. It was the first time since surgery that I feared for Sebastian's life, compounded by Sam's absence. Despite my apprehension, the social worker's presence and comforting conversation eased some of my fears, promising ongoing support during surgery.

Sam, on his way back from Cairns with the girls, was similarly distressed, considering an earlier return to Brisbane. However, after consulting with Sherie, we agreed to wait and assess the situation in the morning, highlighting the unpredictable nature of our life at QCH.

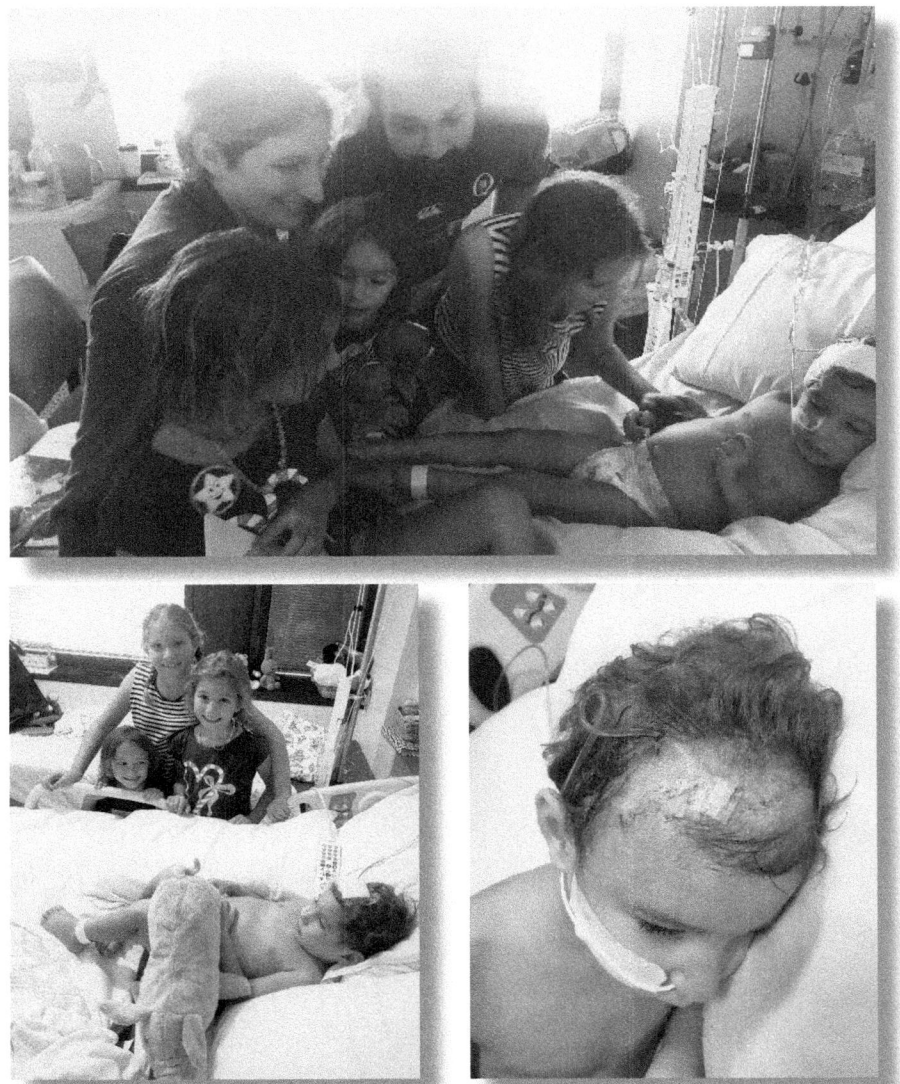

Reunited with our girls on 19 January 2020 and our first look at Sebastian's surgical wound on 22 January 2020

7

UNSTABLE

5:30am, Thursday 23 January 2020

Sebastian's heart rate has finally come down to 115 or lower. His temperature is now also down between 37 and 38 degrees but does return to above 38 occasionally, so he remains febrile. There have been no further leaks from his EVD site since about 2:30am. He slept well from 3-5am and considering he's having hourly neuro obs which include checking his pupil dilation, I think that's pretty good. He seems really settled and not in pain, just tired.

9:36am, Thursday 23 January 2020

Early this morning I was met by the surgical team, including our lead Neurosurgeon, Gert. The team believes Sebastian responded well to antibiotics overnight despite the spikes in temperature and heart rate and observed Sebastian in a generally settled state at the time of his visit. Gert explained that he is reluctant to remove the EVD this morning as he is not 100% convinced that the leak and symptoms last night were from the EVD, rather he believes they're being caused by an infection somewhere in the body. His recommendation was based on clear results for all of his tests last night, except a spike in his white blood cell count which are the bodies infection fighting cells. Gert has decided to leave the EVD in today, continue antibiotics and allow Sebastian's brain to recover from yesterday's events. If a leak occurs again, he plans to remove the EVD and watch what happens. It will either leak (indication his brain needs a shunt ASAP) or his brain will pick up the slack and begin to absorb the fluid on its own.

I have requested a meeting with our Neurological Nurse, Jason, to clarify some areas of concern Sam and I have after speaking with Gert. We also await advice from the Infectious Disease team to gain their opinion of the results from last night's tests.

12.23pm, Thursday 23 January 2020

I have just met with Jason who has answered so many of our questions and explained a lot more about our options today. As always, I took some notes and I'd like to share them with you as they gave me so much more clarity and understanding.

1. 'Hardware' (EVD) in Sebastian's body is always going to be a source of possible infection; one of the reasons Gert would rather remove the EVD than replace it unnecessarily.

2. If Gert does replace the current EVD, it'll be sterile and shouldn't cause the infection to linger or reoccur.

3. The need for a shunt is not taken lightly. Once it's been in the body for three months, the brain will cease to drain on its own and won't ever regain that function again.

4. Gert noticed this morning that Sebastian's brain fluid in the EVD was very yellow in colour. This indicates that there may be 'debris', blood or 'bugs' present in his body. Until the fluid returns to an off-white/clear colour, Gert would prefer not to operate.

Jason also mentioned that Sebastian's fasting status had been lifted but not to stress *if he doesn't want to eat. He is on IV fluids and nightly feeds can recommence via the NG tube at any time if necessary. He reiterated that if there's any sign of another leak from the EVD site, we are to recommence fasting in preparation for surgery, as a precaution. Also, Jason assured me that these types of hiccups when challenging the EVD are quite common. All children react differently, depending on the status of their brain tumour. Sebastian's tumour is low grade so it gives Gert flexibility with the challenge and more time if the EVD is removed. One of our main concerns is Sebastian's negative response to the EVD challenge and him having to endure that a second time. Jason explained that evidence of Sebastian's brain failing to drain fluid on its own will present with a lump under the old EVD site. The fluid will take the path of least resistance and follow the old drain line, looking for an exit. From that point, Gert will want to take a look at the site and make a decision based on how much time has passed since the removal of the EVD and the symptoms Sebastian has at the time. This information settled our concerns and reaffirmed our trust in the team. At times, Sam and I felt overwhelmed with the massive amounts of information we receive, and rarely have time to digest the information and deliver our questions before the team leaves the room. We talk to the nurses often and they are able to give us some clarity but it's such a relief to now have a relationship with Jason who knows the intricate ins and outs of Sebastian's medical portfolio.*

Sebastian himself, is awake mostly but very lethargic. In all my best efforts to cheer him up, I'm still only getting forced smirks, very occasionally. I just fed him some yoghurt after he asked for ice cream and he immediately turned grey and started to gag. No vomiting as yet but it's clearly too soon for him to be eating.

Aunty Julie and Hannah have just turned up so I've taken myself out for a coffee, the first break I've had from Sebastian's bedside in about 24 hours. It's been a huge stint but I've been so reluctant to leave Sebastian while he's so unstable. We've had a lot of curve balls thrown at us today that have taken me by surprise but as usual, the staff have been amazingly supportive and informative which fills us with confidence and comfort.

Everyone's well wishes this morning were so important even though surgery didn't go ahead as planned. Knowing so many people are thinking of Sebastian and sending him so much love gives us strength to stay positive. I'm looking forward to some rest hopefully tonight, here's hoping it's nothing like last night.

Lots of love, Sam, Crystal & Sebastian xoxo

By late afternoon, Sebastian's urine output was up to 12.9 and as a result, his fluid input had increased substantially. The Endocrinology team ordered more tests on his sodium levels and blood culture as Sebastian was also still very lethargic. I was assured that this was just a precaution as lethargy is expected after last night's events. There were also no further leaks from the EVD site so all testing was being conducted as precaution and to keep Sebastian safe. I was advised by nursing staff that the entire operating team was now available at QCH and Sebastian was at the top of the emergency list, should things go pear-shaped that night. I was assured that intervention would be swift and before he has time to get distressed, he will be in theatre.

> *"Turn your wounds into wisdom."*
> -Oprah Winfrey-

8

MENINGITIS

6:15am, Friday 24 January 2020

After a bloody fantastic night where Sebastian and I got 6 hours sleep, at around 5:00 that morning, Sebastian's EVD accidently came out after getting caught on the bed rail whilst our nurse Rachel and I were changing Sebastian's bed linen. It wasn't until I noticed brain fluid pouring out of the EVD site that we realised something had gone terribly wrong. Sebastian became very distressed and began to scream, which created more pressure and a heightened level of sensitivity and pain at the EVD site. As you can imagine, it wasn't a nice experience for Sebastian but after a few minutes and application of a pressure bandage to his head, he began to settle.

By 7:30am, Sherie had sedated Sebastian, in preparation for stitches. Within the next hour, Sebastian had relaxed and the wound site was stitched up as we began to wait and watch what Sebastian's brain's response would be to the absence of the EVD.

Results came through just before noon from the Infectious Diseases team that revealed the infection source was the EVD site, which had developed into Meningitis inside the brain. In response to this new finding, the EVD would have been removed swiftly that morning anyway. The infection formed on 22.1.20 (Wednesday), which supported Gert's advice that Sebastian becoming unwell on Wednesday was a result of the infection, not the EVD challenge. Disaster averted. An antibiotics schedule was put in place and Sebastian was given some additional pain relief in anticipation for headaches to return due to the new stitches in his head.

Throughout the remainder of the day, Sebastian had no signs of fluid retention in the brain which would have presented as 'pooling' or weeping under the skin at the EVD wound site. He remained well and showed only a few signs of headache and pain.

Sebastian's appetite had failed to return after becoming unwell so was placed back on the nightly feeds through the NG tube. He had been very lethargic, particularly since noon so the Neurosurgical team took Sebastian for a CT scan at 6:00pm which was all clear, with no change since surgery except for a pocket of air around the EVD wound site. It was of no concern at that stage as these pockets of air commonly appear after surgery and clear on their own quickly. He was ordered to take an additional dose of steroids that night, firstly to reduce swelling/inflammation/pressure on the brain and secondly to 'perk' him up a bit after being so lethargic for so long. He was expected to rest well during the night, despite blood and urine tests being ordered for midnight.

Further CT scans would be done in the coming days to keep an eye on the brain fluid. The last couple of days were really tiring and quite intense with every change in behaviour and movement closely scrutinized because of the EVD removal. It had however been a good day, with all signs pointing to Sebastian's brain passing the current EVD challenge. Confirmation of this wouldn't come for a few days yet but I was trying to focus on every little win along the way.

By nightfall, Sebastian's obs had been reduced to 4 hourly, which I hoped would allow him to sleep better. It did however mean that I suddenly didn't have a nurse with me at bedside anymore, so there was little hope for sleep for me. More than ever, I looked forward to Sam's return, when I'd finally get some rest.

8:54pm, Saturday 25 January 2020

Sebastian had a really rough night last night with almost no sleep. He had another episode of vomiting and high blood pressure at around 6am. He was assessed quickly by the Paediatrician and Neurosurgeon who agreed that the vomiting and high blood pressure were evidence of his body fighting the infection. Thankfully he began to improve slowly and by noon he was relaxed and able to rest well. Our Neurology team also confirmed that sudden swelling and redness in Sebastian's right eye is just a side effect of the work done on the right side of his brain and should clear up in the next few days.

The Oncology team have also come to see Sebastian this morning. Treatment for his infection has been started with a 10-day course of antibiotics, evaluated every three to four days with blood tests to ensure dosages are sufficient.

Dr Louise Conwell from the Endocrinology team has confirmed diagnosis of Diabetes Insipidus and an Adrenal Gland Disorder. The 2 conditions often go hand in hand, and are usually related to damage to the pituitary gland.

Diabetes Insipidus is a disorder where the body cannot regulate fluid, which is unlike the more commonly known Diabetes Mellitus where the body cannot regulate and manage levels of insulin. Diabetes Insipidus sufferers drink excessive amounts of water in an attempt to quench an unquenchable thirst. The fluid is then expelled from the body, also in excessive amounts, via the bladder. The condition puts the sufferer's kidneys at risk as well as dangerously low levels of sodium and electrolytes in the blood. With the use of Desmopressin, Diabetes Insipidus is manageable but is usually a permanent condition.

On the other hand, the Adrenal Gland disorder may be temporary and improve as Sebastian's brain recovers from surgery. The Adrenal Glands are located just above the kidneys and have many functions including the production of the Cortisol hormone. In Sebastian's case, his Cortisol levels are very low which puts the body at risks when under stress (injury) or trauma (surgery). The disorder is managed with a steroid called Dexamethasone.

Treatment for both conditions have begun today and we have already begun to see improvement. Daily blood tests will monitor the status of the conditions and dosages of Desmopressin and Dexamethasone will be altered accordingly.

It is a huge relief to receive these diagnoses and begin treatment. We are learning very quickly how important the brain is to the whole body and how trauma can alter so many 'normal' and healthy bodily functions. We feel so fortunate to have such specialist teams engaged to manage Sebastian's body.

Sebastian's NG tube was removed earlier in the morning during an episode of vomiting but was replaced in the afternoon so that night feeds and pain relief could continue to be administered. He had had very little to eat in the previous three days but the Paediatrician assured us that his lack of appetite could be from the introduction of the new antibiotics and should return soon.

We were now roughly 36 hours post EVD removal with still no sign of failure which was really exciting. Sam and I were counting each hour as a win and huge achievement. A follow up CT scan would confirm the success of the challenge so we looked forward to that in the coming days.

Sebastian was generally very tired and lethargic and had had quite significant physical regression in the last 24-48 hours. He would quietly watch TV or just sit and look around but for most of the day he would rest. We were still sitting in a darkened room with little noise and stimulation so it made for long days when he wasn't well enough to interact with Sam and I. He wasn't talking much more than 'Mumma' 'Dadda' and 'ice cream' and wasn't sitting up or eager to have cuddles out of bed. We were assured this behaviour was temporary and all part of the ups and downs expected after such significant brain surgery. We looked forward to the return of our cheeky, noisy and active little boy but were also really concerned. He had seemed to go downhill suddenly and we were unsure what it all meant.

At 7pm on 26th January, just as the Australia Day fireworks began outside our Hospital window, Sebastian fell very unwell. Until then, we had probably our best day with Sebastian since surgery where he was stable and well rested after about 6 hrs sleep the night before. It was frightening to witness his abrupt decline where he screamed in pain and became very irritable. Thankfully the Neurology Registrar ordered a CT scan within the hour and reviewed the results from his last blood tests earlier in the day. After consultation with the Endocrinology team, it was revealed that there was almost no sign of the antibiotic in Sebastian's blood stream. Louise (Endocrinologist) explained that this could be caused by his high quantity of urine bypass but it wasn't a definite or final explanation and the Oncology team would need to investigate further. The absence of the antibiotic would cause Sebastian great discomfort as his Meningitis was basically being left untreated. Pain relief was administered soon after his symptoms began and an increased dose of his antibiotic allowed him to settle and go to sleep.

The following morning, we anxiously waited to meet with the Oncology team regarding a plan going forward for the treatment of Sebastian's Meningitis. Immediately after the CT scan was conducted, the Neurology Registrar told us that there was nothing alarming or urgent to be concerned about and that all looked similar to the previous CT scan conducted 2 days earlier. I guess the anxiety was mostly around finding out why his body wasn't accepting the antibiotics and if an alternative was available.

At that point, it had been just past 72 hrs post EVD removal, which was something positive to remain focused on.

6.41pm, Monday 27 January 2020

Our visit with Sherie from Neurology this morning was really positive. Sherie said that Sebastian's CT scan last night didn't show any areas of concern and remained unchanged since our last CT. We are now day 4 since the EVD came out and

Sebastian's brain still appears to be processing brain fluid on its own, which is great news! Sherie also let us know that we can look forward to giving Sebastian a bath, possibly next week! It's been a long 15 days without being able to watch him enjoy bathing in water. Overall, the team is really happy with his progress and the ups and downs we are facing are all expected after such major brain surgery.

Oncology is still concerned, however, about the status of the infection. The increase in antibiotics overnight seem to be doing the job and have helped Sebastian to have a very relaxed day. We are day 5 of 10 with the antibiotics now so at the half way point and hopeful they are doing their job.

Louise, our Endocrinologist, is still closely monitoring Sebastian's fluid input, urine output and sodium levels in his blood. She believes she is getting closer to the correct dosage of Desmopressin and the hormone replacement drug to get this under control. The levels seem to have stabilised today but have otherwise been very up and down.

The highlight of our day was moving back to a private room after 15 days in the Acute Observation Ward on level 11a. We are all far more comfortable and are enjoying the more relaxed and quieter environment. Room 24 is our new home, for anyone wanting to visit - still on level 11a.

Good night all, hope you enjoyed the public holiday.

Lots of love, Sam, Crystal & Sebastian xoxo

Inside level 11a, Sam and I would often bump into other parents in the 'family room'. A place where we were able to heat up a meal, make a coffee, meet with family and friends or just use the space to escape the all-too familiar walls of the Hospital rooms.

All of the parents I encountered were in their own vortex of worry and heartbreak for their sick child. Every now and then however, we'd just stop and connect. Knowing that each of us understood the pain and fatigue we were enduring. Most often, conversation circled around the progress or set-backs our children were currently experiencing but it was also a chance to share survival strategies and helpful advice on all things related to long-term Hospital stays. It was here that I learnt about UberEATS, alternative medicines and pain relief tips, free events for families and general chit-chat about how to keep our inpatient children entertained.

Occasionally, conversations would break down walls, open our minds and allow us to feel human again. To talk to someone other than the medical teams and Hospital staff was refreshing. To be able to open our hearts and have sympathy for the endless tales of children enduring mis-diagnosis, inadequate medical care in rural Hospitals and treatment complications that would inevitably land the children in Hospital, sharing our stories with strangers, living through a similar nightmare and surviving against all odds. It shifted focus for just a moment in time and cruelly provided us all with comfort that we weren't alone. The most surprising realisation for me was just how indiscriminate childhood illness and disease is. Our children were now a statistic and in so many ways, a medical 'experiment', with complications unseen before and treatments never tried, before leaving us parents helplessly hovering over our children, asking ourselves 'why?' and 'how?'.

As the lyrics go in the song "Bless the Beasts and The Children" by The Carpenters, 'Bless the beasts and the children for in this world they have no voice, they have no choice.' I often thought about this song and how relevant the lyrics were to us parents there on level 11a.

*"Bless the beasts and the children
for in this world, they have no voice,
they have no choice."*

-The Carpenters-

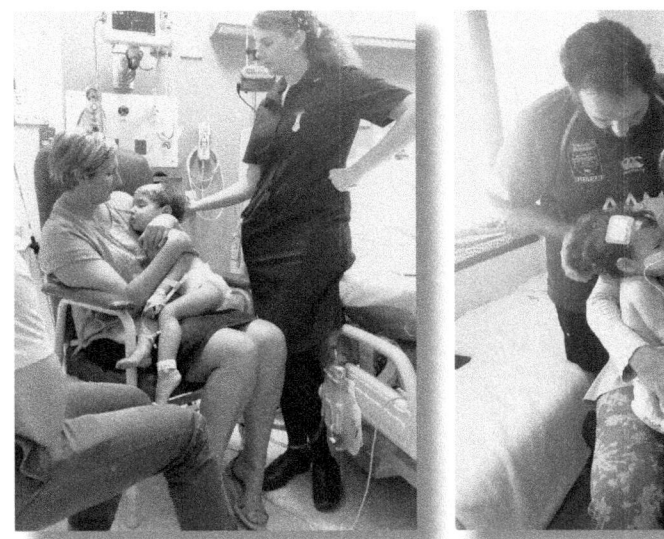
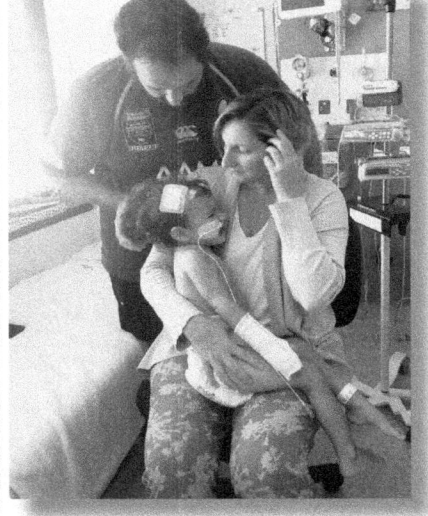

Having our first cuddles with Sebastian post surgery

9

10 MORE DAYS

7:47pm, Tuesday 28 January 2020

On Tuesday, 28th January, we had our first meeting with the Oncology team, led by Dr. Wilson, whom we had nicknamed 'Happy' due to his consistently serious demeanour. Although he rarely showed emotion, his commitment to Sebastian was evident, and over time, we saw his genuine concern for our son. Dr. Wilson's dedication extended beyond his formal responsibilities, often checking in on Sebastian even though he wasn't his primary doctor. Such dedication was reassuring and highlighted how Sebastian's presence touched everyone around him.

We faced a new challenge with Sebastian's infection. The current antibiotics weren't effective, as evidenced by their absence in recent blood tests. This led the team to initiate a new 10-day course of Bactrim, a potent antibiotic harsh on veins. Concerns about further stress and trauma from multiple blood tests prompted Dr. Wilson to question why Sebastian didn't have a PICC line (Peripherally Inserted Central Catheter) already. His advocacy led to the decision to insert a PICC line, alleviating the need for frequent needle pricks and easing Sebastian's discomfort.

The PICC line would be inserted above the bend in his elbow and used for blood tests and administering medications, making it a crucial but unwelcome step.

Despite our reluctance for more surgery, it was necessary to address the Meningitis effectively. The new cannula placed that morning would only serve temporarily while Sebastian began his new antibiotics regimen.

This setback with Meningitis affected Sebastian's ability to participate in his daily Physiotherapy and Occupational Therapy sessions. He was too unwell to even sit up in bed. To engage him, we used touch-and-feel books, flap books, and tickling games to gently encourage movement without causing discomfort. It was clear Sebastian was very ill, with every slight movement causing him pain and reminding us of his fragile state.

Additionally, we struggled with managing Sebastian's Diabetes Insipidus. His urine output remained irregular, leading the Endocrinology team to increase the frequency of his medication to three times daily to better control the disorder.

7.25pm, Wednesday, 29 January 2020

Good evening everyone, well it's been a big day for our little champion. This afternoon Sebastian had surgery to insert a PICC line into his left arm. He came out of theatre at 5pm and was a little sore and sorry but happily ate dinner before falling asleep.

He was really bright and chirpy this morning, and very cheekily throwing toys off the bed and playing games with Sam and I. It was lovely to see him interacting so happily with us after being so stationary and unwell for so long. All a great indication that the new antibiotic is really giving the Meningitis a nudge.

For tonight, we hope that Sebastian continues to recover without any further complications.

Good night and lots of love to you all. Lots of love, Sam, Crystal & Sebastian xoxo

10

FINALLY, FREEDOM

7:20pm, Thursday, 30 January 2020

Hello! Today has been a really positive day in our Hospital world.

All eyes are still on Sebastian's Meningitis. The PICC line is working well and not bothering Sebastian at all. He does seem better again today, so it appears the change in antibiotic is working well. Sebastian recovered from his little surgery yesterday and slept well last night so has been really happy today.

Sebastian's Physiotherapy and OT sessions also went well today. For the first time since his EVD removal (7 days) he got out of bed! He didn't like trying to stand but he was more than happy to sit on my lap or on the floor and play with some toys. Tomorrow, the Physiotherapist would like to get him to sit unaided, however he has lost a lot of muscle strength and coordination in his legs so it will be a very gentle process.

Sebastian's night time feeds via his NG tube have ceased as his appetite returns, however he will still receive fluids via the NG tube to ensure he doesn't dehydrate. Due to the constant increase in his Diabetes Insipidus medication, Desmopressin, his thirst seems to have subsided. The Endocrinology team are keeping a close eye on his sodium levels and adjusting hydration accordingly.

Sebastian has begun to talk more and is really enjoying silly games and belly laughs. His smile seems to be extending a little on his left side now which is so exciting to see. Although his crooked smile is cute, I miss his full, bright smile he had pre-op.

I hope the good news and progress continues tomorrow.

Lots of love, Sam, Crystal & Sebastian xoxo

Friday 31 January 2020

As the end of January approached, the days seemed to blend together, consumed entirely by our focus on Sebastian's condition and the medical challenges at hand. We were oblivious to the world outside the Hospital, absorbed in every aspect of his care. However, on the 31st of January, I was finally able to share some positive news: for the third consecutive day, Sebastian showed remarkable improvement. His progress was exceeding our expectations, driven by his determination to recover.

It was clear that the new Bactrim antibiotic was making a significant difference. His progress had suddenly accelerated, and we were witnessing notable improvements in his condition.

7.37pm, Friday, 31 January 2020

Today we watched Sebastian sit up on his own during his Physiotherapy session, and remain there for about 30 minutes. He is occasionally using his left hand and arm to prop himself up, or assist in lifting something heavy. He is not given much opportunity to strengthen his left leg yet, as he is still too weak to stand. We attempted to stand with him but it was still a bit much for him. The more movement he does, the stronger he will get so we continue to work with him daily. The Physiotherapy sessions are good for all of us as it allows Sam and I to feel more involved in Sebastian's recovery. We often feel helpless as we watch all the professionals guide his body to health with all their medicines and expertise.

On another positive note, The Neurology team have been happy with Sebastian's clinical status over the last 36-48 hours so have given us the ok to bath him and take him to the Hospital garden on level 5 as often as we like. This news came with great excitement for Sam and I, who had been struggling with the confinement of the Hospital room, almost as much as Sebastian. So, we ventured out to the garden and spent about 10 minutes in the shade before Sebastian had had enough. The added stimulation a change of environment has on Sebastian's brain was very exhausting for him at this early stage, so we looked forward to visiting the garden again soon but only for short sessions. The benefits of fresh air and sunshine I hope will make a huge difference to Sebastian's mental and physical health.

Reflecting on January 2020, I feel a profound sense of relief that it's finally over. Reading back through my notes and journal entries is deeply unsettling, as it swiftly transports me back to those harrowing moments. I experience physical discomfort and intense emotional sadness knowing that our family endured such tragedy. We lived through a devastating ordeal that happened to good people, and I hope that the worst is behind us, a chapter we won't have to relive. The coming months promised new obstacles and medical challenges, and we hoped February would bring more positive and progressive changes. Unfortunately, our threshold for enduring pain was tested not just in February but throughout the months that followed.

Timeline of Events: January 2020

08.01.2020	MRI Cairns Hospital – Discovery of tumour & cysts.
09.01.2020	Arrive at Queensland Children's Hospital (QCH) via Royal Flying Doctors.
10.01.2020	CT Scan at QCH.
12.01.2020	Surgery at QCH – Debulk tumour by 50% and investigate cysts.
13.01.2020	Moved from PICU to level 11a Acute Ward.
14.01.2020	Physiotherapy begins.
16.01.2020	Juvenile Polycytic Astrocytoma (JPA) diagnosis. Chemotherapy confirmed as treatment.
19.01.2020	Girls and Mum arrive in Brisbane.
20.01.2020	EVD challenge begins. Occupational Therapy (OT) begins.
22.01.2020	EVD challenge fail. 1st signs of infection, antibiotics administered & CT Scan completed. Sam & girls return home.
24.01.2020	EVD removed accidently. Infectious Diseases confirms Meningitis caused by 'bug' found in EVD wound site. CT Scan.
25.01.2020	Diabetes Insipidus diagnosis, treatment begins. Adrenal Gland disorder diagnosis, treatment begins.
26.01.2020	Discovery of no antibiotic in Sebastian's blood so doses doubled. CT Scan.
27.01.2020	Moved from Acute Ward to Room 24, level 11a.
28.01.2020	Oncology decides to cease antibiotics & begin 10 days of Bactrim to fight Meningitis.
29.01.2020	PICC Line surgery, QCH.
30.01.2020	1st attempt at standing since surgery on 12.01.20.
31.01.2020	Sat up unaided, out of bed. 1st visit to QCH garden.
Total COVID-19 cases confirmed in QLD as at 31.01.2020 = 2	

> "The most wonderful places to be in the world are:
> In someone's thoughts. In someone's prayers.
> An in someone's heart."
>
> -Unknown-

On January 22nd, Australia confirmed its first case of COVID-19. The patient was a man from Wuhan, China, who had flown into Melbourne on January 19th. The first COVID-19 case in Queensland was diagnosed later in January 2020, involving another man from Wuhan who arrived on the Gold Coast on January 28th via Melbourne. During these early months, COVID-19 was barely mentioned within our Hospital world. Visitors to the Acute Ward were loosely advised to sanitize and wear face masks only if unwell. Australia could not have anticipated the virus's ferocity in the following months or the profound impact it would have on those who were vulnerable or had underlying health issues. I admit we were completely unaware of the extent to which COVID-19 would affect Sebastian's Hospital experience and our family journey through this already challenging time. It was an unexpected and cruel twist that tested my emotional and mental resilience.

Once Sam and I began updating our family and friends on Sebastian's progress, we were overwhelmed by the outpouring of love and support. The messages we received after each update were filled with encouragement, questions about our well-being, and concern for Sebastian. We felt the comforting embrace of home, particularly from our small community in Julatten. I had never sought support to such an extent before, and it was both humbling and heartwarming to receive such love from so many. I want to share some of these messages here as a way of expressing my gratitude to those who uplifted us and filled our hearts with love during such overwhelming times.

Messages of Love

"Our hearts are with you. Be strong for each other."

"Hi Crystal, I am so sorry to hear that Sebastian is about to have surgery. I just did a prayer for you and Sebastian. I am sending you all my love and support. You can do it. You are a super strong mother and your love will get him better. Much love."

"He is a very brave beautiful boy, a credit to you both. He is only that way because of you and Sam, you are both brave and beautiful too. Children are amazingly resilient and strong. He will come through this with flying colours and become an amazing man, just you wait and see!"

"Thank you for the update Crystal. Photos are great. He looks calm, settled and knows his mother has him close to her heart. Baby steps... don't have too much expectation, just go with the flow. I have been telling people about what's going on with the Leonardi family. I'm getting the same reaction... lots of tears but most of all concern for little Sebi. They all want to know what they can do. Do the cattle need tending? Feed to get? Fences need checking? Tractor stuff? Lots of people here just wondering what they can do to help. Have a think... give Sebi a kiss for me."

"Awww Crystal, I wish I could just give you a great big hug right now and make this all go away. Thinking about you guys all the time."

"We are all praying for our little man Crystal and we believe you and Sam are doing an amazing job."

"We have such admiration for you Crystal. That piece of good news about the EVD is wonderful... hoping for more good news after the CT Scan. Your little bubba is doing so bloody well, and so are you and Sam. Super special people. With love from us to you."

"Oh, what a brave little boy he is bless him... just a quick message to say that Josie had a great first day back, she was very excited to be there and entered the classroom this morning with a big smile and a lovely greeting. It was good to see her participate in all aspects of the classroom activities all day without any glimpse of an issue. We are now only a Prep/1 class which is beneficial for all concerned, it is a great working area for everyone and all kids seem to be happy. The new teacher is great too and the kids have taken to her just nicely. The year 1's are loving being the eldest and are showing the Preps the ropes. Sorry l didn't get to see too much of Antonia today except when she came in with your Mum, Josie and Alyssa this morning but she seemed super keen to get started too so that was nice... I hope both you and Sam are taking care of each other and getting some well-deserved rest in between your busy schedule with little Sebi. Hope everything is still travelling as smoothly as possible for the situation at hand. Sending big hugs for you all, talk soon."

"Your girls were absolute angels today. I think they had a great day. They were full of smiles as they arrived today. Wishing you all the best with little Sebby. Take care down there... your girls are in great hands with your Julatten family."

"Such great news guys. He's one strong little boy! Just like his parents."

"Oh, how wonderful!!! That's really fabulous news. And how fantastic to see you all outside. Such beautiful photos. Nothing in this world ever beats a mummy cuddle! Gosh he must have loved to have ventured outside. And to be sitting up on his own. Wow! He is one determined and strong little guy."

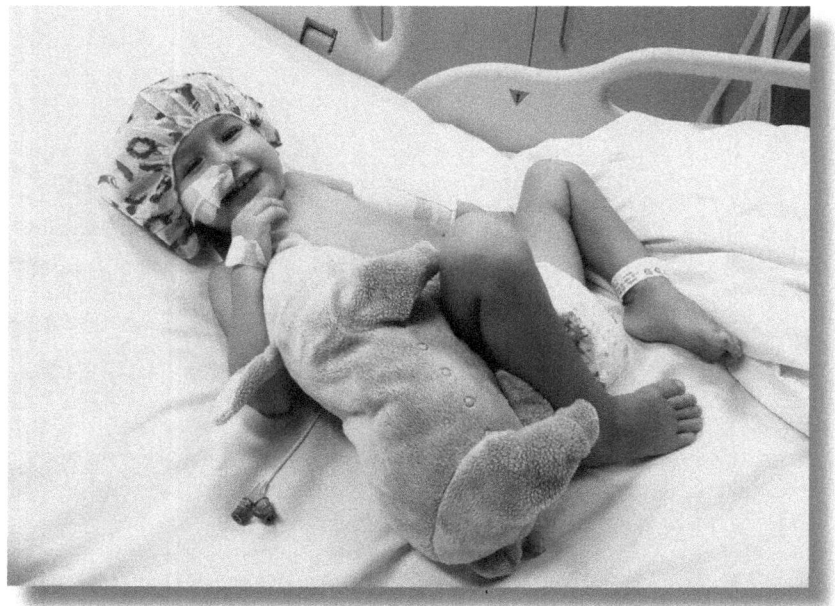

Sebastian prepped and ready for PICC Line surgery on 29 January 2020

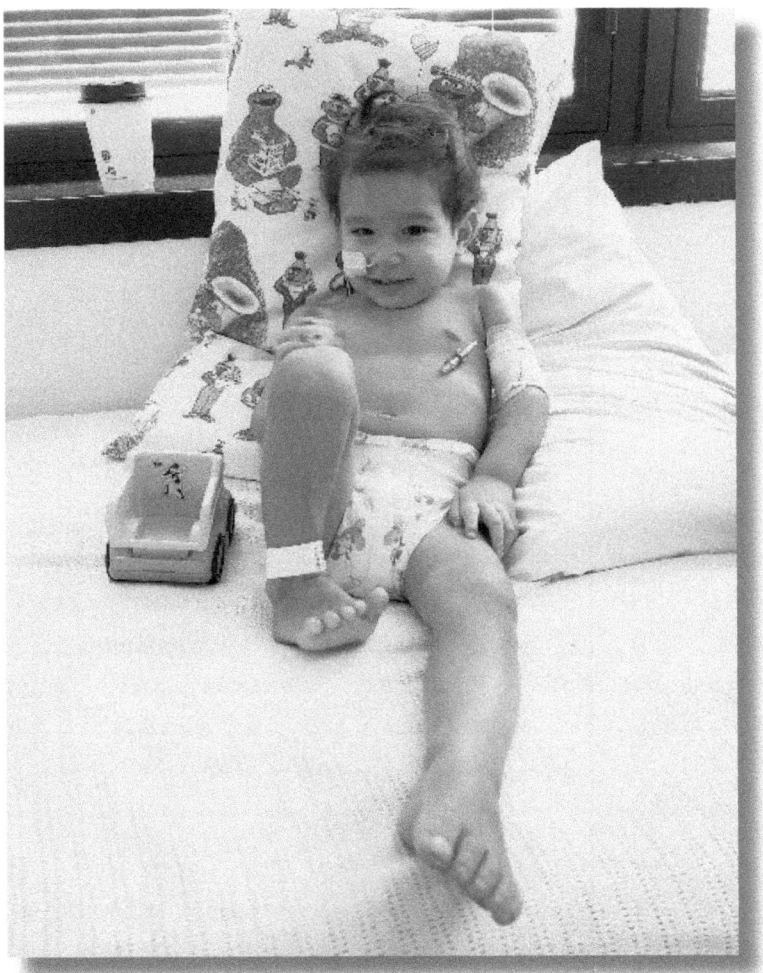

Far more comfortable in his own room (#24) and out of the Acute Ward.
31 January 2020

PART 2

Fact: As of 2023, on average, approximately 1,000 children aged 0-14 years are diagnosed with cancer each year in Australia, with around 100 to 120 children estimated to die from the disease annually.[2]

11

LEAPS & BOUNDS

On Sunday, February 2nd, we were on day 5 of the team's second attempt at treating Sebastian's Meningitis. With each passing day, he became increasingly stable, bringing us a welcome respite from the constant influx of new information and concerns from Surgeons, Doctors, and Specialists. Instead, Sam and I spent our days and nights by Sebastian's bedside, managing Physiotherapy, conducting 4-hourly observations, and adhering to a complex medication schedule of 16 doses every 24 hours. We quickly became walking and talking medical journals for Sebastian, advocating fiercely on his behalf.

Sebastian was now considered 'stable'. Although he still struggled with sleep, mostly due to being woken for medication and observations, he was generally happy and alert. He had started speaking more and was using new words in the correct context each day, which was encouraging.

With Sebastian's condition improving, Sam and I were able to establish a sleep and self-care routine. We realised that full night shifts were too exhausting

---

[2] Australian Institute of Health and Welfare (AIHW) Cancer Data.

given the emotional and mental toll of the Hospital environment. Instead, we opted for three-hour sleep shifts at night and rest periods during the day if Sebastian was asleep. There was a bed in Sebastian's room, so if he did sleep, whoever was with him could also get some additional rest. I had already adapted to sleep deprivation over the past 18 months, so it felt like an extension of our life at home.

Dr. Tim Hassall, the lead Neuro-Oncologist at QCH, encouraged us to take Sebastian out of the Hospital for short periods to benefit his mental and physical well-being. We managed to find a wheelchair and took Sebastian outside for the first time in 21 days. However, our walk down Stanley Street didn't go as planned. While Sebastian had previously been fascinated by cars, bikes, and buses, the noise and commotion of the outside world were overwhelming for him. Every bump and turn in the wheelchair seemed to cause him pain, and it was disheartening to see his discomfort, which starkly contrasted with our hopes that he'd enjoy the city's sights and sounds.

At 21 days post-surgery, we were given the chance to bathe Sebastian in water. We looked forward to this return to normality, but Sebastian did not. Ann-Marie King, Sebastian's Physiotherapist, explained that the droplets of water in the shower could be painful for him and suggested sitting him in a body of water instead. Sitting in water could also be therapeutic for his sore and sensitive limbs, which would be beneficial once Chemotherapy began. Despite only having access to a shower at both the Hospital and Ronald McDonald House, it was still a relief to give Sebastian a wash. He had bed hair, adhesive residue from bandaging, and his skin was stained with pink solution from the surgical procedures.

Some people had noticed from my photo updates that Sebastian was rarely clothed during his Hospital stay. This was because his body struggled to regulate its temperature due to the tumor's location. It became a running joke with the nurses who would repeatedly tuck Sebastian in only to find him kicking off the blankets moments later. The Hospital rooms were freezing at night, and even I struggled to stay warm, so it was unusual to see him dressed in only a nappy and lying on top of all the blankets. The nursing staff must have initially thought we were irresponsible parents until they felt his warm skin and realised that keeping blankets on him was a losing battle.

We were now focused on Friday, February 7th, when Sebastian's 10-day course of Bactrim would end and tests would confirm whether the Meningitis had been successfully treated. As Sebastian's stability improved, our updates to family and friends decreased. It was a relief to shift our focus from challenges and obstacles to celebrating Sebastian's slow but steady improvements.

7:09pm, Tuesday, 4 February 2020

Today we've had lots of meetings with almost all areas of Paediatrics. It feels good to be having these conversations as we begin discussing strategies for when Sebastian leaves Hospital; an equally positive and terrifying notion.

Sebastian's OT, Anshu Sharma, is really impressed by his daily improvements and enthusiasm to move his body. We have been referred to an Orthotist to get Sebastian some Orthopaedic shoes to assist with the limitations in his left foot and leg. Sebastian is already independently throwing his legs and feet forward in an effort to take steps. He is getting stronger every day and is getting closer to holding his own weight (he's not standing unaided yet). When aided (holding both of his hands to help hold his body weight), he is happy to 'walk' around the room and sometimes out into the hallway to 'chase' his Daddy. Obviously, this is something that can't be rushed so we continue to follow Sebastian's cues and allow him to do as much or as little as he can each day.

Today we also met with Claire Radford, Sebastian's Speech Therapist. Claire was impressed by Sebastian's ability to eat unaided, explaining that often facial palsy can take a lot of therapy to enable the sufferer to eat independently. She also expressed that her main area for concern is Sebastian's cosmetic challenges due to the facial palsy. Claire demonstrated some facial exercises we could encourage Sebastian to do as well as making sure he has food like steak and apples, that require his jaw and facial muscles to work hard and therefore strengthen. At this stage, Claire is happy with Sebastian's progress since surgery and doesn't feel that intervention is required at this early stage. She has booked in to review Sebastian in three months' time, to allow for further recovery from surgery and therefore improvements in his facial palsy and speech.

Sebastian is slowly enjoying our outside time more. We managed to find a stroller so we can now walk down to South Bank each afternoon. He's becoming more like his old self each day which is so encouraging and wonderful to see. Lots of love, Sam, Crystal & Sebastian xoxo

> *"Fate whispers to the Warrior;*
> *'You cannot withstand the storm.'*
> *And the Warrior whispers back; 'I am the storm.'"*
> —Unknown—

8:12pm, Thursday, 6 February 2020

Today has been a huge day in our Hospital world with lots of progress and talk about Sebastian becoming an outpatient of QCH.

Firstly though, Sebastian is continuing to improve in leaps and bounds. He is generally happy, hungry and full of cheek. Overall, the medical team is really impressed with his progress and happy to see him looking so well. Sebastian had his NG tube removed yesterday so is not only feeling great but looking great too.

All teams involved in Sebastian's surgery, recovery and treatment have given him approval to become an outpatient of Oncology tomorrow, once his final Bactrim antibiotic is administered at 4pm. The schedule for the next couple of weeks at QCH in Brisbane is as follows:

Friday 7.2.20 - Blood tests, discharge

Monday 10.2.20 - Blood tests

Wednesday 11.2.20 - PICC line removal, meeting with Rick (Oncology) to get blood results

Friday 14.2.20 - Surgery to insert Port-a-cath

Wednesday 19.2.20 – Begin weekly Chemotherapy at QCH and remain in Brisbane for first 5 weeks of treatment. Sebastian can then return home for weekly Chemotherapy at Cairns Hospital, only returning to QCH for Chemotherapy every 28 days, until February 2021.

We will also be required to continue with Sebastian's Physiotherapy and OT sessions, twice a week for the next five weeks here at QCH.

In essence, Sebastian was required to stay in Brisbane for the next 6 weeks as an outpatient of Oncology. Regular tests and treatments necessitated the delay of our return to Cairns Hospital. While Sam and I were cautious not to get ahead of ourselves, we were quietly excited about the prospect of the freedom that being an outpatient would offer. It marked a new chapter where we would need to learn how to navigate life outside the Hospital with a childhood cancer patient, and we felt ready for this transition. As always, I approached this change with more hesitation and trepidation than Sam, but his and Sebastian's bravery inspired me to embrace it.

This phase marked the beginning of our new role as Sebastian's real-world 'medical team'. We were being educated by the QCH team on medications, dosages, administration, emergency plans, schedules, and appointment requirements. We had spreadsheets and procedures printed out for daily use and emergency situations. We would be staying at Ronald McDonald House, conveniently located across the road for proximity to emergency medical assistance.

We had been 'practicing' medicating Sebastian in the Hospital with the support of the nursing staff, but transitioning to managing this on our own was like stepping into a role for which we felt unprepared. It required significant confidence, and I was grateful that Sam's courage carried us both through this challenge. I admired him deeply for his strength and felt incredibly fortunate to have him by my side during this ordeal. The greatest fear in this journey was the unknown, but like the days before, we were prepared to listen, adapt, manage, and remain hopeful.

Remarkably, we were receiving wonderful reports from home about the girls. Both Antonia and Josie had received Student Awards at school, and Alyssa was thriving at kindergarten. Their strength and achievements surprised us daily and filled us with pride.

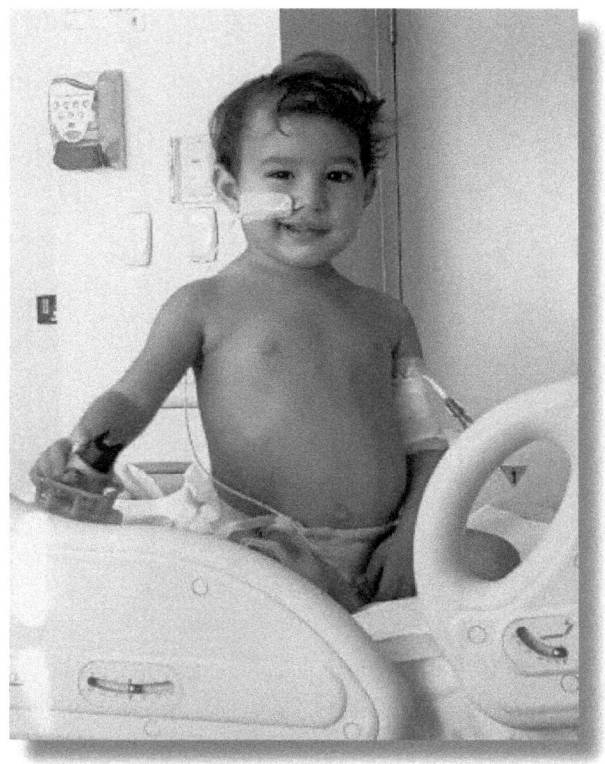

CLARITY - BOOK I

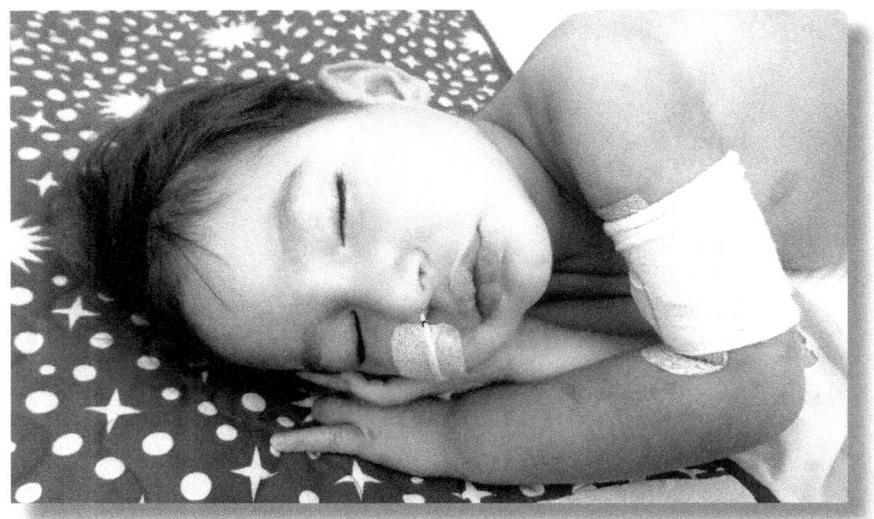

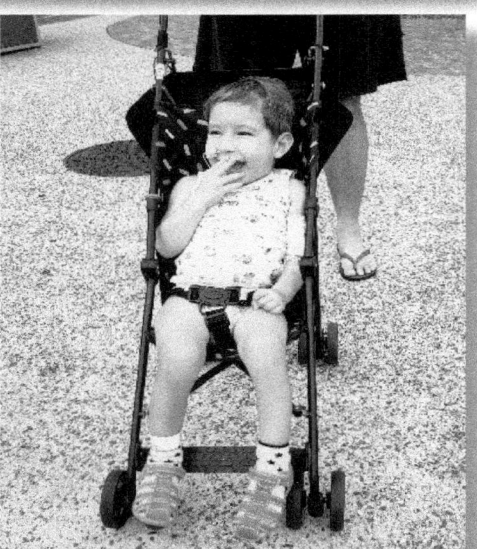

12

PREPARING FOR BATTLE

10:10am, Saturday, 8 February 2020

Well, we made it through our first night out of Hospital without a glitch. We all slept well and Sebastian is loving the more relaxed environment and the absence of the medical staff. We are keeping a low profile and a close eye on him, whilst we await the blood results to confirm that he has successfully recovered from Meningitis.

Yesterday at QCH, we met with the Orthotist who has taken a mould of Sebastian's left leg and foot so he can make him an Orthotic 'boot'. Sebastian is crawling well and pulling himself up into sitting and standing positions but still a way off walking. He should have his Orthotic fitted on Tuesday so we hope he will progress really well next week.

Lots of love, Sam, Crystal & Sebastian xoxo

Tuesday, 11 February 2020

On Tuesday, 11th February, Sebastian had been an outpatient for 4 days and was showing daily improvement. We were hopeful that his blood results would soon confirm that the Meningitis and any infections had cleared, with results expected within the next 24 hours.

The previous day was a mix of emotions as I officially checked Sebastian into Oncology as an outpatient. We were introduced to the chemotherapy ward and met Gemma, our chemotherapy nurse, along with many other friendly faces from Paediatric Oncology. I felt a whirlwind of apprehension and enthusiasm, still struggling to grasp that we were beginning this daunting new chapter in Sebastian's medical journey. While I aimed to be his pillar of support, I often found myself overwhelmed and unable to fully process or control my emotions. It was hard to accept how drastically our lives had changed.

I was relieved, however, when Gemma performed a PICC Line check and physical examination on Sebastian, which he passed with flying colours.

Sebastian's routine sodium and cortisol tests continued to show positive results, suggesting that his body was producing some cortisone hormone on its own. The Endocrinology team advised us to reduce his hormone replacement doses to once a day and to test again in two days to assess his body's response. This was exciting news, as it meant that if Sebastian's adrenal gland was functioning well, he might not need hormone replacement drugs or Omeprazole, which protects his gut from the artificial steroids. This would also mean a reduction in the problematic symptoms associated with steroids.

The Endocrinology team also decided to increase Sebastian's Desmopressin dosage, as his body was still struggling to regulate its fluid input and output. This adjustment showed immediate results, although we remained cautious due to past difficulties in managing his Diabetes Insipidus (DI). Each case of DI is unique, and we hoped that, eventually, managing it would become easier.

Living at Ronald McDonald House was bringing us a sense of ease and relaxation. We believed that Sebastian's continued improvement was due in part to the comfort of being with Mum and Dad and the absence of strangers, which allowed him to enjoy uninterrupted sleep. Our days were spent walking along South Bank, enjoying the scenery and occasional visitors to lift our spirits.

As we prepared for the next phase of Sebastian's treatment, it felt like gearing up for battle. Nerves were high, time seemed to crawl, and the anticipated cancer 'War' was daunting. We were on the front lines, determined not to back down, even though it felt like we were outnumbered.

12:09pm, Wednesday, 12 February 2020

We are thrilled and overjoyed to let you know that Sebastian is all clear of Meningitis and any infection in his body. As a result, today Sebastian's PICC Line will be removed by the Veins team, in preparation for surgery in two days. The Port-a-cath will be surgically inserted on Friday, at 7am here at QCH. If all goes well on Friday, we can expect Sebastian to begin chemotherapy on Wednesday 19th February.

Thanks to everyone for your continued love and support, for all the calls and visitors and for loving our little boy. Will be in touch on Friday to keep you updated on his surgery.

Lots of love, Sam, Crystal & Sebastian xoxo

Thursday, 13 February 2020

After a successful day on Wednesday, Sam and I decided it was a good time for me to return home to recuperate before Sebastian started chemotherapy. I was deeply missing the girls, and the urge to be with them was becoming overwhelming. When Aunty Julie picked me up for the airport, I felt an intense guilt for leaving Sebastian. It hadn't dawned on me until that moment that I was leaving him behind. I was so focused on seeing my girls that I didn't fully process the separation. I cried all the way to the airport, telling Julie how I felt like a terrible mother for leaving Sebastian when he was so unwell. The conflict of needing to be with my children in different ways was heart-wrenching. Aunty Julie's support helped me navigate my guilt, reminding me that while Sebastian was in good hands with Sam, it was okay to want to be with the girls too.

I was heading home for five days, and the girls had no idea I was coming, making our reunion unforgettable. Alyssa, who was three, was particularly overwhelmed and reluctant to let me go once I was home. Her young age and the impact of my absence were deeply concerning.

Upon reuniting with them, it was painfully clear how troubled they had been. Antonia, who was nine, immediately started crying and apologising for what she saw as her failures to be a "good girl." She expressed deep guilt for not helping enough and for being a "bad sister," which broke my heart. She also shared her distressing nightmares about Sebastian dying and bed-wetting, which she hadn't experienced for six years. Josie and Alyssa had numerous questions about when Sam and I would return full-time and if Sebastian would ever come home. Their worries were overwhelming, and once again, I wished I could take their pain away, just as I wished for Sebastian's.

I answered their questions as honestly as I could, recalling advice from Katie, our Social Worker at QCH, who said that it's crucial to communicate openly with siblings of sick children, as their imaginations often make things worse than reality. While some conversations were challenging, the girls mainly sought comfort and reassurance that one day we would all be together again. I still struggle with guilt about how little we communicated with them initially and wish I had done more to address their fears and offer reassurance. I was afraid of how to answer their tough questions and worried that the truth might be too hard for them to handle. However, I realised that children are often more resilient and braver than adults and can face adversity with remarkable strength.

Being home felt strange. The house seemed larger, and the farm more beautiful than I remembered. The comforting smells of home soothed my soul, and for the first time since January 8th, I felt secure and safe. My perspective had shifted; the need to maintain a clean and tidy home no longer mattered. I wanted to focus on spending quality time with my children, enjoying simple moments, and being a more spontaneous "yes Mum."

When it was time to leave, I arranged for my Mum to stay with the girls at the farm to provide them with a familiar environment. The morning of Tuesday, 18th February was one of the most emotional of my life. Leaving the girls in tears, clinging to their teachers, was heart-wrenching. I knew I had to return to Sebastian, but it was incredibly hard to say goodbye. As I drove to Cairns for my flight back to Brisbane, I was overwhelmed by anger. My sorrow had transformed into a deep, uncontrollable anger at the cancer and its unfairness. I was devastated by how Sebastian had been robbed of his innocence and how I had lost the joy of raising him as I had with my previous children. The reality of being separated from my girls and the uncertainty of Sebastian's diagnosis felt unbearable.

I called my Mum during the drive, unable to escape my negative thoughts. Her understanding and comforting words helped me regain control. She reminded me that Sebastian had the best chance because Sam and I were his parents. Despite the emotional rollercoaster, Sam and I were determined not to give up. The conversation helped calm me, and I arrived back in Brisbane exhausted but eager to catch up with Katie at QCH to discuss the girls and my swirling emotions. I realised that it was okay to let my emotions out and cry. I had cried a lot already, and there would be more to come, but I needed to accept and embrace it.

Meanwhile, Sam and Sebastian were enjoying their "boys' weekend," and updates continued...

8:40pm, Friday, 14 February 2020

Sebastian has completed his Port-a-cath surgery today and is now resting back at Ronald McDonald House, coping well with his new 'hardware'. The Port will be 'accessed' for the first time on Monday during his regular sodium and cortisol level testing at QCH. Also on Monday, the Endocrinology team have ordered another challenge to Sebastian's adrenal gland to check it's response to stress. This will confirm whether or not his body has managed its cortisol levels since the reduction in

Hydrocortisone (artificial steroid) earlier this week.

Almost miraculously, Sebastian has woken this morning with the urge and ability to walk! He is now walking around the room in Ronald McDonald House and using his left hand very well. We were told to expect slow improvements over time with lots of physiotherapy so it is just wonderful and almost miraculous that he is recovering so quickly and feeling well enough to walk. It's astonishing just how much improvement we are seeing in his physical ability since surgery on 12th January. Sebastian continues to surprise us with how strong he is, both physically and mentally.

Lots of love, Sam, Crystal & Sebastian xoxo

5:16pm, Monday, 17 February 2020

Sebastian is doing really well after his Port was accessed this morning for the first time during his blood tests and Cortisol challenge. We should find out the results of these tests on Wednesday when we meet with Rick (Oncology), before commencing chemotherapy.

I return to Brisbane tomorrow after the most wonderful time at home with my girls. We didn't get to catch up with many of you as all three girls had either a cold and/or gastro. It sounds horrible but they are ok and I think their little bodies just totally relaxed and released with the comfort and security they received when I returned home. All three girls are feeling much better this morning, other than feeling anxious about my departure tomorrow. They all said they had butterflies in their tummies and feel sad that I can't stay but we've had lots of chats and cuddles and I think they have more understanding about why I need to be with Sebastian in Brisbane at the moment. They really are being so brave. They'll remain at home on the farm this week with Mum and then return to Mareeba next week with Gail and Sebastian (Snr).

For those of you who we did catch up with, thank you for your warm hugs and listening ears. It's been lovely to feel everyone's support in person after being away for so long.

I am looking forward to returning to Sam and Sebastian tomorrow, back to business and getting our little boy well enough to come home. My focus has shifted to getting our family back together as quickly and safely as possible so I'm hoping with all of my heart that this next chapter in our journey goes smoothly.

Please keep us and our little treasure in your thoughts this week, we need every bit of strength we can get.

Lots of love, Sam, Crystal & Sebastian xoxo

> *"If we all could see the world through the eyes of a child, we would see the magic in everything."*
>
> -Chee Vai Tang-

13

THE BATTLE BEGINS

Wednesday, 19 February 2020

Chemotherapy Cycle I, Treatment #1, Day 1.

It was a significant day for us all. Sebastian managed his first chemotherapy session remarkably well, displaying the resilience of a typical two-year-old despite the circumstances. He began his 12-cycle chemotherapy regimen with the first of four weekly treatments. The intensity of the treatment took us by surprise. It involved administering two drugs, Vincristine and Carboplatin, over about five hours, including three hours of hyperhydration.

Despite the daunting process, Sebastian did incredibly well. He had been premedicated to counteract the common side effects of chemotherapy, such as nausea, vomiting, pain, headaches, and fatigue. We anticipated that he might start experiencing these side effects in the coming days.

Sebastian's chemotherapy schedule is as follows:

Cycle #:	Date Administered:	Drug:
Cycle 1	19 February 2020	Carboplatin & Vincristine
	26 February 2020	Vincristine
	04 March 2020	Vincristine
	11 March 2020	Vincristine
Cycle 2	18 March 2020	Carboplatin & Vincristine
	25 March 2020	Vincristine
	01 April 2020	Vincristine
Cycle 3	15 April 2020	Carboplatin & Vincristine
Cycle 4	13 May 2020	Carboplatin & Vincristine
Cycle 5	10 June 2020	Carboplatin & Vincristine
Cycle 6	08 July 2020	Carboplatin & Vincristine
Cycle 7	05 August 2020	Carboplatin & Vincristine
Cycle 8	02 September 2020	Carboplatin & Vincristine
Cycle 9	30 September 2020	Carboplatin & Vincristine
Cycle 10	28 October 2020	Carboplatin & Vincristine
Cycle 11	25 November 2020	Carboplatin & Vincristine
Cycle 12	23 December 2020	Carboplatin & Vincristine

While in Oncology, we received Sebastian's results from the Cortisol challenge. The results indicated that his body was now producing the stress hormone Cortisol on its own, so he no longer required the drugs Hydrocortisone (a steroid) and Omeprazole (a gut protector against artificial steroids). We could discontinue both medications immediately, as he was already on the lowest dose. Sam and I were thrilled with this outcome; it meant one less concern and responsibility for us as his medical team.

Many people had noticed Sebastian's sudden weight gain—he had gained 5kg in just five weeks—which was a direct result of the steroid medication, fluid retention, and increased appetite. The constant eating was causing him considerable discomfort, so we looked forward to him finding relief in the coming days as the effects of the medication began to diminish.

9:15pm, Thursday, 20 February 2020

Today we've spent a few hours back at QCH after Sebastian had a fever just before noon. Unfortunately, I gave Sebastian some Panadol at this time, which brought down the fever initially. After consulting with Oncology, I was reminded that with Oncology patients, it's important not to treat fevers and to call Oncology only if the fever persists for more than 1 hour. Important lesson learnt today! The return of the fever at 5pm was evidence that the Panadol had possibly masked something more serious. Oncology then requested that we take Sebastian over to QCH Emergency where he was monitored in Triage until his fever dropped by about 8pm. A dose of antibiotics was administered and blood cultures taken as a precaution. We have now returned to Ronald McDonald House but have been asked to present to Oncology in the morning for further monitoring and investigation.

Unfortunately, poor Sebastian is also getting his two-year molars so hasn't had the best of days. He has also been really lethargic after chemotherapy yesterday so we've all managed to catch up on much needed sleep.

Tomorrow we will spend time in the Hospital but otherwise keep a very low profile to ensure Sebastian is given the best chance to recover from yesterday's chemotherapy treatment.

Lots of love, Sam, Crystal & Sebastian xoxo

Monday, 24 February 2020

Over the next few days, Sebastian developed a cold and cough, which might explain the spike in his fever the previous week. Despite this, we managed to meet with Sebastian's Physiotherapist, Ann-Marie, on Friday. She was thrilled to see Sebastian walking for the first time. We were also delighted to have his Orthotic boot fitted on Friday, which showed an immediate improvement in his leg tone and foot flex, particularly in his heel. Although Sebastian had some trouble walking with the Orthotic, he was happy to wear it for the recommended half hour a day.

In general, Sebastian hadn't been himself after his first chemotherapy treatment, particularly on days 1, 2, and 3. He was lethargic at times and quite unsteady on his feet. Despite having bursts of energy typical of a two-year-old, he fatigued quickly and became exhausted with minimal stimulation.

Unfortunately, his Desmopressin medication hadn't been effective since the chemotherapy, contributing to his irritability. He was urinating much more frequently, especially at night, which led to very long, sleepless nights for us all. Endocrinology requested a test of Sebastian's sodium levels. We had been warned that Desmopressin was a particularly challenging drug to manage, but we didn't anticipate how volatile it would be after chemotherapy. It seemed effective for three to four days before requiring further adjustment. Additionally, Vincristine, one of the chemotherapy drugs, can act as a diuretic, potentially affecting Desmopressin's effectiveness. We eagerly awaited the sodium results and hoped the Endocrinology team had a plan to address these issues.

Over the weekend, we had the chance to spend time with Aunty Julie and Uncle Brendan at their home in East Brisbane. It was heart-warming for us all. We missed sharing meals with family and engaging in conversation and banter around the table, so it was wonderful to experience that after so long in Hospitals and Hospital accommodations.

14

ALL OF A SUDDEN, PURE JOY

Wednesday, 26 February 2020

Chemotherapy Cycle I, Treatment #2, Day 8.

By Wednesday, 26th February, I had caught Sebastian's cold, and we were both feeling pretty lousy. Along with his usual medical checks before starting treatment, Rick checked Sebastian's chest, which was clear, so chemotherapy was approved to proceed.

Rick surprised us with the news that we might be able to return home sooner than expected. The Cairns Hospital's Oncology Unit had approved administering Sebastian's weekly Vincristine infusions. This meant we would need to return to QCH for the start of his 2nd cycle on 18th March, but he could receive treatment in Cairns in the meantime. Rick had arranged a 6-week post-op review with Neurology for the following day and agreed to let us return home if the Neurology team was satisfied with Sebastian's recovery and progress.

On Thursday, 27th February, we met with Dr Ahmad, one of the Neurosurgeons who had operated on Sebastian on 12th January 2020. Overall, he was pleased with Sebastian's recovery, particularly the improvement in his left side hemiplegia and the healing of his surgical incisions. Dr Ahmad explained that, based on advice from Oncology, the Neurology team was happy for Sebastian to return home as soon as possible. However, there were a few issues to address first, and the team needed to ensure Sam and I understood what was forecast for Sebastian and the possible complications we might face.

Dr Ahmad showed us Sebastian's last CT Scan images from 26th January, which revealed that one of the brain's ventricles was still being squeezed, either by the tumour or swelling from the surgery. He explained that the brain's four ventricles produce, transport, and remove fluid around the brain and spine. If a ventricle became blocked, it could cause fluid buildup, increased pressure, acute pain, and a rapid decline in Sebastian's health. Additionally, chemotherapy could complicate recovery and potentially block a ventricle due to tumour disturbance. We were advised to monitor Sebastian closely and act swiftly if he became lethargic or unwell. It was crucial to contact QCH anytime if we had concerns to ensure the most effective actions were taken to keep Sebastian safe.

We also discussed the possibility of a shunt, which might be needed if a ventricle blocked completely or Sebastian became clinically unstable again. A shunt could be installed via emergency surgery if necessary, and Sebastian would be airlifted by RFDS to QCH for surgery by Gert. This was a relief and provided comfort knowing we would return to the excellent care at QCH. Ideally, Sebastian would remain stable and have MRIs and Neurology reviews every three months during chemotherapy.

The remaining cyst behind Sebastian's temporal lobe was also discussed. We were informed that Gert was keen to surgically remove the cyst but would wait for the results of the next MRI, scheduled for mid-March. The team hoped the cyst would resolve with chemotherapy, as further surgery would delay treatment until Sebastian fully recovered.

Sam and I left Neurology elated and headed straight to Patient Travel on level 6 at QCH to arrange our flights home. The first available flights were the following morning, so we quickly packed up our room at Ronald McDonald

House and organised paperwork and medications for Sebastian. We were overjoyed to finally be taking our baby home.

9:17am, Friday, 28 February 2020

Once chemotherapy was completed on Wednesday, Sebastian's medical team unexpectedly gave him the all clear to leave Brisbane, so in the early hours of this morning, we boarded a Virgin Australia plane and began our long journey home! Sebastian has now been away from home for 50 days, or 7 weeks and 1 day, so the excitement around taking him home feels beyond triumphant.

Sebastian will now receive chemotherapy treatment in Cairns on a weekly basis, returning to QCH on 18th March to commence Cycle 2 of 12.

Before leaving QCH, Sebastian's thyroid and sodium were tested again and the levels were good. His Diabetes Insipidus is still an ongoing issue but we are doing our best to patiently manage it, with the aid of the Endocrinology team. For now, we are thankful that Sebastian is 'self-regulating' which means he drinks to thirst, preventing dehydration, which can happen very quickly when he has urine outputs of up to 2.6L in a single night. We just hope that the brilliant minds at QCH strategise and come up with a solution to this very complicated condition as soon as possible.

For the first time last night, Sebastian was able to communicate where his pain was coming from by rubbing his forehead when I asked him where it was hurting. He then did the same during the night by rubbing his tummy, I assume because of nausea or stomach pain. This is a huge help and relief to us as his carers as one of our biggest challenges has been the inability to identify where Sebastian's pain or discomfort was coming from.

It's so hard not to feel sorry for the poor little fella these days. He has been faced with so much and evidence of this can now be seen in his hair loss. It seems to be thinning and falling out in patches. For now, we've decided to let him enjoy his hair and let it fall out naturally rather than shave it. As a result, it's looking very ordinary but we don't care, it's the least of our worries.

I will keep sending updates as we have news. Please keep in touch and hold Sebastian in your thoughts as we take him home and reunite with his sisters. Love to you all and especially to everyone who made our stay in Brisbane so comfortable. Everyone's generosity and concern will remain with us forever.

Lots of love, Sam, Crystal & Sebastian xoxo

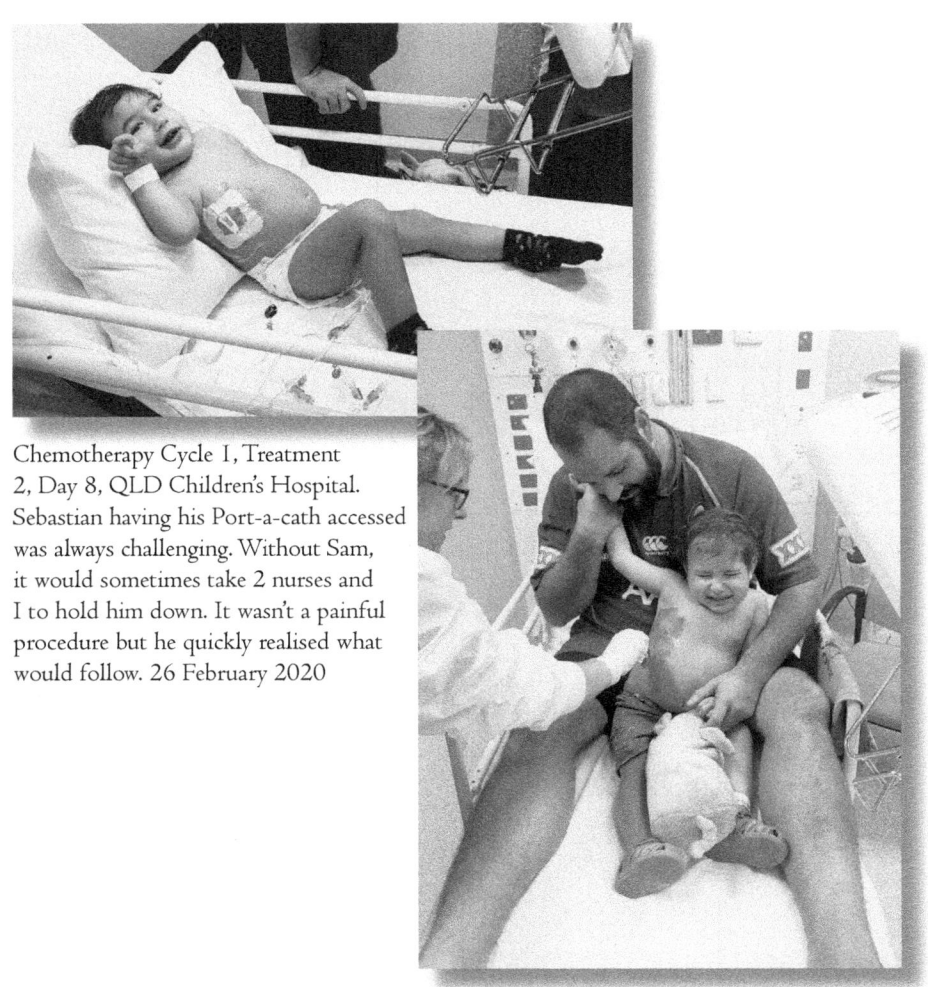

Chemotherapy Cycle 1, Treatment 2, Day 8, QLD Children's Hospital. Sebastian having his Port-a-cath accessed was always challenging. Without Sam, it would sometimes take 2 nurses and I to hold him down. It wasn't a painful procedure but he quickly realised what would follow. 26 February 2020

Timeline of Events: February 2020

01.02.2020	Sebastian's 1st wash in water since 12th January 2020.
02.02.2020	Sebastian's 1st time outside QCH since 12th January 2020.
04.02.2020	Sebastian starts walking around his Hospital room with the aid of someone holding both of his hands. 1st meeting with Claire Radcliffe, Speech Therapist.
05.02.2020	NG Tube removed.
07.02.2020	Orthotist takes mould of Sebastian's left foot and leg. Discharged from QCH, move to Ronald McDonald House
10.02.2020	Check in to QCH Oncology as Outpatient.
12.02.2020	Cleared of Meningitis. PICC Line removed.
13.02.2020	Crystal goes home to Julatten.
14.02.2020	Sebastian walks unaided for the 1st time since 12.01.20. Port-a-cath surgery at QCH
18.02.2020	Crystal returns to Brisbane.
19.02.2020	Chemotherapy begins: Cycle 1, Treatment 1, Day 1.
20.02.2020	Sebastian admitted to QCH emergency after fever, discharged later that night.
21.02.2020	Sebastian and Crystal contract cold.
26.02.2020	Chemotherapy Cycle 1, Treatment 2, Day 8.
27.02.2020	Neurology review - 6 weeks post-op. Sebastian's hair begins to fall out.
28.02.2020	Sam, Crystal & Sebastian fly home to Julatten.
Total COVID-19 confirmed cased in QLD as at 28.02.2020 = 9	

Messages of Love

The messages of support continued to flow. We were so blessed to have so many supportive people in our lives, lifting our spirits and filling our hearts with love and hope.

"They (Antonia, Josie, Alyssa and Sebastian) definitely get their strength from you guys! I said to my husband just the other day that you always manage to frame everything in such a positive way even though you must be out of your minds with worry! You are both absolutely amazing. So happy to hear Sebastian is doing well so far."

"Sebby is very lucky to have such caring, strong and resilient parents. Crystal and Sam, if you ever need anything from us, please don't hesitate to give us a holla. Please continue to keep us updated."

"You guys will do an amazing job. The Hospital is one big security blanket. You guys have been caring and advocating for little Sebby this entire time. You guys have got this! New road ahead but if there was ever a pair to handle it – it's you two."

"Yippee... best news, made my crappy day perfect again!! So happy for you all."

"Love the good news he is as tough as nails. Love seeing him looking so happy."

"Omg Crystal I just had the biggest smile for Sebastian when I opened the message and saw him standing. Hopefully the next few days aren't too rough. Hugs and kisses and all the wishes for you guys x"

"Keep going little champ. Also just letting you know the girls were all smiles at school today. I was a little worried they may be a bit sad, which I'm sure they are in their own way. Definitely not showing it at school, as I'm sure being around their friends keeps them preoccupied for now... they were so blessed to have you home for the short visit to reassure them and have mummy time! All of your babies are amazing, keep going team Sebby. Take time to breathe for now and move forward on this journey."

"Good on ya folks, so lovely to see the little man so happy, that made my day."

"Oh Crystal, what a journey! So much love and strength to you guys. Enjoy being home. I bet it's never felt so good to be home!"

"So happy for you to be taking your little boy home. Being a complete family again will be the best medicine."

"There is no exercise better for the heart than reaching down and lifting people up."
-John Holmes-

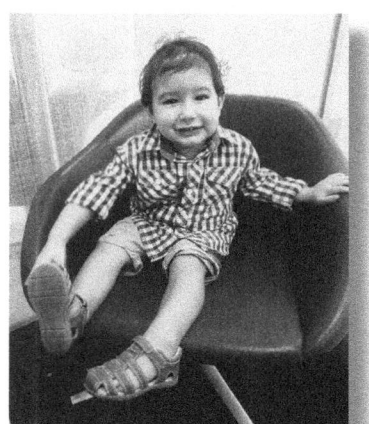

Leaving for home after 50 days away on 28 February 2020 and Sebastian, Josephine and Alyssa enjoying the calm of home on 29 February 2020 (below)

PART 3

Fact: As of 2023, Australia continues to have one of the highest rates of childhood cancer globally, with around 50% of all children diagnosed being under the age of 5. This highlights the significant impact of childhood cancer in this age group.[3]

15

INSIDE OUT & UPSIDE DOWN

1:00am, Wednesday, 4 March 2020

Thank you to everyone for your messages of concern and support since our return home on Friday. For the most part, reuniting as a family has been really healing and much needed for all of us.

Unfortunately, over the last few days Sebastian hasn't been quite himself. On Monday night, after he was difficult to wake after a 5-hour nap, Sam and I decided to get advice from QCH Oncology who recommended we take him into Mossman Hospital. On arrival, a full set of tests were completed under the instruction of QCH and he was admitted for observation until test results were available. By Tuesday morning Sebastian was vomiting, as well as remaining irritable and very lethargic. An X-ray of his chest was completed to check the status of his lungs in light of him having a cold and cough for 10 days now. The X-ray was clear so pneumonia or any other respiratory infections were ruled out. By noon on Tuesday, all other test results had arrived and were clear. By process of elimination, Sebastian's brain was then identified as the area of concern. With lights and sirens and the quickest

---

[3] Australian Institute of Health and Welfare (AIHW) Cancer Data.

trip to Cairns I've ever had, Sebastian was transported via ambulance to Cairns Hospital where he had a CT Scan under sedation as soon as we arrived. Sadly, the CT Scan revealed a spontaneous intracerebral haemorrhage - bleeding in the left lateral ventricle in his brain. As a result, and as predicted by Ahmad only a few days ago, Sebastian was experiencing increased pressure on the brain, which explained his symptoms and steady decline over the past couple of days. The cause of the bleed is still unclear but we will find out when our Neurology team at QCH examine Sebastian today. Now a patient of Neurology at QCH again, Sebastian and I will return to Brisbane via Royal Flying Doctors today. For now, he is in the Cairns Hospital Intensive Care Unit (ICU).

Sam and I have so many questions and are unsure about what this all means for Sebastian. From what information we have been given though, this may mean Sebastian will undergo surgery soon after his return to QCH, to install a shunt into his brain. I will keep you informed as more information comes to hand.

Sam will remain at home to look after the girls who really need some stability in their lives after such a turbulent start to this year already. Unfortunately, this new twist in Sebastian's journey is hitting the girls hard and we continue to hold great concern for them and their emotional wellbeing. Sebastian's decline and return to Hospital was a big blow for the girls, who were really enjoying the comfort and security of having us all back together again. I will return to Brisbane with Sebastian today and make a plan once we have more information about surgery and what impact this is going to have on Sebastian's chemotherapy schedule.

Our minds and hearts are racing with this new diagnosis but we expect to find relief in the expertise of our QCH Neurology and Oncology teams who haven't let us down in the past. As I said, we will keep everyone updated as much as possible and deliver as much information as soon as we can.

Lots of love, Sam, Crystal & Sebastian xoxo

Upon returning to QCH, I was overwhelmed with numbness and shock at the sudden medical emergency we were facing again. I dreaded being back on level 11a (Room 1), as I had mentally closed that chapter and was relieved to have moved past the long, sleepless nights, cabin fever, mediocre food, and endless hours staring out the Hospital room window. It was surreal to be back so soon, but at least the surroundings and medical staff were familiar.

By Thursday, 5th March, we had arrived back at QCH via RFDS. Reflecting on the past 24-48 hours, it was reassuring to acknowledge how well Mossman and Cairns Hospitals followed QCH's instructions during Sebastian's decline. From the nursing staff to the ambulance crew, ICU nurses, and the RFDS team, every individual demonstrated exceptional competence and care. This gave us some much-needed confidence in our local medical services.

Upon arrival at QCH, I had meetings with the Oncology and Neurology teams, who confirmed the results from the CT scan conducted at Cairns Hospital the previous day. The Neurology team expressed concern about the source of the bleed, why it began, and whether it had stopped. Given Sebastian's overnight improvement, it was presumed that the bleed had not completely blocked the ventricle nerve, allowing cerebrospinal fluid (CSF) to continue flowing. An MRI, scheduled for later that day, would confirm this.

Oncology was focused on the risk of continuing as an outpatient during Sebastian's initial intensive chemotherapy treatment (weekly) and whether sending us home again would be viable. Sebastian's recovery, or lack thereof, over the next 24-48 hours would also factor into this decision.

4:43pm, Friday, 6 March 2020

Sebastian's MRI has been completed and has confirmed the site of the bleed to be isolated to the ventricle that appeared to be compromised by the tumour as discussed with Ahmad at our review last week. The blood in the ventricle appears to be 'organising' which means it has oozed (rather that squirted) blood during the bleed and is now converting into something resembling a 'scab'. This is reassuring and indicates that the bleed has now stopped. The source of the bleed appears to be from either the tumour or cyst, both of which have shown evidence of bleeding in the past, as discovered in the CT scan images from 10th January 2020.

Because the bleed has appeared to have stopped, Neurology are monitoring Sebastian's clinical status before they determine a treatment plan. If symptoms were to persist and become unmanageable with basic pain relief (Panadol), the team plan to surgically insert an EVD (External Ventricular Drain) again, to drain any blocked CSF and blood. Unfortunately, it is highly likely that Sebastian would then need a shunt.

Additionally, there is some long-term concern about Sebastian developing Hydrocephalus which is an enlargement of the ventricles due to further blockages of CSF. Realistically, the team believe the development of Hydrocephalus is possible but the probability of it happening decreases with each chemotherapy treatment, which is promising in Sebastian's case.

For now, the Neurology team's advice is that the bleed will be irritating his brain and the addition of protein in his head will cause him pain and discomfort. However, they anticipate that his symptoms should ease over the next few days.

Also included in the MRI report were two positives findings; 1. Sebastian is low risk for a stroke as his 'Circle of Willis' is showing full and flowing arteries inside the brain with no obstructions or clots and 2. because the bleeding is coming from the tumour or cyst, it's also low risk for causing permanent brain damage.

Just as an additional little challenge this week, yesterday Sebastian's Port-a-cath failed while being accessed in Triage at QCH. There are two reasons why a Port-a-cath fails;

1. Thrombosis (blood clot in the catheter) or

2. Mechanical failure. Troubleshooting is ongoing but unfortunately both outcomes would need the Port to be replaced. We are on our final attempt to correct the failure

today, but if it doesn't correct the Safety Team will be called in to assess the Port and it's replacement.

Chemotherapy has been paused for this week but will be made up when treatment recommences.

Sebastian has not been very well today. He has bouts of irritability and fatigue, mixed in with vomiting episodes. It's obvious he is suffering from pain and discomfort so he is really unsettled at the moment. Please keep him in your thoughts, we all need the warmth of your love at this difficult time.

Lots of love, Sam, Crystal & Sebastian xoxo

> "Hard times don't create heroes. It is during the hard times when the hero within us is revealed."
> -Bob Riley-

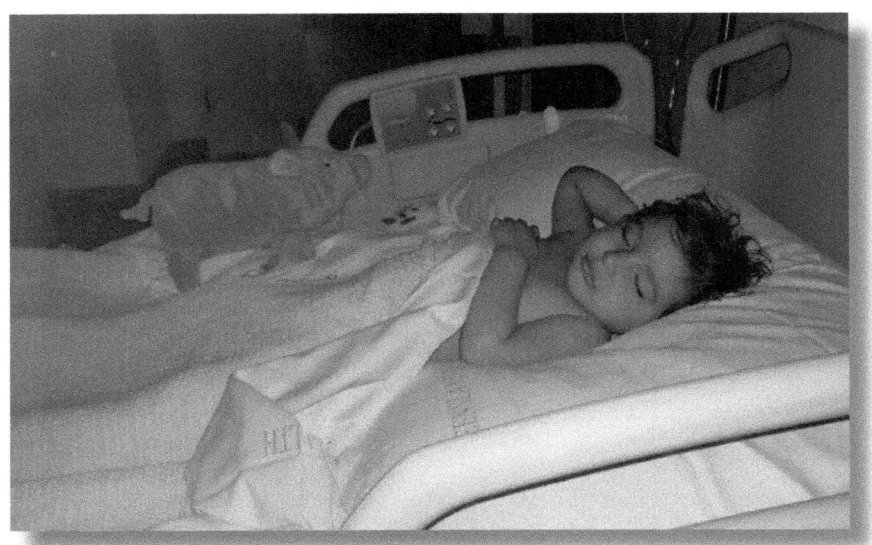

Admitted to Mossman Hospital, 2 March 2020

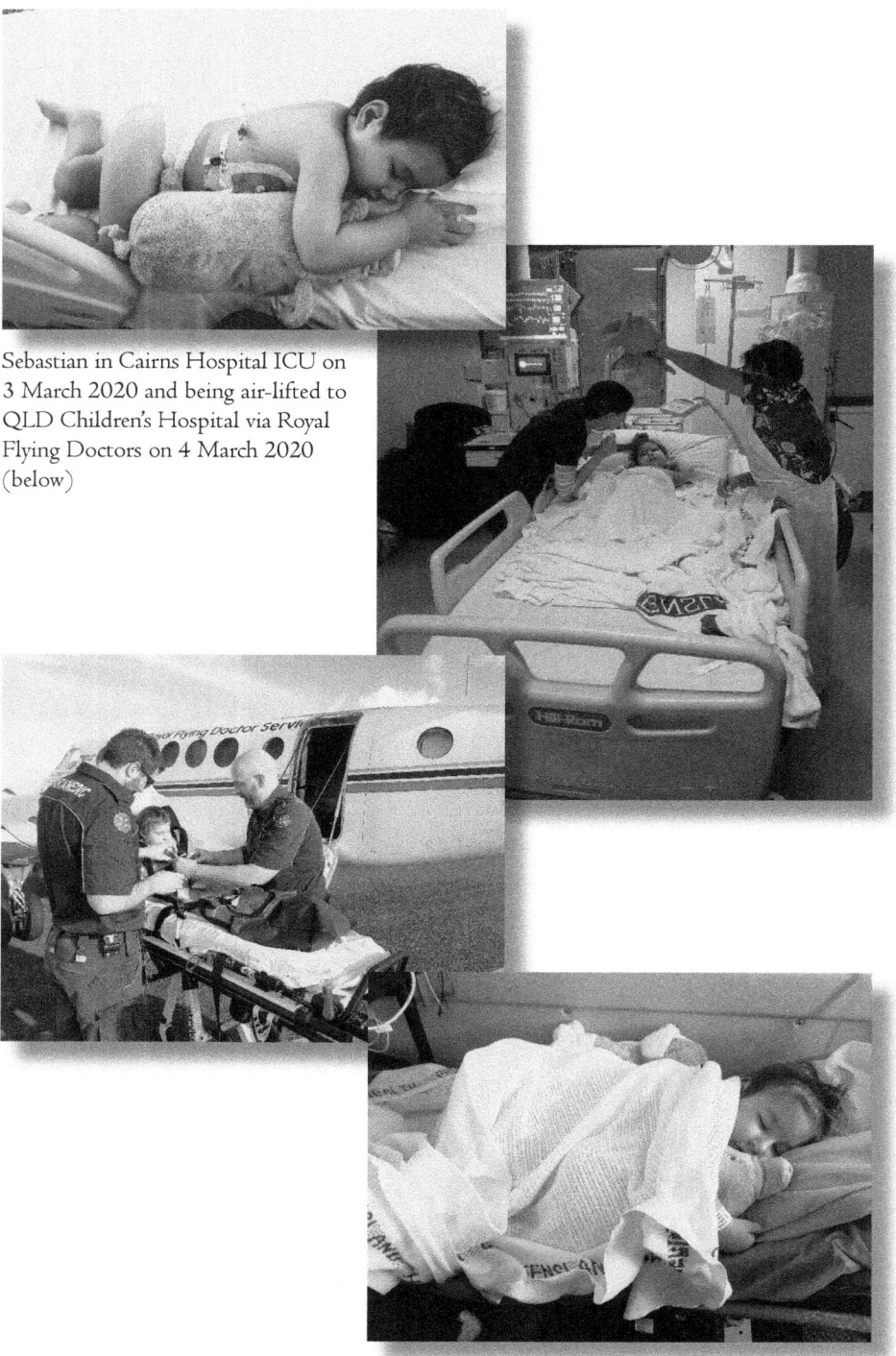

Sebastian in Cairns Hospital ICU on 3 March 2020 and being air-lifted to QLD Children's Hospital via Royal Flying Doctors on 4 March 2020 (below)

Boy of Steel: Little Sebastian's Big Miracle

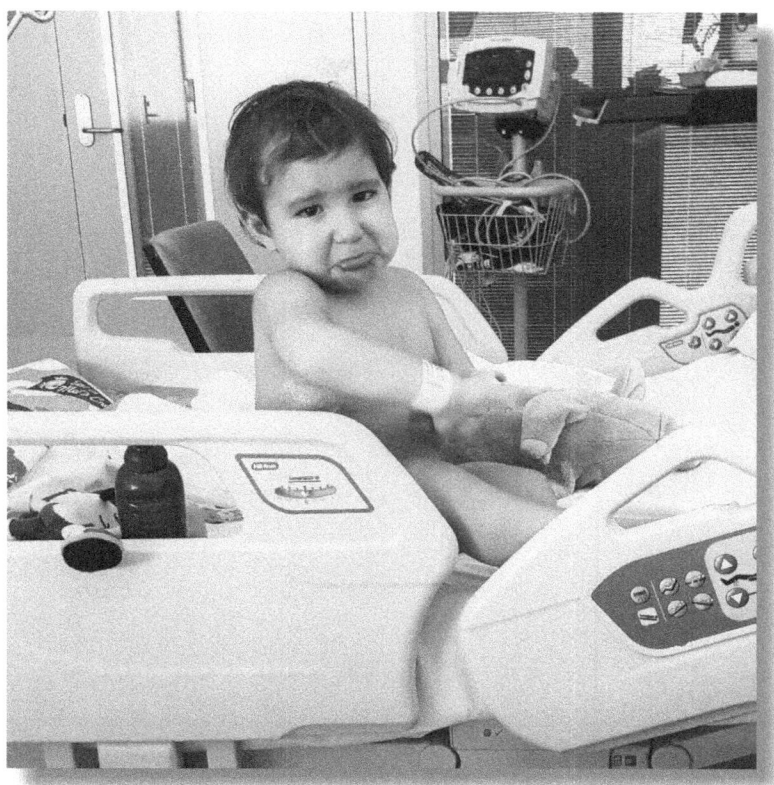

Our sudden and unexpected return to QLD Children's Hospital

16

THE WUHAN EFFECT

Sunday, 8 March 2020

On Sunday, 8th March, we were relieved when the final attempt to correct the failing Port succeeded after clearing a small clot in the line. With the cannula in Sebastian's foot removed, the Port was flowing again, bringing great comfort, especially to Sebastian, who had struggled with the extra cannula affecting his ability to walk.

In positive news, Sebastian's DI treatment showed improvement over the previous 48 hours. The Endocrinology team noted that the absence of chemotherapy this week might have allowed the Desmopressin drug to work more effectively.

Since stopping the steroids, Sebastian's 'puffiness' had noticeably decreased. His taste palette, affected by chemotherapy, had shifted to a craving for mostly salty foods like crackers and Twisties. He still enjoyed cheese, chicken, dry toast, and pasta, but his choices were limited. The Dietician was pleased that he retained an appetite despite the chemotherapy and encouraged me to feed him whatever he was willing to eat.

On 8th March, I also met with Dr. Tim Hassall, the Head of Neuro-Oncology at QCH and Clinical Leader for the Child and Adolescent Brain Cancer Research Centre in Queensland. Dr. Hassall provided valuable reassurance, explaining that in the first 7 days post-ventricle bleed, Sebastian was at high risk for further bleeds. From days 7 to 14, he would need close monitoring for Hydrocephalus (ventricle blockage). With Sebastian 6 days post-bleed and showing no worsening symptoms, the Neurology and Oncology teams agreed the next day (Monday 9th March) that he could safely resume outpatient status with chemotherapy scheduled at QCH on Wednesday, 11th March.

To remain close to QCH while avoiding the Hospital environment and clusters of people due to the rising COVID-19 cases in Australia, we chose to stay with Aunty Julie and Uncle Brendan rather than at Ronald McDonald House. Their home, 7 km from the Hospital, provided Sebastian with a safe space to explore, play, and watch boats, away from the Hospital's confines.

Back home, Sam and the girls were managing well. Pam (my mother-in-law) and Mum were alternating in helping Sam so he could continue working. We received wonderful support and offers of help from local friends, which was greatly appreciated. It was comforting to know that while I was with Sebastian, Sam and the girls were fully supported at home, work, and school.

4:00pm, Wednesday, 11 March 2020

Chemotherapy Cycle I, Treatment #3, Day 22.

This morning I was woken by a sweet little boy giving me a kiss for the first time. He melts my heart with his loving and gentle nature and it's so uplifting to finally see him improving.

We went into QCH this morning and met with Rick before commencing chemotherapy. Unfortunately, Rick had some really upsetting news for us. It took all my strength to hold back the tears when he said that together with the Neurology team, it's been decided that it's not safe for Sebastian to return home until his weekly chemotherapy treatments are complete, therefore cancelling all of Sebastian's scheduled treatments at Cairns Hospital. The reason behind this decision is that unusually, Sebastian didn't make it through his 1st cycle of chemotherapy before a bleed occurred. It leaves them little hope that it won't happen again and places him at high risk, especially during his more intense portion of chemotherapy treatments. Sebastian will have a CT Scan of his brain on Monday to get a baseline status to work from. He will then have the next three weekly chemotherapy treatments here at QCH followed by an MRI to monitor how the tumour and cyst are being impacted. There is no talk of our return home at this stage but based on the chemotherapy schedule, we may be able to temporarily leave Brisbane by 8th April, another 28 days away.

Positivity is the only way to get through this so I have to feel thankful that we have such a diligent and expert team looking after our little boy, ensuring his safety is paramount. We have been approved to stay close by with family, so it's not all bad. Aunty Julie and Uncle Brendan have been kind enough to let us stay on for another month in their beautiful home where Sebastian feels relaxed, safe and comfortable.

If anyone sees my girls this week, please give them an extra tight squeeze. Their little hearts are broken at the news we cannot return home as quickly as we first thought. I just wish I could be there for them, in every sense of the word. Sam's doing an incredible job but all of our hearts are heavy with the seriousness of what Sebastian is going through and the constant changes and unknowns.

Tomorrow Sebastian is having his eye sight checked again with the Ophthalmology team, looking for any changes since his last tests, prior to surgery and the commencement of chemotherapy.

We will also continue Physiotherapy with Anne-Marie King at QCH during our extended stay in Brisbane.

Lots of love, Sam, Crystal & Sebastian xo

To say I felt sad and disappointed about this news is an understatement. I had hoped so much that we would be returning home that week after chemotherapy. My instinct was to pack up and go home, to stop treatment and hide from the cancer with our family. The struggle was becoming overwhelming. With every delay or complication, I felt increasingly helpless and hopeless. My heart ached for Sam and the girls, and I worried about them constantly. The separation and uncertainty were agonising.

Sunday, 15 March 2020

By mid-March, COVID-19 had begun to dominate every news report. In Queensland, there had been only one recorded death, but the daily infection rate was rising rapidly. By 20th March, there were 184 COVID-19 cases in Queensland, a significant jump of 166 cases since 1st March.

It was deeply concerning to think about Sebastian contracting COVID-19 while his immune system was compromised from chemotherapy. The QCH Oncology unit kept us well-informed, with the general consensus being that children were less likely to contract COVID-19. However, all immunosuppressed individuals needed to self-quarantine to avoid any illness, not just COVID-19. Tele-Health or Skype appointments at QCH were becoming preferred over face-to-face visits, which I supported as it meant less travel to the Hospital and reduced exposure to people.

Supermarket supplies were starting to run low, particularly toilet paper and nappies. Thankfully, the Manager at IGA East Brisbane agreed to place a special order of 250 nappies for Sebastian from a Queensland supplier. We received similar support from several local retailers in Brisbane. Their generosity during such a challenging time for all was a significant relief, and I am forever grateful for their help.

Sebastian continued to improve slightly each day, despite feeling unwell and tired from chemotherapy. He had moments of pain and irritability, but these were relatively manageable with Panadol. His typical 2-year-old mood swings and reluctance to cooperate were challenging, especially with his limited verbal communication since surgery. The teams remained confident that his speech would return, but it would take time.

> "Let it hurt, let it bleed, let it heal, let it go."
> -Unknown-

Thursday, 19 March 2020

Chemotherapy Cycle 2, Treatment #4 and 5, Day 29.

At the chemotherapy treatment on Wednesday, 18th March, we had another opportunity to speak with Rick. Our meetings with him had become highly anticipated as the COVID-19 situation continued to escalate. We desperately needed his and our Oncology Nurse, Brooke's, guidance and advice.

Rick reported that he was satisfied with the status of Sebastian's tumour, cyst, and ventricles based on the CT scan images from Monday, 16th March. The 'gaps' and pockets of air that were previously occupied by fluid and/or tumour and cyst had now been taken up by Sebastian's brain, indicating that the brain was 'relaxing' and moving back into its correct position. This was promising as it suggested relief from irritability and pressure that could have been causing headaches. The most encouraging news was that this improvement should continue with each chemotherapy treatment.

However, Rick and the Endocrinology team were concerned about Sebastian's inability to lose weight since completing his steroid medication nearly four weeks prior. Despite the reduction in 'puffiness,' Sebastian continued to gain weight, which was surprising given that the Dietician had advised feeding him whatever he was willing to eat. Rick believed that Sebastian's tumour and/or the surgical procedure might have impacted his hypothalamus function more than initially thought. Symptoms of hypothalamus malfunction include sensitivity to heat, irritability, mood swings, fatigue, difficulty sleeping, and constant thirst and hunger—symptoms that Sebastian was exhibiting. Additionally, individuals with Diabetes Insipidus (DI) often suffer from hypothalamus issues since both conditions rely on the proper function of the pituitary gland. While DI affects fluid regulation, hypothalamus malfunction affects food intake regulation, leading to excess weight gain and Sebastian's brain's inability to signal when he's full. With chemotherapy increasing his cravings for protein and salty foods, weight gain was almost inevitable.

Treatment for hypothalamus malfunction involves adjusting Sebastian's diet to include foods that promote a feeling of fullness for longer (like grains and legumes). Unlike DI, hypothalamus malfunction cannot be managed with medication. I began discussing with Sebastian's Physical Therapy team ways to increase his physical activity to boost his metabolism and burn off excess energy. Moving forward, Rick and the Endocrinology team would closely monitor Sebastian's organs and the effects of ongoing weight gain. Meanwhile, I felt overwhelmed by the added challenge of managing this new issue, especially since Sebastian was already struggling with medical interventions, treatments, medications, and fatigue. Although I had complete trust in the team at QCH, the situation was incredibly difficult.

Unsurprisingly, Sebastian was non-compliant during his Ophthalmology appointment earlier in the week, so the testing could not be completed. The appointment was rescheduled for Monday, 30th March, as it was becoming clear that, while undergoing treatment and feeling unwell, Sebastian was very difficult and impatient with medical appointments. Despite being strong and doing well in chemotherapy the day before—only crying when his Port was accessed and de-accessed—Sebastian struggled with the continuous medical procedures. He napped, ate (of course), and happily watched TV without complaint. It was challenging to remain strong and focused for both of us, and I found it hard to accept or feel grateful for the life lessons this experience was teaching me. I couldn't imagine ever feeling thankful or enriched by this ordeal.

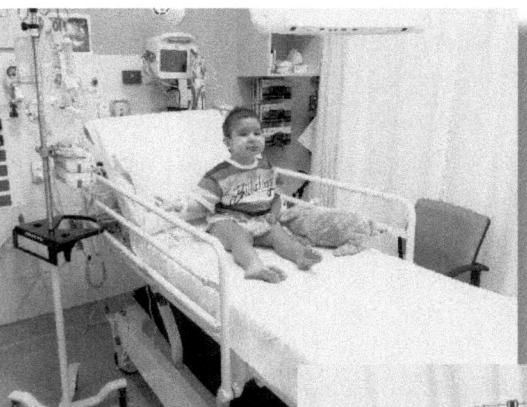

Treatment resumes. Chemotherapy Cycle 2, Treatment 4&5, Day 29, QLD Children's Hospital, 18 March 2020

Chemotherapy Cycle 2, Treatment 6, Day 36, QLD Children's Hospital, 25 March 2020

17

CHOOSING TO FIGHT, NOT FLY

"Having children is like having your heart walking around outside your body."
-Barack Obama-

5:58am, Thursday, 26 March 2020

Chemotherapy Cycle 2, Treatment #6, Day 36.

We are slowly but surely getting through these weekly chemotherapy treatments. Sebastian has 1 remaining weekly treatment to go (next Wednesday 01.04.20), and another 11 monthly (every 28 days) treatments to complete. We were originally expecting to return home for Easter on the 8th April (also my birthday) but unfortunately, Rick has decided that it is best for Sebastian to remain in Brisbane until after chemotherapy on 15th April. Sadly, with the rapidly accelerating COVID-19 pandemic, there is too much uncertainty around the safety of Oncology patients, particularly in the children's Hospitals. Currently, there are no known COVID-19 cases in paediatric Oncology patients around the world which gives QCH great reassurance. It's believed that this is due to the increased hygiene practices and self-isolation behaviour that Oncology families partake in, regardless of COVID-19, which limits the child's exposure to illness. Frighteningly, the reality is that COVID-19 is affecting the whole world. Earlier this month COVID-19 was declared a 'pandemic' by the World Health Organisation, the Queensland borders shut to the rest of Australia yesterday and there's now talk of schools closing down. It's out of everyone's control now and the priority of the amazing medical teams around the world is to keep people safe. It's only fair to respect the decisions of Sebastian's medical team and try to ride out the storm with as much patience as possible.

Sam and I are obviously desperate for our family to be together again so after 11 weeks of separation already, another three weeks seems unbearable. Sebastian and I will miss Easter and celebrating my birthday at home which breaks my heart. In such a turbulent time, my only birthday wish is to just be together with my family. I've shed more tears in this last week than I have in my whole life as I'm really struggling now with the emotional and psychological toll our journey is taking on us all. All I want is to hug my parents and my girls and cry on Sam's shoulder. As a mother of a small child with cancer but also three little girls, I feel all of their pain, their fears and their anxieties. Barack Obama said in Press Conference in a 2015 that "Having children is like having your heart walking around outside your body." When it's hurting, you're hurting, when it's breaking, so are you. It's beautiful and torturous all at the same time. I have also heard the saying... "You have to go through it to get through it", so, I guess we have no other choice than to do just that.

This week, I experienced an overwhelming level of emotion that felt beyond the limits of what the human spirit can endure. It became clear to me how desperately I needed the comforting embrace of a loved one more than ever. Even though I was living with family, we were practicing social distancing within the house. Each day, I longed to sink into someone's arms and cry on their shoulder for as long as I needed.

The harsh reality of COVID-19 for me was that I found myself in a city that wasn't my own, in a house that wasn't home. I had nowhere to go, no one to see, and was trapped in a relentless isolation. It felt incredibly cruel, almost unbearable.

On a positive note, Oncology explained today that if COVID-19 becomes out of control in Queensland, they will have no choice but to train all of the regional chemotherapy nurses so that chemotherapy drugs could be administered at patients' local Hospitals. I guess only time will tell.

Over the last week, I've been working hard with Sebastian to get him moving more and increase his physical activity. We do little activities like climbing stairs, short walks and making little running games in the lounge room. It does seem to be paying off, with a 300g weight loss this week.

Our attempt at Skyping our Physiotherapy and OT appointment this week was not a great success. Sebastian is very camera shy and shut down the moment he heard the voices from the Hospital talking to him over the phone. We have decided to persevere and try again next week in a hope that we can get him moving during these sessions, whilst keeping him safely out of the Hospital environment. In the meantime, I will be recording some of Sebastian's movement to show Anne-Marie and Anshu if future Skype appointments don't work.

Alyssa's Kindy has closed this week due to COVID-19 restrictions so she is staying with Sam's Dad in Mareeba while the girls attend school. Julatten State School is still open but we are not sure for how much longer.

We are all experiencing such a surreal feeling of continued loss of control. Everything is put back into perspective on Wednesdays however, when we enter the Chemotherapy ward at QCH. Despite all of the frantic behaviour and frightening uncertainty around COVID-19 amongst the general public, every day there are families sitting bedside with their children receiving lifesaving treatment for cancer. Sadly, we are one of those families. There are so many sick children suffering from cancer, currently 216 at QCH to be exact, all helplessly entrusting their lives in the medical angels that go bed to bed talking us through how we are going to get through this. Yesterday there was a little girl across from us who was about the same age as Sebastian. She looked so unwell, a poster child for chemotherapy - pale skin, no hair, tubes running in and out of her face and head and I just felt so sorry for her little soul. Something I'm thankful for every day is that our little warrior doesn't 'look' sick at all. It allows me to love and care for him without the constant reminder of what his body is going through.

Having an unwell child takes its toll on your emotions so it's a blessing to still have a robust, active and olive-skinned boy who shows few obvious physical signs of cancer. It's all come down to the little things, now more than ever.

Enjoy this rare opportunity to slow down during lockdown and to those still working, please keep safe. Sending everyone so much love, miss seeing you all.

Lots of love, Sam, Crystal and Sebastian xoxo

Taking some time out to play while public parks and playgrounds remain open during COVID-19 restrictions, 30 March 2020

Timeline of Events: March 2020

02.03.2020	Sebastian admitted to Mossman Hospital when hard to arouse after 5 hours sleep.
03.03.2020	X-ray of chest at Mossman Hospital – all clear. Transported to Cairns Hospital via Ambulance. CT Scan at Cairns Hospital revealed bleed in ventricle. Admitted to ICU at Cairns Hospital.
04.03.2020	Transported to QCH via RFDS. Admitted to level 11a at QCH. Chemotherapy #3 paused until 11.03.20. Port-a-cath failure.
05.03.2020	MRI at QCH.
08.03.2020	Port-a-cath corrected.
09.03.2020	Discharged from level 11a at QCH. Outpatient of QCH Oncology once again.
11.03.2020	Chemotherapy Cycle 1, Treatment 3, Day 22 (at QCH). Cairns Hospital chemotherapy cancelled. Stay in Brisbane extended to 08.04.20. COVID-19 – WHO (World Health Organisation) declare COVID-19 a pandemic.
13.03.2020	COVID-19 - 35 new cases & 1st death in QLD.
16.03.2020	CT Scan at QCH. COVID-19 - 69 new cases in QLD & all ANZAC Day ceremonies cancelled in Australia.
18.03.2020	Chemotherapy Cycle 2, Treatment 4&5, Day 29. Kindergarten in Julatten closed due to COVID-19.
19.03.2020	Ophthalmology appointment at QCH – attempt #1 (rescheduled). COVID-19 - Aus. bans all international arrivals of non-citizens and non-residents. Chemotherapy Cycle 2, Treatment 6, Day 36
20.03.2020	COVID-19 - Travel ban in place to remote Aboriginal communities.
22.03.2020	COVID-19 - Gold Coast theme parks closed. Ophthalmology appointment at QCH – attempt #2 (completed).
23.03.2020	COVID-19 - Pubs, clubs and restaurants closed.
24.03.2020	Kindergarten in Julatten closed due to COVID-19.

25.03.2020	Chemotherapy Cycle 2, Treatment 6, Day 36. Stay in Brisbane extended again to 15.04.2020. COVID-19 - QLD borders shut. Australians celebrate ANZAC Day by standing outside their front door at dawn.
30.03.2020	COVID-19 - QLD schools closed – students to be home-schooled with online lessons arranged by the teacher/school. 2 visitor maximum in homes. Travel outside of home banned except for 4 essential reasons; food, medical, work, exercise.
Total COVID-19 positive tests in QLD as at 31.03.20 = 743	

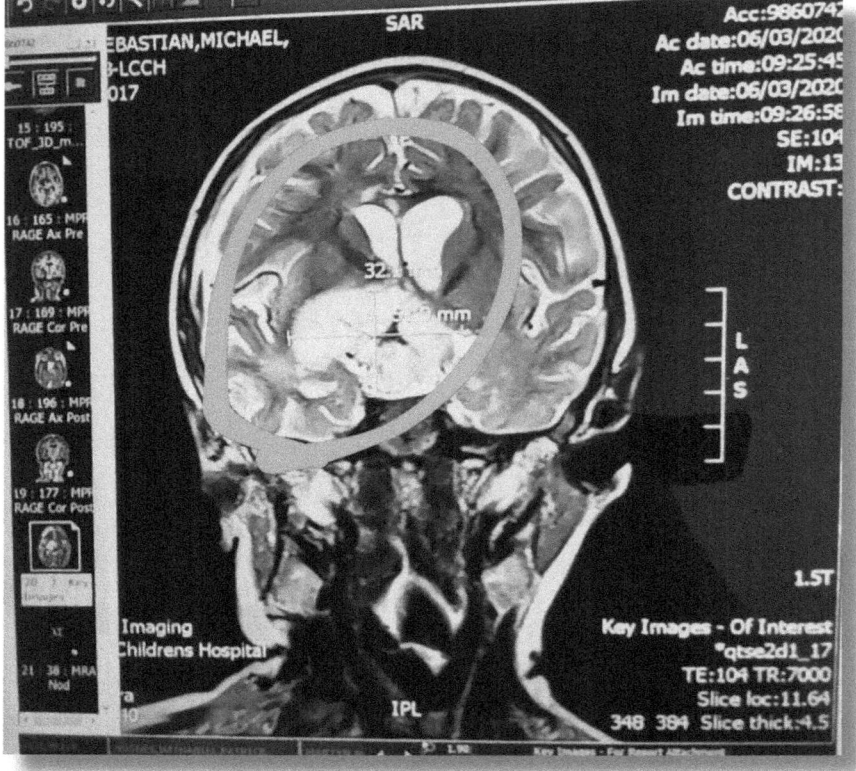

MRI, 5 March 2020

Messages of Love

"Oh my gosh Crystal. Lots of love and positive thoughts with you through this time of uncertainty and deep distress. Hope you get the answers you all need and your family can go back to some sort of normality soon. You are an incredible Mother."

"Spoke with Sam this morning. You two are amazing in every way. Love you and hope the week brings all the answers you seek."

"What a team... positive thoughts for great results today."

"OMG. You guys blow me away... just get him well and his reward is chemo. So tough! No words mate just know we are all thinking of you and hoping for best results each day. Hugs from all of us in PNG."

"Poor Little man. This is all so much for him to manage and for you. I hope you are getting some rest as well. You have a lot of good people all keeping an eye on what is happening with him by the sounds of it. You are the loving arms he needs. Thinking of you and sending you both hugs."

"Legends, the lot of you. Especially Sebby the Lion Leonardi. Hugs guys, big big hugs."

"He absolutely looks great! Keep showing up with trust and positive emotions Crystal. We are all fighting along with you guys."

> *"How we walk with the broken speaks louder than how we sit with the great."*
>
> -Bill Bennot-

PART 4

18

TRUST THE WAIT

"There is nothing certain, but the uncertain."
-Proverb-

Wednesday, 1 April 2020

Chemotherapy Cycle 2, Treatment #7, Day 43.

By Wednesday, April 1st, Sebastian had completed his 1st and 2nd cycles of chemotherapy and was set to transition into monthly treatments at QCH, starting Wednesday, April 15th. Meanwhile, the medical teams were preparing Sebastian's three-month post-surgery report while he underwent several tests that week.

The physiotherapy report indicated that he has a 12-month delay in both fine and gross motor skills, as well as speech development. It's predicted that Sebastian will require physiotherapy, occupational therapy, and speech therapy for several years, as his development will likely be further hindered during chemotherapy and any additional surgical procedures. Further reports from the occupational therapy team were still being prepared.

The ophthalmology report revealed that Sebastian's eyesight had neither improved nor declined since surgery. There was a possibility that his eyesight might improve or worsen during treatment. However, correcting any vision issues wouldn't be considered until he is much older.

There was an anxious wait for the reports from the neurology and oncology teams, which would be based on MRI images taken later that week, on Friday, April 3rd. The MRI results would heavily influence whether the teams would allow Sebastian to return home between monthly chemotherapy treatments. Although flights were limited, COVID-19 was not affecting rural families traveling to and from QCH for chemotherapy treatment. Our hope was that Sebastian's medical status would be stable enough to ensure his safety during the 28 days he would be in a remote location, far from emergency medical assistance. As in previous experiences, it would likely come down to a last-minute approval to travel.

Over the past week, chemotherapy had taken a significant toll on Sebastian's body. He experienced symptoms such as nausea, diarrhea, headache, and vertigo for six days post-treatment, whereas he typically only suffered symptoms for three days. Nonetheless, he continued to soldier on and surprisingly showed signs of recovery. He was becoming more animated and expanding his vocabulary. Some of his new words included "key," "bubbles," "pig," "me," and "bus." This was such positive progress.

Due to feeling unwell, Sebastian hadn't been very active. Aunty Julie and I continued to take long walks daily, with Sebastian in the pram, which he thoroughly enjoyed. If nothing else, the fresh air and change of scenery were beneficial for both of us.

At his pre-chemotherapy medical check-up, Sebastian gained 900 grams in 7 days. This prompted another meeting with the dietician to discuss and plan weight loss strategies for Sebastian. This issue was particularly frustrating in these early days, as it seemed everything was working against us in our efforts to help Sebastian lose weight.

With Sebastian's upcoming MRI, I felt terribly anxious about yet another general anaesthetic (G.A.). Since January 8th, 2020, he'd undergone 11 G.A. procedures and numerous sedatives and very strong pain relief. The thought of him going through that tunnel again felt so wrong, but I also appreciated how necessary it was. It's a lot for such a little boy to endure.

Back in Julatten, the girls were now at home full-time after schools in Queensland closed on Monday, March 30th. Julatten State School was well-prepared, and with the help of parents at home, they had set up online learning sessions each day. Of course, there have been a few technical issues and learning curves, but for the most part, the girls and Sam are managing the new changes and are happy to be safe and in full lockdown.

4:04pm, Wednesday, 8 April 2020

After an excruciatingly long wait, we have finally received the MRI results from Rick. I'm happy to share these results, which are very positive!

- Tumour and cyst are stable. Rick explained that at this early stage of treatment, obvious change and/or shrinkage are not expected so stability is good.

- Remaining cyst is still present but seems to have shrunk. There is no fluid level inside the cyst anymore and the blood seen in previous MRIs (8.1.20 and 5.3.20) has resolved independently. This in itself is sensational news, more than any of us could have hoped for at this early stage.

- The risk of Sebastian having further bleeds in the brain is reducing as chemotherapy continues. Ultimately, chemotherapy will de-vascularise the tumour which lowers the risk of complications. Evidence of de-vascularisation is being seen in the cyst already, so we can assume it's also impacting the tumour.

- The angiogram revealed that all blood vessels and ventricles in the brain are of a good size and are stable.

To summarise, the team are confident that Sebastian is out of the high-risk period where complications such as a bleed are likely to happen. Sebastian's sodium levels have remained consistently good and he has generally been improving a little each week, with each chemotherapy treatment. The team will meet again on Tuesday 14th April but at this stage we have the all clear to return home after chemotherapy on Wednesday 15th April!

The level of relief and joy that Sam and I are feeling after today's news is simply exhilarating. In amongst all the stress of cancer and COVID-19 it feels wonderful to finally have some good news and a rare taste of hope for a brighter future, something I'd almost forgotten existed. The positive news is the best birthday present I could have ever hoped for and I will be sure to celebrate tonight in honour of this good news and our strong and brave little boy.

Sam and I have decided not to tell the girls about our return until after chemotherapy and Sebastian's final medical tick of approval next Wednesday 15th April. They are doing really well and managing home schooling with Sam. They are missing Sebastian and I but are relishing in having Sam home every day with them, which I'm sure is a lot of fun and far more relaxed than if I was the one running the home-schooling program. We continue to Skype each day and talk about all the things we will do when I get home, even though 'the corona' (as Josie calls it) makes life a bit different.

While I was away, I started recording myself reading a book to the girls each day. I borrowed some children's books from Aunty Julie's neighbours since libraries were closed due to COVID-19. I would send the recordings to Sam via WhatsApp, and he'd play them on our Smart TV at home for the girls to watch before bed. Sometimes, Sam would record the girls watching the stories so I could also enjoy seeing their reactions.

The girls thoroughly enjoyed this little ritual and found comfort in hearing my voice each day. In a very sweet display of empathy, Antonia would occasionally record herself reading some of Sebastian's favorite books from home and send the videos to me to show him before bed. This gesture warmed my heart and was a beautiful way for us to stay connected during this challenging time.

Thank you for all the birthday wishes I've received so far today. It's been the toughest birthday I've ever had – one that I'll never forget - but all the love I've received has kept a smile on my face so thank you!

Lots of love, Sam, Crystal & Sebastian xoxo

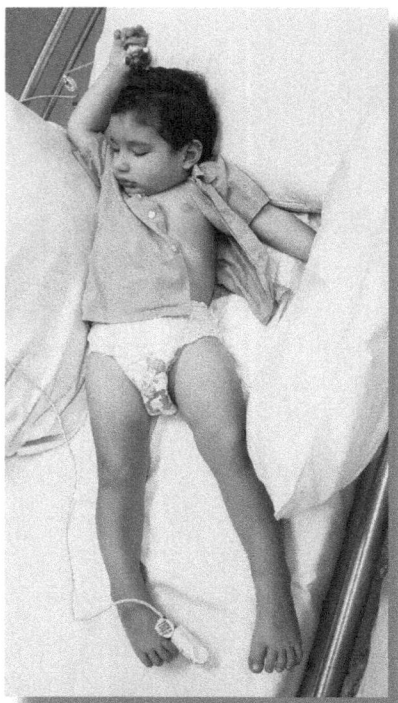
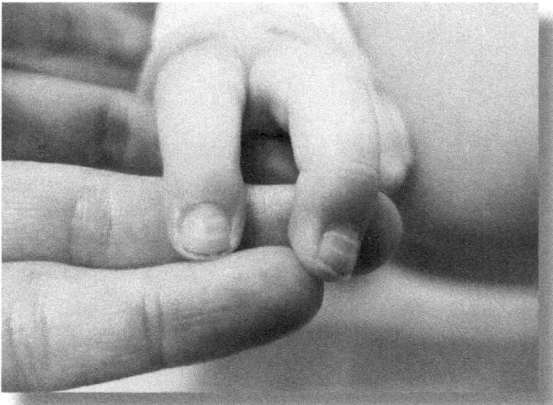
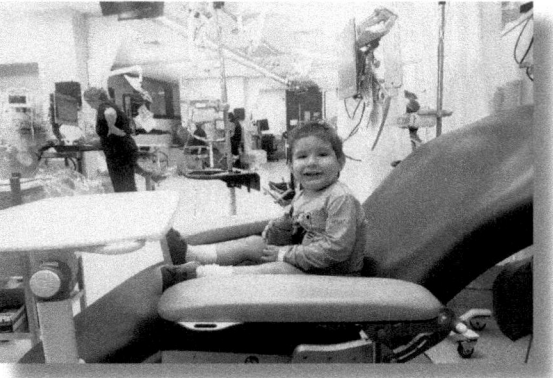

Chemotherapy Cycle 2,
Treatment 7, Day 43, QLD Children's Hospital, 1 April 2020

19

"THERE'S NO PLACE LIKE HOME"
-The Wizard of Oz-

9:58am, Wednesday, 15 April 2020

Chemotherapy Cycle 3, Treatment #8, Day 57.

Since his last treatment, Sebastian had started experiencing pain in his back, legs, and feet, likely a side effect of Vincristine, one of his chemotherapy drugs. We were warned at the beginning of his treatment that such side effects are common once a 'build-up' of the drugs occurs in the body. Sebastian's pain was being managed with Panadol and additional physiotherapy. At the peak of his pain, he was unable to walk and would sometimes collapse when attempting to stand. Despite this, he showed remarkable toughness and resilience, often lying down and waiting for the Panadol to bring relief.

I discussed Sebastian's pain levels with Rick, who believed that the pain should decrease and be limited to the weeks when he has chemotherapy, now that his treatments are scheduled every 28 days.

Otherwise, Sebastian had been relatively happy and cheeky, showing signs of regaining some mischievous behaviours, which was a delight to see. He had moments where he danced, spun around, stomped, and even tried to run when he felt well. He was experiencing extreme highs and lows in how he felt, but generally, he looked healthy and behaved as one might expect a two-year-old in his situation to behave.

On April 15th, we had meetings scheduled with Sebastian's Dietitian, Physiotherapist, Occupational Therapist, and Speech Therapist to continue addressing his physical challenges. He received his adjusted orthotic boot, which would be sufficient for another month before he needed a larger one. I could see improvements in his muscle tone, strength, and gait due to the orthotic.

Sebastian's Diabetes Insipidus continued to be a daily challenge, as his medication was compromised during chemotherapy treatment. He experienced periods of extreme thirst and urination, usually at night, making for long and difficult nights followed by long and lethargic days. This situation was certainly a learning curve and a test of patience for both of us, something we unfortunately had to learn to live with.

3:00pm, Wednesday, 15 April 2020

We have been given the green light to return home after chemotherapy today! Sam and Sebastian (Snr) are on their way to Brisbane via road as unfortunately, we have been unable to book a flight home before 26th April due to COVID-19 and the subsequent travel restrictions. We have gained written advice and consent from QCH Oncology to travel via road and have notified Queensland Police and the Department of Transport Queensland of our intention to travel. All going well, we will return to Brisbane in 28 days via aeroplane to continue chemotherapy treatment. Physiotherapy, OT, Dietician and Speech Therapy appointments will continue on a weekly basis with the QCH teams via telehealth and/or Skype.

I am unsure of exactly when we will make it home as Sebastian typically doesn't travel well. I will keep you updated and will be sure to let you know when we are all safely home.

Lots of love, Sam, Crystal and Sebastian xoxo

5:51pm, Thursday, 16 April 2020

Just before 6pm on Thursday, April 16th, we finally arrived home. Sam and his dad, Sebastian Sr., had driven straight through the night and day to reach Brisbane by 6pm on Wednesday, April 15th. After a meal and several failed attempts to get Sebastian to sleep, we decided to begin our journey home at 9 pm that night. Sebastian traveled exceptionally well, requiring only a few stops to stretch his legs and get some fresh air, which conveniently coincided with our toilet and food breaks. We encountered no issues with law enforcement regarding our authority to travel, which was a great relief and made for a relaxed journey. Sam and his dad drove for almost three days with only short rest periods while the other person took over driving. They did an incredible job, and I am immensely grateful for their courage and determination to get us home as quickly as possible.

3:58pm, Sunday, 10 May 2020

By 3:58pm on Sunday, May 10th, as I updated friends and family, I was processing a flood of overwhelming emotions. Once the chaos of the past few months had settled and we were all home, I was overtaken by a wave of post-traumatic stress. I had continually adapted to change and had no choice but to adjust to uncertainty. For months, I had oscillated between hope and hopelessness, leaving me feeling stuck in time, unable to move forward or envision a brighter future.

Most nights, I found myself crying myself to sleep, overwhelmed with doubt and fear that Sebastian's health might deteriorate despite our best efforts to keep him safe. My deep-seated parental protectiveness had sustained my strength during all those months away from home, but now that the immediate crisis had passed, his vulnerabilities became painfully clear.

I initially confided in Sam, but I felt it was time for us to start processing our grief separately. We were, after all, very different individuals who, despite weathering the same storm, had distinct ways of coping. I turned to reading when I couldn't sleep and quickly found solace in online grief counseling and support groups.

It became apparent that I hadn't fully accepted Sebastian's diagnosis nor had time to process it before Sam and I watched helplessly as the little boy we knew and loved was suddenly thrust into a fight for his life. After his surgery on January 12th, Sebastian didn't look the same, he didn't act the same, and it felt like we had lost the child we once knew. His diagnosis was a confrontation with death that continued to haunt me, even though he was now past the worst of it medically.

I missed the "old" Sebastian and felt immense guilt over it. It was as if he went into surgery as one person and came out as someone completely different. I was grieving for my son who was still alive. I felt blessed and full of love and admiration for the "new" Sebastian, but I longed for the "old" Sebastian who was innocently unaware of the trauma cancer had inflicted upon him. The cancer had stolen his innocence and had taken away the son I had known and loved so perfectly.

The emotional turmoil—fear, anger, guilt, sorrow, devastation, disbelief, terror, and more—swirled in my mind, keeping me awake at night. Sleep only returned when I discovered grief management meditation sessions online, which I listened to as I fell asleep. Talking to social workers from the children's Hospital and connecting with other parents who had experienced similar challenges also helped. However, I had to be cautious, as hearing stories about the deaths of children with conditions similar to Sebastian's could sometimes trigger my grief.

It wasn't an easy journey, but my little survivor Sebastian motivated and empowered me to overcome the grief with his strength and determination to recover. After all, he was also grieving the loss of his health, on top of everything else.

Happy Mother's Day to all my fellow Mums, I hope your day has been special.

Thank you to everyone who has called or sent messages since our return home. I'm sorry if I haven't replied to your message yet, we've had a full on three or so weeks.

For the most part, Sebastian has been very happy to be home in a familiar and comfortable environment. Unfortunately, until about three days ago, he was quite unwell so we really haven't got much to report. We have attempted to continue physiotherapy and OT through telehealth but haven't had much success due to Sebastian being unwell. I hope to catch up with our rehab team in Brisbane this coming week to make an alternative plan going forward. At times when Sebastian has felt well, he is walking and moving independently and speaking more and more each day. We believe the chemotherapy is the cause of his discomfort as all blood tests are trending as they have been previously.

Unfortunately, we've had no reprieve from the sleepless nights due to Sebastian's DI. It has been great to be home in this regard, where I have a team mate (Sam) to help with the night shifts, which sometimes mean only 1 or 2 hrs sleep. We expect DI to remain difficult to medicate whilst chemotherapy is in play so we try our best to take it one day at a time.

Tomorrow Sebastian and I return to Brisbane for chemotherapy on Wednesday 13th May. Unfortunately, we couldn't get a flight home until Saturday 16th May due to the COVID-19 impact on domestic travel. We will be staying with Aunty Julie and Uncle Brendan again which we are both looking forward to.

In other home news, we've been very busy home-schooling with Antonia, Josie and Alyssa. Thankfully, this week, Prep, Year 1, Year 12, vulnerable children and children of essential workers were welcomed back to school and Kindergartens re-opened. So, I have Antonia at home Mondays-Wednesdays, Alyssa home on Mondays and Fridays and Josie at school 5 days a week again. This easing of COVID-19 restrictions has come as a great relief as the home-schooling experience since my return home, has been very challenging for us. With Sebastian being so high needs at times, following a routine or schedule is very difficult and adds a lot of pressure to my day.

I'm so thankful to have had the opportunity to experience a second 1st day of school with the girls, even if it was during the COVID-19 pandemic. We did our usual photos outside the school and Kindy and for the 1st time in a long time I was happy to pack a lunch box. Josie also lost her first tooth this week so it's been a very special week all around and I'm so happy I was here to experience it all with them.

I will be in touch again after chemotherapy this week. Stay safe.

Lots of love, Sam, Crystal & Sebastian xoxo

8:15pm, Wednesday, 13 May 2020

Chemotherapy Cycle 4, Treatment #9, Day 85.

Upon returning to QCH for chemotherapy, most of our discussions with the team focused on managing Sebastian's pain. He had spent three out of the past four weeks suffering from nausea, vomiting, diarrhea, pain, lethargy, and an inability to sleep.

Children who experience physical trauma or extended periods of pain can develop hyper-alertness, becoming extremely sensitive to even small amounts of pain. Rick explained that in Sebastian's case, his body was in a state of constant pain even before his diagnosis, as hemiplegia is very damaging and stressful on the body. With multiple surgeries, chemotherapy, and a brain haemorrhage, it's no surprise that Sebastian's body had endured significant pain. When the body is hyper-alert, even minor pain can disturb or wake a child from sleep.

Sebastian consistently complained of lower back, hip, leg, and foot pain, which Rick believed might be nerve-related. Rick highlighted several key points:

Left-sided hemiplegia adds stress to the right side of the body. As Sebastian's left side recovers and develops muscle, his weight will increase.

Hip, back, leg, and foot pain can also be related to rapid weight gain in short periods. In Sebastian's case, weight gain began with artificial steroid medication.

Since January 8th, Sebastian has grown 6 cm in height and gained 11 kg. This rapid growth in itself can cause discomfort and pain.

Sebastian may have some nerve damage from incorrect use of his hips, legs, and feet in the months before his diagnosis, when his hemiplegia was at its worst. Our paediatrician, Tim, diagnosed Sebastian with hypermobility, allowing him to manipulate his body despite his hemiplegia. Hypermobility can damage nerves and muscles if the body is not used correctly or manipulated, as in Sebastian's case.

Rick also noted that a rapid increase in height and weight, regardless of the cause, could promote muscle development and strength, especially on his left side where he had increased mobility. There could also be a genetic component, suggesting Sebastian was naturally on track for a growth spurt at this time. Regardless, Rick prescribed stronger pain relief to help Sebastian function day-to-day, reduce pain, and improve sleep. We decided to trial this new medication for the month between chemotherapy treatments and discuss its effectiveness with Rick upon our return to Brisbane on June 10th.

Rick remarked that Sebastian looked fantastic considering what he was going through, and our strict diet regimen over the last couple of weeks had made a significant impact. At Sebastian's weigh-in, he gained 1.2 kg in a month, a great improvement from his recent average of 1 kg weight gain per week. Sebastian's dietitian was also pleased with the changes we had made and thrilled with the slower rate of weight gain. She noted that it might take a few months to get back on track, but so far, so good.

The endocrinology team continued to monitor dosages of Desmopressin to manage Sebastian's DI. A review with endocrinology was scheduled for the following week via telehealth.

I felt relieved to have some clarity and direction on making life easier and pain-free for Sebastian moving forward. Aunty Julie told me that her sister-in-law had also undergone Vincristine chemotherapy and experienced severe pain in her feet, describing it as feeling like walking on broken glass. Hearing this, I realised Sebastian might be experiencing similar sensations, as he looked like he was walking on something sharp. This insight was invaluable, giving me a better understanding of what Sebastian was going through. The physiotherapist recommended compression therapy with tight socks or warm water baths to soothe the pain.

We still had a long way to go with treatment, and there were still days when Sebastian couldn't walk or sleep due to pain, making the days and nights blur together. However, it was reassuring to know that we were being guided by a great team at QCH. It was one day at a time, and as Sam often reminded me, 'It's just wonderful to still be parents to this amazing little boy; everything else we will figure out.'

20

"28 DAYS"

6:50am, Thursday, 21 May 2020

Sebastian and I returned home on Saturday and it still feels surreal to be home after treatment and have the freedom to leave Brisbane for the first time.

Sebastian's new pain medication (Gabapentin) is giving him so much more relief and allowing him to move more freely during the day. Sadly, it hasn't helped much with his sleep, however it is nice to know he's not waking in pain anymore and that it's some other complication that's keeping him from sleeping. His inability to sleep remains difficult to manage but is part in parcel with having brain cancer - the presence of pressure and a foreign object (the tumour) at the middle of his brain would be generating a lot of discomfort. The more reading I do on other cases, the more I realise that sleep is something that a lot of brain cancer patients report they don't or can't get. We keep Sebastian comfortable, loved and supported during the long nights and wait for the day when chemotherapy starts to make enough of an impact on the tumour that we can all finally get some sleep.

Otherwise, Sebastian is doing well. He travels really well on the aeroplane, sleeping most of the way. He loves being at home in his own environment and enjoys the company of his sisters and all of our pets. The girls have been terrific. I have not once had to remind them that sometimes Sam and I have to be attentive to Sebastian only and that his health is still up and down. Their spirit and resilience have continued to surprise me and has made our transition to home life so easy. They all adore Sebastian; he is definitely one loved little boy and it's so nice to watch them all enjoy each other's company now that we're home. The girls are doing really well at school and kindy and due to easing of COVID-19 restrictions in Queensland recently, the girls are officially all back at school on a full-time basis from today. Hooray! My appreciation for Queensland Education and all the educators has skyrocketed after this little online learning/home-schooling experience.

Lots of love, Sam, Crystal & Sebastian xoxo

6:27am, Saturday, 30 May 2020

We are now two weeks post chemotherapy and Sebastian has managed his last treatment really well. The addition of his new pain medication has made a world of difference. The highs and lows are both improving and Sam and I are spending far less time managing Sebastian's pain.

This week, Sebastian had a review with the Endocrinology team regarding Sebastian's Diabetes Insipidus. Once again, the team have changed his desmopressin dosages which has helped on some nights but not on others (about a 50% success rate). Sebastian had blood tests done yesterday to check on his sodium and thyroid levels which will confirm that the new desmopressin dosages are safe. We expect these results by Tuesday 2nd June.

Yesterday we also had a telephone meeting with NDIS. NDIS provides funding for children with disability and/or developmental delays. We hope that this kind of funding will allow us to be able to afford to send Sebastian to private Physiotherapists, OT, Speech therapists and any other therapies he may need, as well as purchasing things like orthotics and equipment suitable for children with hemiplegia.

I've been in contact with another mother in Mareeba (Katie) after I saw a story about her 4-year-old son, Nate, in the Cairns Post. Nate was diagnosed with brain cancer at two years old and has been treated by Dr Charlie Teo. Katie has been a great source of information and although Nate's brain cancer is different to Sebastian's, she's been able to connect me with other parents of older children with an Astrocytoma tumour, like Sebastian's. It's been really interesting and helpful to read about how their children felt after surgery and is helping me to understand what Sebastian may be feeling when he's in pain. They've also given me some insight into what may be ahead of us regarding treatment options down the track. I'm really thankful for the support other parents of oncology and/or brain cancer kids have given us, it's very comforting to know someone else out there has experienced what we're feeling and managing on a daily basis. This thing, childhood cancer, it's not only a tough pill to swallow but it has the ability to destroy your spirit and grab hold of your heart and mind. And all the while, your physical being is circling your sick child, trapping you in a vortex where all the focus is on them and nobody else. So, the comfort these other parents give to each other is so important to our 'long-game', to keep us strong and to give us hope.

It's been wonderful to see Sebastian come out of his shell a little more when he has felt well in the last fortnight. He is trying to talk more and interacts happily with his sisters. He really misses them when they're at school and kindy but still fatigues quickly and struggles to keep up with their energy when they are home. His energy levels will hopefully continue to improve as he recovers and gets older.

Sebastian's next chemotherapy treatment is on 10th June and Sam will be accompanying him this time. Until then, we are working on catching up with family and friends after not seeing so many of them for almost 6 months. The familiar and loving faces of the 'constants' in Sebastian's life are also so important to his development, recovery and emotional well-being. It will be lovely to physically be in the same space as our loved ones, even if we are still only allowed to elbow tap or say hello from a distance.

Lots of love, Sam, Crystal & Sebastian xoxo

> *"I may not be there with you,
> but I'm always there for you."*
> -Unknown-

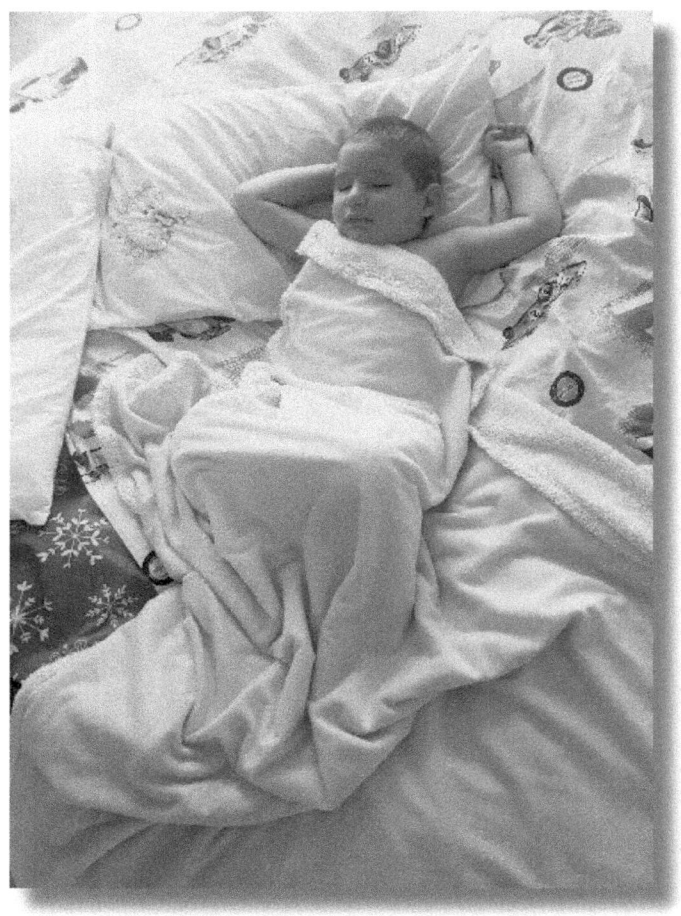

Timeline of Events: April 2020

01.04.2020	Chemotherapy Cycle 2, Treatment 7, Day 43. Physiotherapy & OT Report - 12-month delay in fine and gross motor & speech. Ophthalmology Report – No change. Pain begins to intensify for Sebastian, lasting 3 weeks post-treatment. COVID-19 – 40 new cases in QLD.
02.04.2020	COVID-19 – National parks closed in QLD. COVID-19 – 57 new cases in QLD.
03.04.2020	MRI at QCH. COVID-19 – 39 new cases in QLD.
04.04.2020	COVID-19 – 27 new cases in QLD.
05.04.2020	COVID-19 – 9 new cases & 1 deaths in QLD.
06.04.2020	COVID-19 – 14 new cases in QLD. COVID-19 – Testing for COVID-19 expanded to include anyone with respiratory symptoms in hotspots of Brisbane, Gold Coast and Cairns.
07.04.2020	COVID-19 – 14 new cases in QLD.
08.04.2020	Neurology & Oncology Report – Tumour stable & evidence of cyst shrinkage. COVID-19 – 13 new cases in QLD. COVID-19 – All Cruise Ships in QLD waters ordered to leave by midnight.
10.04.2020	COVID-19 – 22 new cases in QLD.
12.04.2020	COVID-19 – 18 new cases in QLD.
13.04.2020	COVID-19 – 4 new cases in QLD.
14.04.2020	QCH Teams meet to discuss Sebastian leaving Brisbane.
15.04.2020	Chemotherapy Cycle 3, Treatment 8, Day 57. Approved to travel home after chemotherapy. No flights so Sam & his Dad decide to drive to Brisbane to bring us home.
16.04.2020	Sebastian and Crystal arrive home.
17.04.2020	COVID-19 – 10 new cases in QLD.
18.04.2020	COVID-19 – 7 new cases in QLD.

20.04.2020	COVID-19 – 1st day of Term 2. Schools open for vulnerable children or children of essential workers only. All other students to be home-schooled. Kindergartens open and free for all children. Education QLD website crashes as thousands of students start online learning from home. COVID-19 – 5 new cases in QLD.
21.04.2020	COVID-19 – Virgin Australia enters voluntary administration.
22.04.2020	COVID-19 – 5 new cases in QLD COVID-19 – 130,000 jobs lost in QLD due to COVID-19 pandemic.
26.04.2020	COVID-19 – 1st easing of restrictions. 50km drive from home and picnics ok. COVID-19 – 6 new cases in QLD.
28.04.2020	COVID-19 – 3 new cases in QLD.
Total COVID-19 confirmed cases in QLD as at 30.04.20 = 1,033	

Timeline of Events: May 2020

01.05.2020	COVID-19 – 0 new cases in QLD for 2 days in a row.
02.05.2020	COVID-19 – non-essential shopping ok.
04.05.2020	COVID-19 – 5 new cases in QLD.
06.05.2020	COVID-19 – 5 new cases in QLD.
07.05.2020	COVID-19 – 2 new cases in QLD.
10.05.2020	COVID-19 – Up to 5 visitors allowed in homes.
11.05.2020	Sebastian and Crystal fly to Brisbane. COVID-19 – Prep, Grade 1 and Grades 11 & 12 students welcomed back at school.
13.05.2020	Chemotherapy Cycle 4, Treatment 9, Day 85. Gabapentin prescribed to Sebastian for pain relief. Sebastian's weight gain reduces to 1.2kg in 28 days, down from 1kg gain per week.
15.05.2020	COVID-19 – 9 new cases in QLD. COVID-19 – Nursing Home in Rockhampton in lockdown after nurse tests positive.
16.05.2020	Sebastian and Crystal fly to Cairns. COVID-19 – Pubs, clubs, restaurants, cafes and beauty parlours open to up to 10 patrons at a time. COVID-19 – 1 new case in QLD.
18.05.2020	COVID-19 – 2 new cases in QLD.
25.05.2020	COVID-19 – All remaining grades return to schools.
27.05.2020	COVID-19 – 1 new case in QLD.
31.05.2020	COVID-19 – Unrestricted travel ok within QLD for QLD residents only.
Total COVID-19 confirmed cases in QLD as at 31.05.20 = 1,058	

Messages of Love

"That's fantastic news Crystal. This has made my day."

"Hey Crystal, thanks for the update and pictures. You're doing great. You and Sebastian are in my thoughts every day, especially tomorrow."

"Amazing news! Goodness knows your family deserves it! I am so so so happy that you guys are finally receiving some positive news. Sebastian is one strong, determined, resilient young man! Gets it from his parents! Well done team."

"That's such wonderful news Crystal, what a great birthday present indeed. I hope the return goes as planned, the girls will be so delighted to have you and Sebastian back."

"Oh, my goodness! I'll be thinking of you all coming back together as a family and how wonderful and happy that will be for you all. I'm sure there will be many tears of joy. Sending so much love to you all. Safe travels on the road beautiful."

"Crystal, such great news on many levels. So glad the trip home is happening. The girls will love having you both home. Sebby is a true fighter and I'm always astounded by the resilience kids show in these times. Keep the updates coming, we love sharing them."

"Thank God, tears of joy!"

"Oh wow! I'm in tears. Can't imagine there is a dry eye."

"Happy Mother's Day to the bravest, most amazing Mum I know! Love the photos. Sorry to hear Sebi has not been well recently. All the best with chemo this week."

"He's such a trooper!"

"Thinking of little mate today for his chemo."

"Hugs for you all, Hang in there Mumma bear, you are doing amazing."

"He is a tough little bugger. I miss and love you all. Mind you, when I say little bugger, probably only 2 birthdays before he's as tall as me."

"This little boy forever amazes me."

PART 5

21

DREAMING OF SLEEP

"And so rock bottom became the solid foundation on which I rebuilt my life."

-J.K. Rowling-

11:55am, Saturday, 10 June 2020

Chemotherapy Cycle 5, Treatment 10, Day 113.

Sebastian and Sam returned to Brisbane for a seven-day stay as Sebastian underwent another round of chemotherapy on June 10th. It's hard to believe that our little champion is steadily progressing through his chemotherapy schedule, consistently amazing us with his resilience. Remarkably, chemotherapy symptoms seemed secondary to his other health issues, a reality that felt surreal. We continued to navigate sleepless nights, manage pain, and attend countless meetings with the medical team to improve Sebastian's quality of life as much as possible.

The million-dollar question that we and many others were asking was, "Why doesn't he sleep?" Unfortunately, there were many potential reasons but no definitive answer at that time. We knew that brain tumours could cause insomnia, headaches, vertigo, and a sensation of tightness in the head. Additionally, Sebastian's tumour, located near the pituitary gland and pressing on the optic nerve, was affecting his hormone function and vision. Something I found particularly interesting during my research was how the brain controls the body's internal clock. The human body has tiny clocks operating all over it to keep everything running smoothly, but the 'master clock' resides in the brain and regulates the circadian rhythm. This circadian rhythm is the body's 24-hour cycle, controlling body temperature, hunger, bowel movements, and sleep. The body clock operates in an area of the brain called the suprachiasmatic nucleus (SCN), situated above where the optic nerve fibres cross. It's plausible that Sebastian's inability to maintain a regular sleep pattern is due to the location of his tumour, potentially disrupting his circadian rhythm.

Adding to the complexity was Diabetes Insipidus (DI). Unlike Type 1, Type 2, or Gestational Diabetes, which involve issues with insulin or glucose levels, DI affects the body's ability to regulate salt and water balance, leading to intense thirst and heavy urination. All forms of Diabetes are incurable and often require lifelong management. While Sebastian was undergoing chemotherapy, his medications, including those for DI, were compromised, leading to sporadic and intermittent failures. This situation often resulted in him waking up several times a night in a wet bed.

Tragically, even on nights when the DI medication was effective, Sebastian often suffered from other symptoms associated with his brain tumour. This left him with little rest. Sam and I struggled to understand all the complexities of Sebastian's condition, often finding ourselves going in circles trying to pinpoint why he couldn't sleep. We learned to appreciate any sleep he managed, realising that while the brain tumour was still present, consistent sleep might be unattainable. It was challenging for us as parents, but it was nothing compared to the discomfort and confusion Sebastian must have been experiencing.

I had to constantly remind myself that we were told to expect at least a 24-month delay in Sebastian's fine and gross motor developmental skills, so it was remarkable to see any improvement, especially considering his lack of sleep. He sometimes appeared lethargic and struggled with energy levels, but we also witnessed bursts of energy and moments of his loud, cheeky, and bossy personality. It was as if we could see all the words and movements trapped inside him, as he tirelessly tried to communicate and keep up with his sisters. From an early age, he demonstrated incredible patience and determination, traits that were serving him well during this incredibly challenging time for his mind and body.

We were fortunate to add a trampoline to Sebastian's at-home physiotherapy activities, thanks to my mother-in-law's generosity. She bought Sebastian a Vuly trampoline, which he approached with enthusiasm and some hesitation, as the feeling under his feet was likely unsettling. However, his courageous nature shone through as he sat and bounced along with his sisters, who entertained him. Trampolining, horse riding, and swimming were recommended by Physiotherapist Ann-Marie King as the best therapies for left-side hemiplegia, so having a trampoline at home was a wonderful addition to his therapy options. We were still working on the swimming pool and a horse...

Our daily 'routine' at home was still largely non-existent, revolving around Sebastian's sleep—or lack thereof. This often meant running late or forgetting things, but it also taught me to relax and focus on what truly mattered: being together as a family, despite all the medical challenges. Before Sebastian's diagnosis, I prided myself on being super organised, completing the kids' homework on time, and always doing that little bit extra. My world revolved around running on time, checklists, and endless housework, like many stay-at-home parents. Having my world turned upside down was perhaps the shake-up I needed to truly appreciate how lucky I was to have four beautiful children, a loving, hardworking husband, and a beautiful life. It made the neglected piles of laundry, running late, and forgotten homework seem less important. While I wasn't completely transformed into an unconventional, carefree mom, I was learning to embrace a more relaxed and slower-paced home life.

Sam and I had been thrust into an incredibly challenging year, but we were determined to rise above the chaos and find stability. Although there was always an element of fear and uncertainty regarding Sebastian's future, for now, he was here, strong, and making us all proud. Not all brain cancers are terminal, but all are treated as life-threatening, a reality we faced daily. The constant awareness of this was exhausting, but fortunately, our sleep deprivation left little time to dwell on it.

For the remainder of June, we had Sebastian's six-month neurology review and the commencement of physiotherapy and speech therapy with locally appointed therapists.

Sebastian, 21 June 2020

22

NO STONE LEFT UNTURNED

12:21pm, Wednesday, 8 July 2020

Chemotherapy Cycle 6, Treatment 11, Day 141

Sebastian has had an awesome month with the positive impact of chemotherapy really starting to show now. We are seeing a more confident and entertaining Sebastian, continuing to return back to his 'normal self'. Sam and I are revelling in watching him enjoy the company of his sisters, spending more time outdoors, singing along to his favourite songs and just being cheerful in general.

From a medical side of things, we've had further confirmation this month that Sebastian's body is producing an excessive amount of growth hormone, which explains his rapid growth since surgery on January 12th. We will spend a day in Cairns Hospital next week with our Cairns Endocrinologist, Dr Dyanne Wilson, to undergo further tests and begin to make a management plan for this condition moving forward. If further testing reveals that Sebastian does in fact have permanent damage to the brain, resulting in excessive growth in his early years, Dr Wilson is confident Sebastian can be medicated for this condition, commonly known as Gigantism.

Sebastian's next chemotherapy treatment is scheduled for 5th August. Our time in Brisbane will also include his three-monthly MRI and hopefully some good news regarding the status of Sebastian's tumour.

Today marks 6 months since Sebastian's brain tumour was discovered during an MRI at Cairns Hospital. A monumental journey that has touched each and every one of us. Thank you all for the love and support that has lifted us up through the darkest months of our lives.

Lots of love, Sam, Crystal & Sebastian xoxo

1:39pm, Monday, 27 July 2020

Over the next fortnight, we continued to observe signs of Sebastian's brain recovering from surgery. He began talking more, attempting to sing and dance, and returning to his cheeky, mischievous self. Additionally, we saw improvements in the effectiveness of his Diabetes Insipidus (DI) medication, Desmopressin. Whether this improvement was coincidental and short-term or another sign of his brain's recovery, we couldn't yet determine, but we welcomed the positive change. We experienced nearly two weeks without a wet bed at night, a significant relief as winter temperatures dropped. Following advice from Dyanne, our Cairns endocrinologist, we began adjusting Sebastian's Desmopressin dosages, aiming to eventually eliminate the midnight dose, which he no longer seemed to need. Despite having dry nights, Sebastian still woke up during the night, but these episodes were shorter and less frequent.

On Monday, July 27th, I spent the day at Cairns Hospital with Sebastian for further tests related to his growth hormone levels. Our goal was to determine the extent of the hormone imbalance and whether intervention was necessary. We learned that growth hormones control the pace at which bones and organs grow, and excessive growth could cause various health issues. If intervention was required, the hope was that establishing an appropriate treatment plan would provide Sebastian with additional pain relief and allow his body to grow at a normal rate. Gigantism, like DI, is treatable but rare in children, presenting unique treatment challenges. The results from the day's tests were highly anticipated and closely monitored by Sebastian's entire medical team, both in Cairns and Brisbane. It was always reassuring for Sam and me to know that Sebastian was being guided by the best medical professionals available, leaving no stone unturned in his care. We believed this comprehensive approach was giving him the best chance to identify and overcome any challenges his body faced.

The following week, we looked forward to another trip to Brisbane for chemotherapy treatment and to receive the results from the tests conducted at Cairns Hospital.

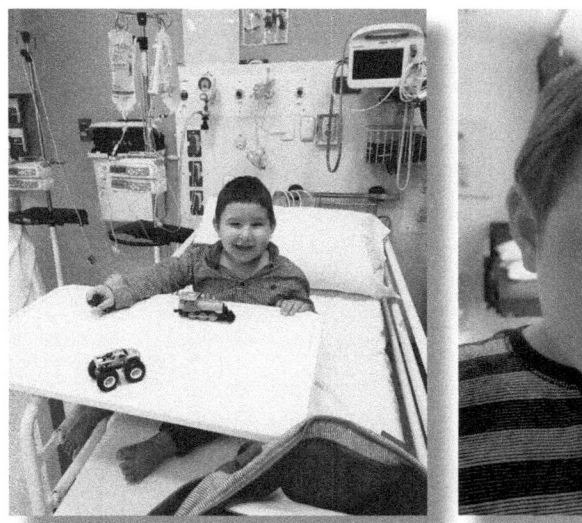
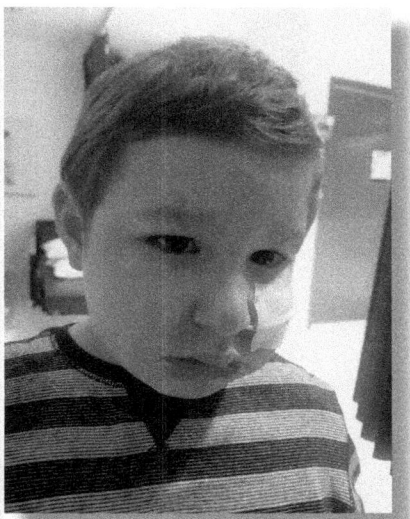

Chemotherapy Cycle 6, Treatment 11, Day 141, QLD Children's Hospital, 8 July 2020 and a sad little boy at his hormone investigation appointment at Cairns Hospital, 27 July 2020

23

WATCH & WAIT

4:55pm, Wednesday, 5 August 2020

Chemotherapy Cycle 7, Treatment 12, Day 169

Sam has accompanied Sebastian to Brisbane this week to complete his chemotherapy treatment today at QCH. Sebastian's monthly health check showed good health and continued to trend as it has been with weight gain and a height increase. Our next trip to Brisbane is booked in for 5 days commencing 30th August, which includes an MRI on Tuesday 1st September, followed by chemotherapy the next day.

Sebastian's test results from his day in Cairns Hospital on 27th July have all come back relatively normal. An unexpected result but certainly a relief. The tests included levels of growth hormone and how it reacted to the Glucose Tolerance Test, Type 1 and 2 Diabetes, thyroid and cortisol levels. What these results indicate is that Sebastian's hypothalamus function is the source of his inconsistent levels, rather than a problem with his growth hormone. This condition is commonly experienced by people with Diabetes Insipidus as both conditions rely on the correct function of the pituitary gland. Furthermore, Rick explained last week that because we are taking Sebastian's thirst sensation away with the use of Desmopressin, his brain is becoming confused in a way, i.e. instead of feeling thirsty, he feels hungry. Add chemotherapy treatment into the mix and you're left with an awfully complicated mess, each little discrepancy having a domino effect on the satisfactory function of Sebastian's brain. Going forward, Rick and Dyanne have advised that for now all we can do is keep making healthy meal and snack choices for Sebastian and do our best to keep him comfortable while he receives chemotherapy. These results have somewhat come as a relief to Sam and I, albeit a tad frustrating. In some ways, a definitive diagnosis would have been preferred as at least then we could make a management plan and work towards improving the condition immediately. In this case, and so many others so far, we must watch and wait and feel disappointed that we can't do more to help Sebastian.

Unfortunately, the improvements we were seeing with Desmopressin last month were short lived and we continue with the usual ups and downs related to DI, including wet beds and little sleep during the night.

> *"There's winning and there's losing, and in life you have to know that they both will happen. But what's never been acceptable to me is quitting."*
>
> -Earvin 'Magic' Johnson-

We continue to work on finding Sebastian suitable therapists here at home, away from QCH. We have engaged with a new Physiotherapist, Dr Joanne Backer (Jo) from Cairns who comes to our home every month to work with Sebastian and us as parents to improve mobility and strength in Sebastian's left side. Sebastian is a little cautious around Jo but warms to her quickly as she involves him in lots of play-based therapy with new and exciting toys. Jo is a great source of information, guiding us to make purchases of teaching aids to have at home which help Sebastian in his daily activities. She has also invited us to a Playgroup in Yorkeys Knob (Cairns) that caters to children with disability and has Physiotherapists, OT and Speech Therapists at each session to assist the children whilst they play. We look forward to going to our first session tomorrow morning and continue on a weekly basis. We are so grateful for such a fantastic initiative and the support this service provides to all children with a disability. Jo has also recommended that Sebastian try a couple of different support orthotics for his left leg and foot, now that he has grown out of his orthotic boot. She noted that his left foot still needs a lot of work and that it's important that his brain and muscles retrain themsleves correctly, and not create new, incorrect muscular memory. I plan to look into this further next week.

Speech therapy has continued with Evyenia Michellis (Nia) from the Cairns Hospital who comes up to Mossman Hospital to see Sebastian each fortnight. Nia is really terrific and again, Sebastian enjoys his time with her. Fortunately, we've also been introduced to a Speech Therapist who comes to the Julatten Community Centre each fortnight. We will have our first session with Laura Nelson this coming week and all going well, we will transition to Laura on a full-time basis. This will keep our therapies here in Julatten which is convenient and far less travel and disruption to Sebastian and the family.

We have successfully applied for a Disability Parking Permit which is making life so much easier, especially when parking at Hospitals. It also makes life a lot easier when having to transport Sebastian from the car to a store or business.

Sadly, the stress and trauma of the past seven or so months has started to take a toll on the girls. All three of them are having a lot of separation anxiety issues on a daily basis but especially every 28 days when one parent and Sebastian return to Brisbane for treatment. Nightmares about Sebastian dying have also returned so they are waking up quite distressed and tired from emotional fatigue. Even just dropping them off to school in the morning is met with at least one of the girls in tears, just feeling overwhelmed with fear for no particular reason. I've had advice from the school to engage with the Guidance Councillor, Diane Hoy, to figure out the best way to help the girls work through their emotions and fears. Diane's brother was diagnosed with Leukemia when he was 7 years old so she has first-hand experience with how traumatic Sebastian's diagnosis would be for the whole family. She will meet with the girls at school on 12th October and we'll go from there.

Lots of love, Sam, Crystal & Sebastian xoxo

Wednesday, 18 August 2020

After returning home from Brisbane last month, Sebastian and I both fell ill with a cough and cold. Sebastian complained of a "hot head" and sore tummy and was notably bloated and irritable. After seven days without improvement, we underwent a COVID-19 test at the Mossman Showgrounds on August 14th, which came back negative within 24 hours. We fully recovered after another two weeks. Despite feeling unwell, we watched in awe as Sebastian continued to improve beyond our expectations in August.

Receiving a childhood cancer diagnosis is a tough pill to swallow, and entrusting your child's survival and treatment to a team of specialists can feel overwhelmingly helpless. While chemotherapy seemed to be working as we had hoped, it brought many challenges. It took Sam and me quite some time to accept that there wasn't much we could do for Sebastian beyond waiting and allowing time to work as the best medicine. It was difficult to have no control over our child's health, especially when traditional remedies like Panadol, chicken soup, extra cuddles, a day in bed, or ice cream couldn't make it all better. We felt blessed to have a strong and happy little boy who surprised us every day. Despite everything he was going through, he continued to improve and still managed to make us laugh with his cheeky and typical two-year-old behaviour.

CLARITY - BOOK I

Timeline of Events: June 2020

02.06.2020	COVID-19 – 1 new case in QLD.
06.06.2020	COVID-19 – 2 new cases in QLD.
10.06.2020	Chemotherapy Cycle 5, Treatment 10, Day 113.
12.06.2020	COVID-19 – 3 new cases in QLD.
15.06.2020	COVID-19 – 1 new case in QLD.
17.06.2020	COVID-19 – 1 new case in QLD.
18.06.2020	COVID-19 – Aged Care facilities limited to 2 visitors.
20.06.2020	COVID-19 – Up to 2,000 fans allowed at Lang Park and The Gabba.
21.06.2020	COVID-19 – Up to 10,000 fans allowed at Lang Park on 27.07.20 in time for Broncos NRL Match.
25.06.2020	COVID-19 – 0 new cases in QLD for 1 week.
26.06.2020	COVID-19 – 1 new case in QLD.
Total COVID-19 confirmed cases in QLD as at 30.06.2020 = 1,067	

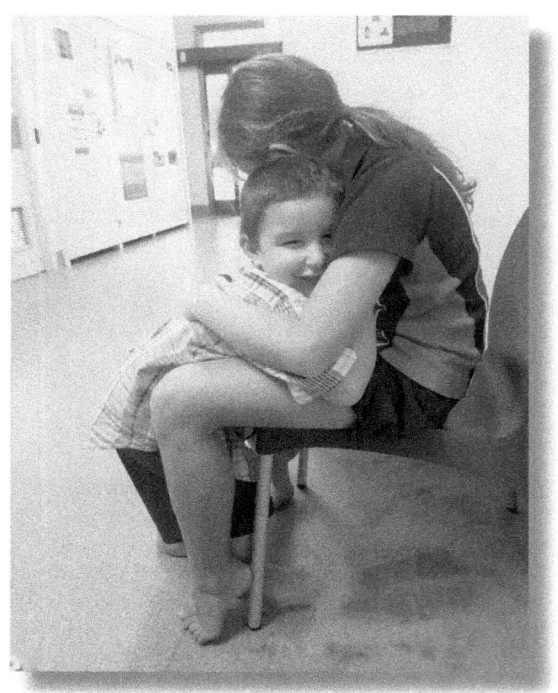

Timeline of Events: July 2020

03.07.2020	COVID-19 – Public bars open without restrictions. COVID-19 – Queenslanders returning from VIC forced to quarantine in a hotel for 2 weeks at own expense.
08.07.2020	Chemotherapy Cycle 6, Treatment 11, Day 141.
09.07.2020	COVID-19 – 1 new case in QLD.
10.07.2020	COVID-19 – QLD Borders open to all states except VIC.
14.07.2020	COVID-19 – 2 new cases in QLD. COVID-19 – QLD blocks entry to NSW residents from hotspots of Campbelltown and Liverpool after new cluster of cases in Sydney.
16.07.2020	COVID-19 – Up to 100 mourners allowed at funerals.
22.07.2020	COVID-19 – 2 new cases in QLD.
24.07.2020	COVID-19 – 3 new cases in QLD.
27.07.2020	Hormone investigations conducted at Cairns Hospital.
29.07.2020	COVID-19 – 3 new cases in QLD. COVID-19 – Parklands Christian College, YMCA Chatswood Hills State School & Outside School care closed after 2 travel companions from VIC test positive.
30.07.2020	COVID-19 – 3 new cases in QLD.
Total COVID-19 confirmed cases in QLD as at 31.07.2020 = 1,082	

Timeline of Events: August 2020

01.08.2020	COVID-19 – 1 new case in QLD.
02.08.2020	COVID-19 – 1 new case in QLD.
05.08.2020	Chemotherapy Cycle 7, Treatment 12, Day 169. Guidance Councillor engaged to help girls. Dr Joanne Backer (Jo) appointed as Sebastian's local Physiotherapist. Laura Nelson appointed as Sebastian's local Speech Therapist. Disability Parking Permit approved. COVID-19 – 2 new cases in QLD.
08.08.2020	COVID-19 – QLD Borders shut again to VIC, NSW & ACT after outbreaks. COVID-19 – 1 new case in QLD.
10.08.2020	COVID-19 – 1 new case in QLD.
14.08.2020	Sebastian and Crystal test negative to COVID-19.
20.08.2020	COVID-19 – 4 new cases in QLD.
22.08.2020	COVID-19 – 10 new cases in QLD.
23.08.2020	COVID-19 – 2 new cases in QLD.
24.08.2020	COVID-19 – People in SE QLD urged to wear face masks outside homes. COVID-19 – 1 new case in QLD.
26.08.2020	COVID-19 – All Correctional Facilities in QLD locked down due to positive test result at Training Academy. COVID-19 – 2 new cases in QLD.
27.08.2020	COVID-19 – 2 new cases in QLD.
Total COVID-19 confirmed cases in QLD as at 31.08.2020 = 1,110	

Messages of Love

"Wow! Half way already. What a journey for everyone. You are all doing an amazing job and Sebastian is a little trooper! Thanks for the updates we are always thinking of you guys."

"He's just the bravest little man I know. I adore him."

"Thanks for the update. It is always good to hear how things are progressing. You must be so exhausted yet somehow you manage to find positives in things. You really are a remarkable woman and mother."

"Crystal, I think of you often. If you ever need a break from the brave face or a moment of letting it go and not coping, I'm just down the road. You are doing such an incredible job and being so brave for everyone it must be exhausting at a level I can only imagine. Please take care of yourself! Big hugs to you all."

"You and Sam are absolutely giving your little boy the very best chance! What an amazing team the two of you make. His big smiles in the photos are so beautiful."

"Crystal, thanks for the update and beautiful photos. Sebi is very lucky to have you and Sam as parents. Take care of yourselves."

"Hi Crystal, lovely to hear from you and receive Sebastian's update. What welcome relief the dry nights must be for you! Wishing for continued progress for him! He is definitely looking very happy which is lovely to see."

"Strong tuff little man. Keep up the good work mum and dad. Gorgeous photos."

"Such beautiful photos. What a strong little boy with awesome parents and siblings. You are doing an amazing job."

"Beautiful photos Crystal and Sam. Many thanks for the update. Just a few days ago I was thinking of you all and now your wonderful text has arrived. You all are doing great work under very difficult circumstances and keeping very positive. This is just fantastic. Our love to you all. Again – never be afraid to contact me if you need anything. I am basically retired and can help anytime."

"You two are amazing... keep up the good work."

"I look so forward to your texts Crystal and so appreciate the time and effort you put into keeping us all up to date on Sebastian's health issues. I often think of speaking to you instead of texting but I know your free time is about nil so for the time being texting will suffice until you have time to 'chat'. Loved the photos particularly the one of Sam and the children under the tree. Sebastian looks well and happy despite all he has to cope with. He is such a lucky little boy to have you and Sam as parents who love and nurture him as he bravely tackles each step ahead of him. Love you all dearly."

> Winnie the Pooh: "How do you spell love?"
> Piglet: "You don't spell it. You feel it."
> -Winnie the Pooh & Piglet-

Sebastian in happy times during June, July & August 2020

PART 6

24

MATTERS OF THE HEART

"You may have to fight a battle more than once to win it."
-Margaret Thatcher-

By September, Sebastian was playing freely and happily without inhibition, which was a joy to see. He had become increasingly adventurous in his play, eager to explore and try new things. His favorite activities included taking rides in the buggy, bull catcher, motorbike, ute, or any machinery in the shed.

Although still somewhat robotic, Sebastian's speech had become more fluent. Due to his recent progress, Speech Therapy sessions had been reduced to monthly rather than fortnightly. We transitioned to Laura Nelson, who met with Sebastian at the Julatten Community Centre for his sessions. Laura was impressed and excited that Sebastian was already using verbs and adjectives and expanding his vocabulary each fortnight. By mid-September, Sebastian could say phrases like, "Mummy, me go aeroplane," "Mummy, me need help," and "Mummy, me read train book." The expansion of his vocabulary made life easier and less frustrating for all of us, especially for Sebastian.

Our physiotherapist, Jo, was also impressed with Sebastian's progress in September. Sebastian was now engaging his left hand more freely and subconsciously, using it not just as a "helper hand" but as an active participant in two-handed play. I still hadn't made time to look into support wear for Sebastian's left foot, but Jo encouraged me to do so as soon as possible. We also noticed more symmetry in Sebastian's face, especially noticeable in photos. Jo was pleased with Sebastian's progress and decided to reduce the frequency of his sessions to every six weeks, a tremendous achievement considering the progress since daily physiotherapy sessions only seven months ago.

Astonishingly, we had also seen further success with Desmopressin in recent weeks. For five nights in a row the previous week, Sebastian managed to go without a wet nappy. Although the success was still sporadic, this improvement was something we never expected, given Sebastian's current condition. While the return of dry nappies didn't eliminate sleepless nights, it greatly improved the situation.

All of this positive news was wonderful to share with our family and friends. When we stood back and put everything into perspective, it was important to recognise that improvements were expected to increase rapidly now that we were almost eight months post-surgery and two-thirds of the way through chemotherapy treatment.

3:18pm, Wednesday, 2 September 2020

Chemotherapy Cycle 8, Treatment 13, Day 197

Today Sebastian and I are at QCH for chemotherapy and I've met with Rick to receive the full report from Sebastian's MRI yesterday. There was both good and bad news. Firstly, the good news was that since Sebastian's last MRI on the 6th March, the size of the tumour has reduced in size and become 'cystic'. Our greatest hope at this early stage was for no change to the tumour so we are absolutely thrilled with these results. Since its surgical reduction of 50% on the 12th January, the tumour has now decreased in size by 0.9mm from top to bottom and 3mm from left to right. The tumour has also now 'come away' from the hypothalamus, which should have resulted in Sebastian's growth to slow, not accelerate as it had been. It is now evident however that the hypothalamus has been severely damaged by surgery. In short, Rick explained that there appears to be a very limited line of communication between Sebastian's brain and stomach and that if Sebastian's growth continues at the same rate, he is at risk of cardiovascular collapse. Alarmingly, Sebastian's heart is now of more concern to the medical team than the status of his brain tumour.

This news was such an unexpected curveball! For so long, Sam and I had been feeding Sebastian limitless amounts of food, believing that keeping his weight up was essential for his health during treatment. While at QCH, we were surrounded by sick children who appeared pale and emaciated, their bodies almost skeletal. In contrast, we were proud to have a robust, chubby toddler. We never imagined that an issue could arise in this cancer journey that would put Sebastian at greater risk than his brain tumour. The potential risk to his organs from weight and growth gain had always been at the back of my mind, but I never thought it would have such a negative impact so soon.

Our next step was to further restrict Sebastian's food intake, effective immediately. Together with Dietician Aria Kerz, we established meal plans to slow down his weight gain before his next chemotherapy treatment in 28 days. We worked with the Australian Dietary Guidelines Serving Recommendations and quickly realised that while the quality of the food we were feeding Sebastian was great, we were simply allowing him to eat too much.

Although this news is overwhelmingly concerning, I am feeling optimistic that we have a lot of room for improvement regarding Sebastian's diet and that we will start to see improvements relatively quickly. We will also need to have more frequent check-ins with Sebastian's Dietician in Cairns to keep a close eye on his progress. Ultimately, Aria would like to see Sebastian's weight to sit around 20kg (he is currently 28kg), by slowly reducing his weight gain, rather than focusing on weight loss. Our goal for the next 28 days is to reduce Sebastian's weight gain from 2kg to 500g – 1kg, as Aria doesn't believe it's possible to stop his weight gain all together at this early stage.

Rick is concerned that the hypothalamus issue will be a lifelong battle for Sebastian but like every complication, we have a plan of attack, clear goals and benchmarks to work towards and an amazing medical team keeping Sebastian safe. I have such a surprising sense of optimism today, despite receiving this news. Perhaps proof is in the pudding and the positive progress we're seeing in Sebastian is starting to outweigh the new challenges we're faced with. Anyone who comes in contact with Sebastian and gets to witness his cheeky, funny and happy personality would agree he's moving mountains in terms of recovery. It makes it an honour to be on his team.

We still have stacks of work to do and our resilience grows with each new challenge. Thank you for all your support and well wishes. I'm pleased and so proud to share another month of smiles from Sebastian.

Lots of love, Sam, Crystal & Sebastian xoxo

25

ANAPHYLAXIS

9:39pm, Wednesday, 30 September 2020

Chemotherapy Cycle 9, Treatment 14, Day 225

Hello to you all. I'd like to start with the good news as right up until chemotherapy treatment today, Sebastian had had a dream month.

He has once again exceeded our expectations by embracing the changes to his diet. I'm delighted and very proud to report that Sebastian has lost 1.9kg in 28 days, since his last visit to QCH. This result has come as such a huge relief to us as parents as we've quickly remembered how tricky introducing new foods, especially vegetables, can be with a toddler. From a medical perspective, Sebastian's body's ability to drop the weight suggests that his suspected hypothalamus dysfunction may only be mild or even temporary. Dyanne our Cairns Endocrinologist, explained that it is still far too soon to accurately diagnose the extent of the damage to Sebastian's hypothalamus and pituitary gland so to continue managing his symptoms as we are.

Within two days of starting his diet, Sam and I noticed Sebastian's bloating and puffiness had reduced significantly. Within two weeks, his sleep improved dramatically. He slept for most of the night and on nights when he did wake, he settled back to sleep quickly. It was at this two-week mark that we also noticed that

Sebastian was becoming less reliant on his Desmopressin medication for DI. He is now taking two rather than four doses each day, making a huge difference to us all, especially now that the midnight dose has been eliminated.

Also due to his weight loss, Sebastian has been more active, agile and is increasingly more independent. At home, we are seeing more of the 'old Sebastian'; lots of smiles, lots of cheek and loads of enthusiasm for outside play and 'shed time' with his dad. His vocabulary is improving and his pronunciation of words is more accurate also. All in all, we were really thrilled with the results and eager to arrive in Brisbane and share the good news.

This week, Sam accompanied Sebastian to Brisbane for another chemotherapy treatment at QCH on Wednesday 30th September.

Once Sebastian's medical was complete, Sam's first meeting was with Aria Kerz, Sebastian's Dietician. She was really impressed by Sebastian's weight loss and other than a few little tips to help with further weight loss, she encouraged us to continue what we're doing. Swapping out chicken nuggets for plain steamed chicken, and white bread for multigrain bread, were some examples of how to help Sebastian feel fuller for longer and assist with digestion. Sebastian's poor bowels had been so overworked prior to commencing his diet. He would sometimes have several bowel movements every day but he was now down to 1 every other day. It was very devastating to realise just how much impact Sebastian's weight was having on his recovery and to think, Sam and I thought we were doing the best for him by feeding him as much as he could eat. We were in fact, almost killing him with kindness.

Rick is away on leave this month so Sam next met with Dr Jordan Hanford who was stepping in during Rick's absence. Again, attention was on Sebastian's progress this month and Sam received lots of very positive feedback and praise. Chemotherapy therefore started on time and up until the last hour of his Carboplatin infusion, Sebastian was his usual relaxed, sleepy self during chemotherapy.

Just after noon, Sam messaged me to ask if Sebastian's face was usually "puffy" after sleeping. I said no, but didn't think too much of it since Sam mentioned Sebastian had been sleeping on his face for the last couple of hours. About 15 minutes later, Sam called and asked if Sebastian's breathing was usually loud during sleep and whether it was unusual for him to be coughing while asleep. I asked Sam to put me on a video call so I could see Sebastian, and just as the call connected, Sebastian woke up and sat up. I noticed his face was swollen, especially around his eyes and mouth. I started to tell Sam to call a nurse when one walked in and said she was going to get assistance as his coughing and facial swelling were concerning.

Unfortunately, Sam had to hang up the phone when the medical staff arrived, leaving me pacing around my kitchen, anxiously wondering what was happening. I felt helpless, unable to support Sam and Sebastian, and now, I was in the dark about what was going on. Once again, my son's welfare was in the hands of medical professionals, and I wasn't there to provide information or be there for Sebastian emotionally. I feared Sebastian was having an adverse reaction to the chemotherapy, and since this was a new experience, I had no idea what it meant or how it would end.

** This excerpt from Sam's Carer Impact Statement in 2024 provided a more detailed recollection of what unfolded that day...

'The trauma I experienced from seeing what happened to my son will never be forgotten. I truly hope that one day the memories of it all will fade for him, that the pain will lessen, and that I can carry more of his burden.

I won't detail every single incident, but one that stands out was when he became allergic to his first course of chemotherapy. His speech was improving, allowing him to communicate. He was on a harsh regimen—12 months of carboplatin and vincristine, administered monthly. Our neuro-oncologist had warned us that it was rare for a child to complete the full 12 months; most become allergic. The month before the treatment in question, he developed a rash around the needle site, and the general consensus was that he probably had only one more treatment left, as his body was beginning to reject the chemo.

The following month, when I accompanied him, we prepared for his chemo as usual. This time, however, we were placed right next to the nurses' station. There was no panic or alarm, but a nurse did mention to me before they started administering the chemo that I should keep a close eye on him and let her know if I noticed anything unusual. They began pumping the chemotherapy into my son, and after a short while, he gave a slight cough. It was nothing serious—just a little cough—but it was something I hadn't heard before. Erring on the side of caution, I poked my head out the door and asked the nurse to come take a look.

She walked in, took one look at Sebby, and literally knocked me out of the way to press the emergency button. Within 30 seconds, no less than ten staff members arrived—one nurse with an oxygen mask, another with an adrenaline needle, and many others, all there for reasons I still don't understand. Our neuro-oncologist was also present and insisted that for Sebby's sake, they needed to complete the administration of the drug.

I held my son down while a nurse placed an oxygen mask over his little face. He was screaming in terror, repeating, "Daddy, me go home! Daddy, me go home!" I will never forget those words for as long as I live. I can't think about them, even today, without crying.'

Unfortunately, during Sebastian's chemotherapy infusion earlier today, he has had a moderate anaphylaxis episode to Carboplatin, one of his chemotherapy drugs. The alarm was raised when Sebastian's face became swollen, his airways narrowed causing him to cough constantly and after a full medical, he also had swelling and a rash to his abdomen, ears, neck, face and head, as well as nausea. He was promptly treated with an additional dose of Dexamethasone (steroid) and Zyrtec *(antihistamine) which very quickly improved his symptoms. It was very frightening, even though we had been warned about anaphylaxis back in March, as it was a rather common side effect in children receiving chemotherapy treatment. Thankfully Sebastian had already completed his Carboplatin infusion and was having the last of his post-chemo hyperhydration infusion so remained clinically stable during the episode. He was discharged from Oncology later in the afternoon, once the team were satisfied that the swelling had reduced and his airways were clear. His symptoms have now almost completely gone and Sebastian is sleeping peacefully. Sam and I on the other hand are struggling to relax after quite a frightening experience.*

With Rick being absent today, it's hard to know what this means for Sebastian's chemotherapy treatments in the future. Our clinical nurse Brooke, has advised that usually, Dexamethasone and Zyrtec would be administered prior to chemotherapy infusions beginning, to reduce the risk of further allergic reactions in future. Sebastian has received medical clearance to travel and his Oncology referral for the next scheduled chemotherapy treatment on 28th October, so we assume we will find out more on our return to QCH next month.

For now, I look forward to being able to relax once Sam and Sebastian return home tomorrow.

Lots of love, Sam, Crystal & Sebastian xoxo

This was all happening in the school holidays so I had sent the girls to stay with Mum in Cairns whilst Sam and Sebastian were in Brisbane. I thought some uninterrupted time on my own would be lovely but unfortunately it just felt weird. The house was so empty and quiet and I felt like my days had no purpose. I must say however, I'd enjoyed staying up late and getting a few odd jobs checked off a long list of neglected chores. I had to really strain to see the positives in the situation though, finding myself longing for the return of my usual chaotic and bustling home, filled with children. We still had another week of holidays ahead of us so I vowed to enjoy every minute and make the most of the time with all 4 of my beautiful children together.

Wednesday, 28 October 2020

Chemotherapy Cycle 10, Treatment 15, Day 253

Sebastian was unable to complete his chemotherapy treatment today due to another anaphylaxis episode, this time at the commencement of the Carboplatin infusion, so a much quicker reaction than the last. On commencement of chemotherapy today, Sebastian was medicated with Dexamethasone and Zyrtec as expected but unfortunately it didn't have the desired effect. The episode was an improvement on the last however with his breathing remaining normal and swelling and rash to his neck, face and lips not as severe. At the onset of anaphylaxis symptoms, additional medication stabilised Sebastian's body very quickly. We were required to remain at QCH for a little longer than usual today due to the episode, but Sebastian was eventually cleared for travel and we received his Oncology referral for next month. Rick was concerned but didn't believe the risk associated with continuing chemotherapy despite the mild anaphylaxis was high enough to delay the next scheduled chemotherapy treatment.

Sebastian's recovery from his chemotherapy treatment on September 30th was slower than usual due to the anaphylaxis episode. However, overall, the month leading up to his next chemotherapy on October 28th was good. Sebastian struggled more with his diet than in the previous month, which we later learned was due to a growth spurt. He grew 1.7cm in height while still managing to lose 1.1kg in the 28 days since his last check-up. Rick and Sebastian's dietician, Aria, were thrilled with his progress and encouraged us to continue with his diet.

Sebastian's Diabetes Insipidus (DI) also began to stabilise in October, resulting in fewer wet nappies and a bit more sleep during the night. This was a significant turning point for Sam and me, as we started feeling much better with the increased rest. We continued to work with the endocrinology team to fine-tune Sebastian's Desmopressin dosages, aiming to help his body maintain the reduction of symptoms.

In other life news, we are all looking forward to finishing off this year with Sebastian's final two chemotherapy treatments at QCH. The children and Sam and I are feeling extremely exhausted after the events of 2020, a feeling I'm sure is being felt around the world due to COVID-19. We look forward to getting through an always busy 4th term at school and Kindy and starting the long 6 weeks of Christmas holidays in early December.

Wishing you all so much love and thanks for your continued support. It's comforting to know we have a huge team cheering Sebastian on in this fight for his life.

Lots of love, Sam, Crystal & Sebastian xoxo

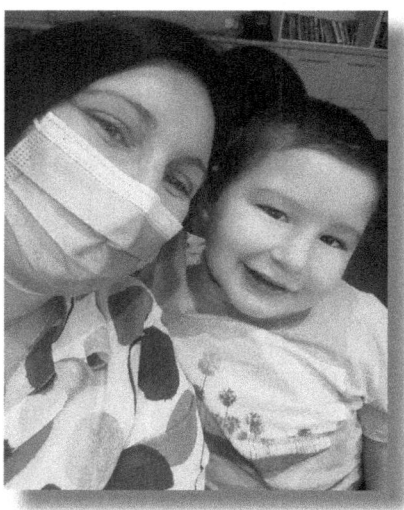 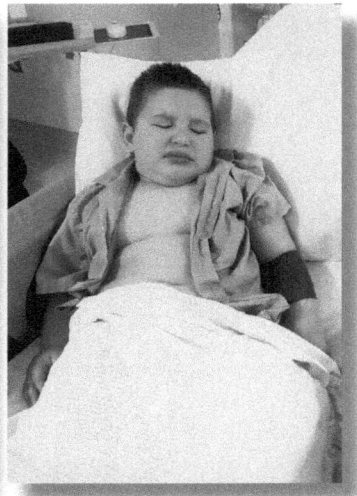

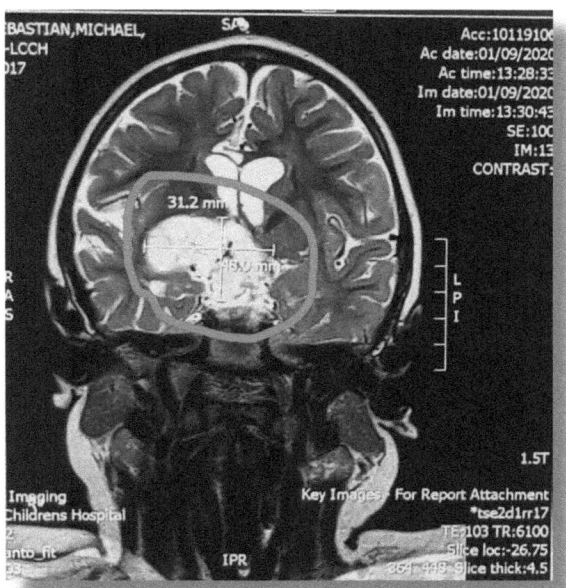
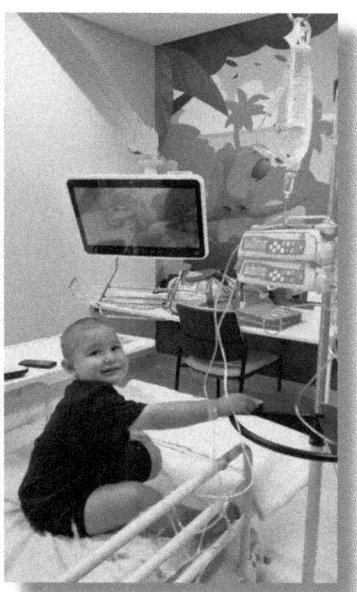

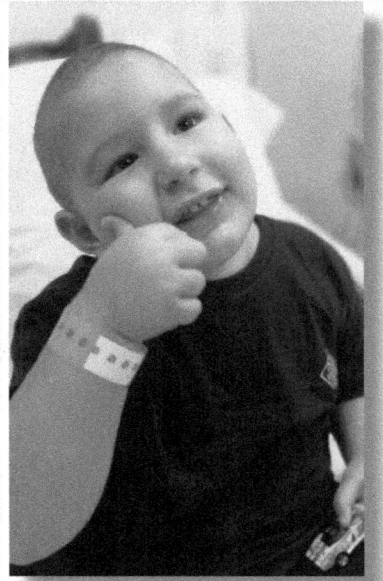

The highs & lows of September & October 2020 including Sebastian's MRI on 1 September 2020

Fathers Day, 6 September 2020

26

MORE LOVE THAN FEAR

9:41pm, Wednesday, 25 November 2020

Chemotherapy Cycle 11, Treatment 16, Day 281

Sam accompanied Sebastian to Brisbane for chemotherapy treatment today, his 2nd last session before his next Neurology Review in January 2021. Prior to chemotherapy commencing, Sam met with Rick for Sebastian's monthly medical and catch up. I received a call from Sam to say that results from Sebastian's tests this morning revealed his platelet blood count was at a concerningly low level and Rick had postponed Sebastian's final chemotherapy treatment until 6th January 2021. Rick was confident that Sebastian's bone marrow would have enough time to recover his platelet count by 6th January and that the extra time would allow his body to receive his final chemotherapy treatment. Sebastian's platelet count is at 120, much lower than the healthy count in children of between 150 and 400. This discovery gave us some explanation as to why Sebastian had not been himself in the last 28 days, where he often complained of feeling sick, was extremely lethargic and just a bit 'off' in general.

I became particularly concerned on Thursday 19th November when Sebastian had been sleeping a lot more than usual during the day. He had also been irritable that morning and had mild swelling around his mouth and eyes, before and after sleep.

With advice from Oncology at QCH we presented Sebastian to Emergency at Cairns Hospital but after further investigation and a few tests, he was cleared to return home. We put his lethargy down to his body's slower than usual recovery from chemotherapy due to the anaphylaxis episode and the additional drugs he had received to manage it. We now know however, that his low platelet count was struggling to keep up with the stress a build-up of chemotherapy was putting on his body and that recovery would be a long and slow process.

Chemotherapy then started on time this morning and all was going well until about midday. Sebastian was about ¾ of the way through his infusion and had had his pre-meds of Dexamethasone and Zyrtec to minimise the risk of anaphylaxis occurring but sadly it didn't work. Sebastian's airways narrowed to a point where he was coughing constantly, struggling to catch his breath and his abdomen swelled severely. Once Sam alerted a nurse, all hands were on deck and Sebastian had assisted breathing with oxygen and an assortment of drugs to bring the anaphylaxis under control. Sam said a team of around 10 medical staff, including Rick worked on Sebastian and successfully took total control of the reaction within about 30 minutes. The swelling to his abdomen was so severe that his Port was no longer holding a 1-inch needle so couldn't be accessed any longer to complete the chemotherapy infusion. Rick ordered the infusion to stop immediately and concluded that Sebastian's body was telling us that it couldn't handle any more.

His low platelet level was not allowing his body to fight the anaphylaxis on its own and therefore the treatment was deemed too dangerous. By 1:30pm Sebastian was breathing on his own and being encouraged to drink water, in an effort to complete the required level of hydration his body needed after a chemotherapy infusion. By 1:45pm Sebastian had hydrated enough to satisfy Rick and was relaxed and medicated enough to fall asleep.

During this entire episode, I anxiously awaited by the phone, receiving sporadic messages from Sam with only bits of information. Once again, I felt completely helpless and deeply saddened that I wasn't with Sebastian during this battle. I had full faith in Sam, but it was always harder being the one left behind, separated from Sebastian when things went wrong. I was beside myself with worry, frantically googling everything about anaphylaxis caused by chemotherapy in children. It was possibly the longest 30 minutes of my life. Thankfully, the crisis passed, and Sebastian was okay. The emotional trauma, however, took me almost 24 hours to recover from, and it was tough to deal with on my own. Sam and I had a long debrief that night, which helped, but it wasn't until our conversation the next morning that I found true solace. Sam's words soothed my heart when he said, "It's okay, today he gets to start the rest of his life," referring, of course, to the completion of Sebastian's chemotherapy treatment, albeit prematurely. In that moment, I felt an immense sense of peace. Completing chemotherapy, regardless of the circumstances, meant that Sebastian would finally have time to heal, recover, relax, and blossom into the boy he was meant to be. He hadn't known a life without a brain tumour, potentially never knowing a life without pain either. I felt sudden relief that we were about to enter the next chapter of his childhood, and the trauma and pain I had experienced in the previous 24 hours slipped away. There was suddenly more hope than despair, more to look forward to than fear, and more love than anxiety.

Sam had to wait until Sebastian stabilised before he was able to leave the Hospital at 5pm. Sebastian is ok, just totally exhausted, traumatised and heavily medicated. Today's events conclude Sebastian's chemotherapy treatments for now. Rick said that it's not ideal but very common for children to struggle to complete their entire schedule of treatment due to similar complications. Thankfully, Sebastian was strong enough to get through 11 of his 12 cycles, completing 16 of 17 chemotherapy treatments. I feel disappointed that we didn't get to the end of treatment and ring that bell, and that it wasn't a clean finish. I am grateful however for what we were able to achieve and just hope that it's enough. A likely date for Sebastian's MRI is around 11th January where the images will provide the team with a baseline to go by for future reviews in 2021 (every three months).

Now, we just wait and watch Sebastian recover from what has been an absolutely traumatic year. Today marks day 281 since chemotherapy started, 323 days or 11 months and 17 days since this whole nightmare began. It's now time for us all to breathe a sigh of relief, hang up our boots and begin to heal, from the inside out.

On a positive note, Rick shared some encouraging information with us regarding the effects of chemotherapy on brain tumours, particularly Juvenile Pilocytic Astrocytomas like Sebastian's. We learned that chemotherapy could potentially cut off the blood supply to the tumour, effectively 'killing' the cancer. Remarkably, this process could continue for up to 18 months post-treatment. Until now, Sam and I had understood from early discussions with the medical team, shortly after the surgery on January 12th, that chemotherapy could not completely 'kill' Sebastian's tumour but could only slow its growth by destroying any dividing cells within it. So, this clarification from Rick was incredibly exciting, giving Sam and me hope for the first time that Sebastian might go into remission, a possibility we hadn't dared to consider due to the complexity of his cancer and its location in the brain.

Alternatively, Rick mentioned that tumour growth could recur within 6-12 months after treatment completion, which, while not ideal, was a relief compared to the uncertainty of it returning unpredictably years later. The fear associated with Sebastian's initial diagnosis continued to haunt us, even months later. The scheduled MRIs in 2021 would monitor the tumour's progression and determine which direction Sebastian's condition might take.

I am very happy to report that Sebastian no longer suffers from Diabetes Insipidus. We have not medicated him for 21 of the last 28 days and he has maintained good sodium levels whilst his body manages its fluid intake and output on its own. Such a huge relief! The sudden 'disappearance' of DI is thought to be due to shrinkage of the tumour and the proximity of the tumour to the pituitary gland. It also confirms that the onset of DI initially was due to aggravation to the pituitary gland, not damage and time has recovered the pituitary gland of that aggravation.

Obviously, Rick was very pleased with this outcome and was thrilled that Sebastian's weight and growth had continued to stabilise. Sebastian lost a further 550g and only grew 0.2cm in the last 28 days. All further evidence that the hypothalamus function was also returning to normal and the issues we'd had post-surgery were due to trauma or aggravation to the brain, not permanent damage.

Sebastian has been cleared for travel tomorrow so he and Sam will return home as planned.

Thank you for reading this very long update and if you have, thank you for caring and loving our little boy.

Lots of love, Sam, Crystal and Sebastian xoxo

4:18am, Friday, 25 December 2020

Merry Christmas to you all, our amazing friends and family.

Well, we made it to Christmas! Sebastian is now 30 days post chemo and doing really really well. He turned 3 this week so it's a wonderfully happy time for us.

Sam and I are so grateful for all of your love and support this year and hope 2021 brings us all lots of good health, better luck, lots of love and loads of laughs.

Lots of love to you all from us, Sam, Crystal, Antonia, Josie, Alyssa & Sebastian xoxoxo

5:12pm, Thursday, 31 December 2020

Sam and I would like to wish you all a very happy, safe and exciting new year. 2020 was a challenge to say the least, but my wish is that we can all look back on the year that has strengthened our resilience, reminded us how lucky we are to be Australians and taught us to focus on what's really important – our relationships with each other. Thank you all for reminding us how much love you have for our little family and for wrapping us up in support when we needed it most.

Sebastian has been thriving, now 36 days post chemo. We continue to work through sleepless nights and a very hungry toddler at times but are overall excited about how well he is. He is not being medicated at all, other than his routine antibiotics to cover for illness whilst his immune system remains compromised. This is an overwhelmingly positive and unexpected outcome after expecting Sebastian to live a life that relied on medications to control a long list of health issues. This all contributes to keeping a positive outlook for the future where time will hopefully correct the issues he is having with sleep and his body clock, all believed to be a direct result of the brain tumour, which unfortunately is still there.

On 17th December, we had a Neurological review with lead surgeon, Dr Gert Tollesson. He was pleased and surprised to hear how well Sebastian is, so soon after surgery (2-year recovery time expected for Sebastian's brain surgery). Gert was happy to leave us in the capable hands of Oncologist, Rick over the next 12 months, whilst Sebastian undergoes 3 monthly MRIs. Gert explained that if there is any concern regarding growth or change to the tumour, his recommendation would be for another cycle of chemotherapy, rather than surgery as a preferred treatment plan. Gert also recommended that we continue to have Sebastian's eyesight and hearing checked regularly as another insurance that nothing sinister is developing inside Sebastian's brain. Gert has booked Sebastian in for an MRI on 12th January 2021 at QLD Children's Hospital. We will then meet with Rick on 13th January to discuss the MRI findings and blood results. Sebastian and I hope to be in Brisbane on 11th-13th January, for a short and sweet visit whilst the girls are home on school holidays. I will be sure to update you on our next appointments at QCH and hope to report good things.

However you are celebrating the end of 2020 tonight, please be safe and have fun! Sam and the kids and I are enjoying lots of rain at home and hope more than anything for a decent night's sleep to see in the new year. May 2021 be an extraordinary one!

Sam, Crystal, Antonia, Josie, Alyssa & Sebastian xoxo

"*Try to be a rainbow in someone's cloud.*"
-Maya Angelou-

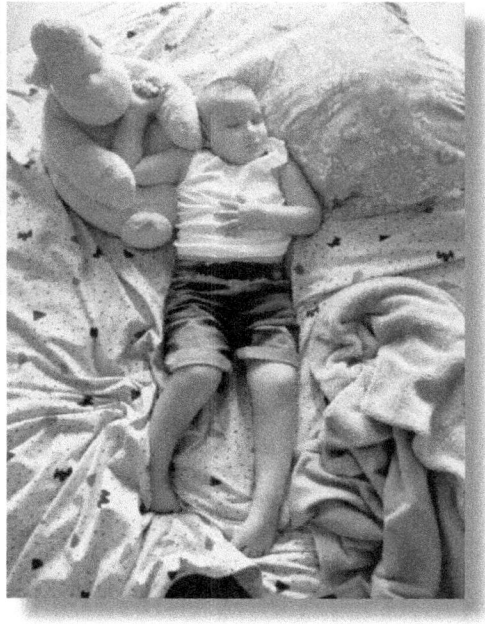

Timeline of Events: September 2020

01.09.2020	MRI at QCH.
02.09.2020	Chemotherapy Cycle 8, Treatment 13, Day 197. Meetings with Dr Rick Walker and Dietician Aria Kerz to receive MRI results and establish meal plans for weight loss.
08.09.2020	COVID-19 – 1 new case in QLD.
09.09.2020	COVID-19 – 8 new cases in QLD.
12.09.2020	COVID-19 – 3 new cases in QLD.
15.09.2020	COVID-19 – 1 new case in QLD.
26.09.2020	COVID-19 – 3 new cases in QLD.
30.09.2020	Chemotherapy Cycle 9, Treatment 14, Day 225. 1.9kg weight loss during first 28 days of restricted diet 1st Anaphylaxis reaction (mild) to chemotherapy.

Timeline of Events: October 2020

28.10.2020	Chemotherapy Cycle 10, Treatment 15, Day 253. 2nd Anaphylaxis reaction (moderate) to chemotherapy.

Timeline of Events: November 2020

04.11.2020	COVID-19 – 2 new cases in QLD.
19.11.2020	Sebastian admitted to Cairns Hospital after being irritable and lethargic all day. Released from Hospital at 11:00pm, after stabilising.
25.11.2020	Chemotherapy Cycle 11, Treatment 16, Day 281. 3rd Anaphylaxis reaction (severe) to chemotherapy Chemotherapy treatment ceased.

Timeline of Events: December 2020

17.12.2020	Neurological review with Dr Gert Tollesson.
18.12.2020	COVID-19 – 3 new cases in QLD.
23.12.2020	Sebastian's 3rd birthday.
25.12.2020	COVID-19 – 2 new cases in QLD.
28.12.2020	COVID-19 – 5 new cases in QLD.
30.12.2020	Cancelled - Chemotherapy Cycle 12, Treatment 17.
31.12.2020	COVID-19 – 3 new cases in QLD.
Total COVID-19 confirmed cases in QLD as at 31.12.2020 = 1,253	
Total COVID-19 confirmed cases in QLD as at 31.12.2021 = 13,863	

Messages of Love

"God how scary! That aside – Sebby is kicking this out of the park. Go boy. So happy to hear he is improving and being more of his happy little self!"

"Hello beautiful, I love receiving your updates of all this good news (except for chemo experience). It fills my heart to hear how well Sebastian is doing. Thanks too for sending all the photos. Oh my, just beautiful seeing Sam and Sebastian cuddling and all the boys out working. Sending you all loads of love."

"It often feels like two steps forward and one back with Sebastian's health so I can imagine it feels very challenging for you and Sam. Enjoy what is left of the school holidays. Thinking of you."

"Oh Crystal, so happy Sebby is just smashing through this so well! What a trooper! Sending love love love love."

"Gosh Crystal, what a monster of a day. Thank you for sharing this update with us. I read it aloud to the family and my stomach reacts each time I read the next section. I honestly cannot imagine what it's like to be in your shoes as parents. You are all incredible, and Sebastian is just so strong to deal with these challenges. We send you all so much love and care."

"Thank you for the update Crystal. Another month of ups and downs for your family. I was in tears reading your message. What your family has been through is just beyond words. You can definitely see in the last photo that Sebastian has slimmed down. All our prayers are with you that the chemo he has under his belt will work to blast that tumour!"

"Thank you for such an intensive update. It must be very hard on you writing them (or maybe it helps get things straight in your mind?) sending you biggest loves. Sebastian is such a strong little boy but his body says NO now. Sounds positives about his Diabetes Insipidus and such a relief. Now to let his body and brain heal itself in a circle of love. Hope to see you all at Christmas time."

"You beautiful gorgeous Leonardi family. We are all so thankful and grateful that little Sebastian is home and doing well and able to have a family Christmas with you all together. Merry Christmas to you all. Sending huge love and hugs."

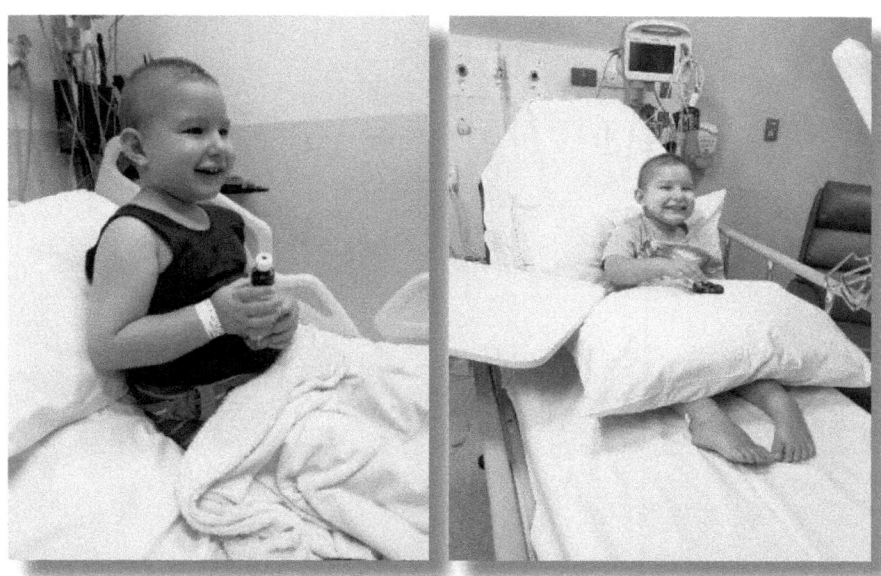

At Cairns Hospital on 19 November 2020 and at Chemotherapy Cycle 11, Treatment 16, Day 281 at QLD Children's Hospital, 25 November 2020

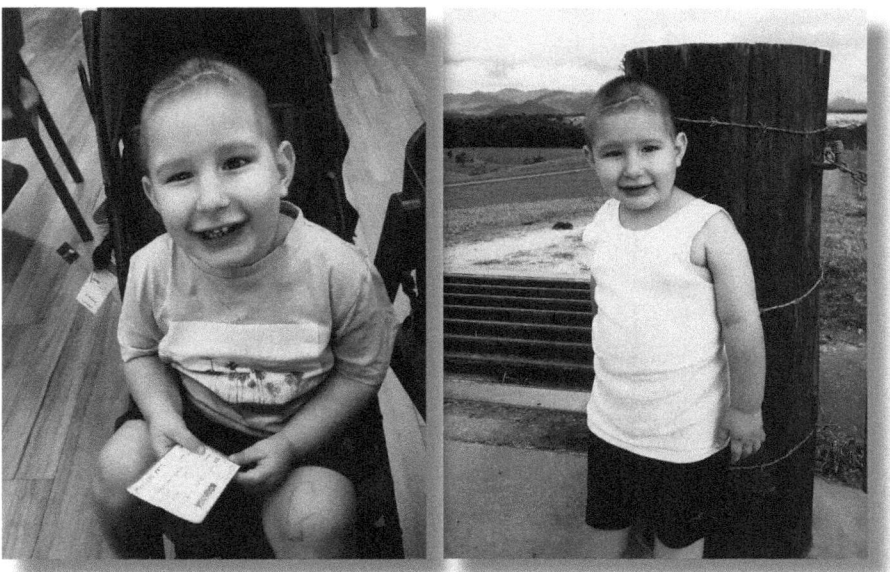

Celebrating Antonia's 10th birthday on 30 November 2020, Sebastian's 3rd birthday on 23 December 2020 and the kids on Christmas Day 2020

PART 7

Fact: As of 2023, around 84% of children diagnosed with cancer will survive at least five years after their diagnosis, a significant increase from 72% in the early 1990s. This improvement is largely attributed to advancements in treatments and early detection methods, highlighting the progress made in paediatric oncology.[7]

27

ONE YEAR ON

Without a doubt, COVID-19 intensified the challenges we faced in 2020. As the world welcomed a new year, Australians looked forward to a better 2021, buoyed by the fact that the pandemic was relatively under control in our part of the world. With minimal community transmission and positive cases mainly linked to travellers, health care workers, and hotel quarantine staff, the public began to relax and reconnect on a community level.

However, on January 8, 2021, Queenslanders were jolted by a new development when a positive case of the more contagious UK strain of COVID-19 was detected in the community, believed to have escaped from hotel quarantine in Brisbane. This heightened threat led to a 3-day lockdown affecting more than 2 million residents in the Greater Brisbane area. With just 3 days left before Sebastian and I were scheduled to fly to Brisbane, our concerns for our safety escalated rapidly.

---

[7] Australian Institute of Health and Welfare (AIHW) Cancer Data.

Despite the lockdown, Cairns Hospital and Queensland Children's Hospital had not advised cancelling essential medical or oncology procedures. This meant that Sebastian and I would be entering what felt like a 'war zone,' a situation Sam and I had hoped to avoid unless absolutely necessary. We relied on the advice from QCH and Sebastian's medical team, who assured us that the risk of traveling into Brisbane was manageable, despite the media frenzy surrounding the UK strain of COVID-19 that had finally reached Australia.

As we prepared to travel on January 11th, I was uncertain whether we would be required to quarantine upon our return home. My resilience to last-minute disruptions had been tested over the previous year, but the ongoing uncertainty served as a stark reminder of our vulnerability.

11:56am, Wednesday, 13 January 2021

We have had a very productive and positive stay in Brisbane after arriving on Monday 11th January, despite entering during the 3-day COVID-19 lockdown. Thankfully we will be able to return home tonight as planned, without having to quarantine.

Yesterday, Sebastian had routine blood tests and Port flush as well as an MRI under general anaesthetic at QCH. Sebastian was very relaxed going into the Hospital and extremely calm once in theatre, allowing the general anaesthetic to work its magic without resistance or fear. Unfortunately, on our arrival at QCH this morning however, Sebastian was very distressed and crying to go home as we pulled into the entrance of the Hospital. He fought me as I tried to get him out of the car and kept screaming to me that he didn't want to 'go in there' because 'they hurt me'. All I could do was choke back the tears as we moved through the routine security and health checks at the entrance of the Hospital and console my little boy who I believe thought he was going into Hospital for a round of chemotherapy treatment.

Thankfully, I was able to calm both myself and Sebastian down with a few phone calls to home and we were able to meet with Rick without any more tears from either of us.

Sebastian's reaction to our arrival at the Hospital that morning really unsettled me, momentarily knocking me off balance. I had believed that we were past the worst of our Hospital visits and that Sebastian's anxiety had diminished, especially after his remarkable display of resilience, courage, and bravery the previous day. However, his response reminded me that, like me, he too had his vulnerable moments. The trauma of the past 12 months was far from resolved, resurfacing unexpectedly and undermining any emotional control we thought we had achieved.

Our highly anticipated results from yesterday's tests and MRI have now been received and I'm so thrilled to report only positive things.

Tumour: Further reduction in overall size. The shape of the tumour has changed due to the continued impact of Gert (Neurosurgeon) cutting blood supply during surgery on 12.01.20. The posterior component of the tumour has 'folded in' on itself, as the bulk of the tumour continues to collapse. This helps to explain the improvement we have seen in the function of Sebastian's hormones as it is now evident that there is less weight on his pituitary gland and hypothalamus.

The tumour overall now appears to be cystic which, in an Oncologist's view, is far more manageable than tumour/cancer growth. Rick explained that if the cysts begin to grow again, they can be drained and probably wouldn't need further chemotherapy treatment, unlike tumour growth. Furthermore, in Rick's opinion, he would be very surprised to see the tumour aspect of Sebastian's cancer to become unstable again due to the evident success chemotherapy treatment has had thus far. However, Rick was unfortunately unable to answer my questions around the likelihood of cyst or tumour re-growth as there are no other cases like Sebastian's that he has treated. This lack of experience to draw on was a little unsettling but mostly disappointing to hear, however I have realised now that having little expectations and hundreds of similar case studies may protect us from disappointments and heartbreak if the worst was to occur in the future. All of a sudden, the unknown has potentially become a safe place.

Cysts: There is strong evidence to suggest that the blood supply has been completely cut as the cysts continue to reduce in size. It is clear from the MRI images that the remaining cyst is now 'empty' and not affecting Sebastian's brain as severely. Simply taking up space inside the brain and impacting on vital glands and blood supply have always been the cysts' most dangerous weapon. However, it is evident that this risk reduces further as the remaining cyst continues to reduce in size and volume.

All of Sebastian's blood tests produced perfect numbers yesterday, including evidence of perfect kidney and liver function. Sebastian is now free of his weekly Bactrim antibiotic also as Rick sees very little reason why he'd be at greater risk of illness than any other 3-year-old, now that he has ceased chemotherapy treatment. Unfortunately, chemotherapy has eliminated the effectiveness of his immunisations to date, so Sebastian will be given the required doses once he is 6 months past his last chemotherapy treatment.

Sebastian's weight and growth have continued on a positive path also. He has had another growth spirt which made him a little hungrier than normal over the last few weeks but has still managed to trend positively on the growth charts, so we're really relieved about that. In the 1 year between diagnosis, Sebastian has grown 11.4cm (double the average) and gained almost 11kg (5 x the average). We do occasionally feel overwhelmed with the impact of so much growth Sebastian's body has achieved in such a short time but to remain positive about the new direction the weight loss is going, we simply look at photographs of Sebastian from 3 months ago to recognise how well he is doing now.

Moving forward, in 2021 our focus is on physiotherapy & OT to further correct Sebastian's left side hemiplegia, speech therapy and 3-monthly MRIs. Our next visit to QCH is booked for 12th April where Sebastian will have an MRI, surgery to remove his Port-a-cath and another Oncology review with Rick.

Overall, we feel that these are exciting times as we look forward to a positive 2021. Sebastian has been extremely well and continuing to improve every day. He still has trouble sleeping but we look forward to addressing this issue in another 12 months' time, when his brain has fully recovered from surgery.

Now that we are able to return from Brisbane, I am really looking forward to the final two weeks of holidays with all four children.

Lots of love, Sam, Crystal & Sebastian xoxo

> *"Life goes on, live it well."*
> -Unknown-

28

IN THE BEGINNING...

In the beginning of this journey, there was immense doubt about whether Sebastian would make it to Christmas 2020. Shortly after his diagnosis, I feared that Christmas 2019 might have been our last with him. Throughout this year, we have lived in constant fear of losing our baby boy, and the pain and trauma associated with that fear have forever changed us all.

Sebastian's story has touched countless lives. His strength has been an inspiration to many, and our story will remain etched in our hearts forever. For reasons beyond our understanding, Sam and I were entrusted with guiding our child through a life-threatening illness, a task that often seemed insurmountable. I believe in fate and destiny, and I am convinced that we were chosen to be the parents with the strength and determination needed to face this enormous challenge on behalf of our son. We are not finished yet; this is merely the first chapter in Sebastian's story. His book still has many pages yet to be written.

I believe Sebastian has a lifetime of happiness ahead of him, despite the inevitable health battles he may face. We are far from finished fighting. We still have an immense amount of strength and resolve, and we will never surrender to cancer. Sebastian has cancer, but cancer does not define him. Should it return, we will be ready with unwavering strength and courage.

Now is the time to celebrate, to experience life through our children's eyes, and to cherish every precious moment with them. Sebastian has brought us closer together and rallied his "troops" like a true leader. We entered a battle we never chose, fought a war we felt unprepared for, and, in the words of Julius Caesar, we "Came, Saw, Conquered."

The steadfast support and compassion from our family, friends, and community throughout 2020 will remain with us forever. Our local community, Sam's employers, and even strangers showed a level of kindness that was crucial to our emotional survival. Our parents became guardians to our three beautiful girls, providing them with love, security, and reassurance when Sam and I lacked the strength. Sam's employer and the school community took a compassionate approach to our situation, alleviating our concerns about the impact of our absence on work and school commitments. For this, we are eternally grateful.

I write this story hoping it will provide what so many parents facing a life-threatening childhood cancer diagnosis desperately need: HOPE. Our story has not been a fairy tale, and we have overcome numerous challenges to reach this chapter. But there are more chapters yet to come. There are still many pages in Sebastian's book that are yet to be filled.

As parents, it is our duty to protect, advocate for, and fight for our children, no matter how daunting the battle. You must find the strength within yourself and be inspired and humbled by your child's resilience. They embody survival, never quitting or giving in. They fight, and they need our voices to advocate for them and our hearts to hold boundless love. Because as long as there is life, there is hope.

At times, I feel as though a part of me died the day Sebastian was diagnosed with cancer. His diagnosis stole our innocence and plunged us into a torturous journey that awakened a profound empathy for suffering and an awareness of life's fragility. Before Sebastian's diagnosis, I naively didn't realise that children could get brain cancer, or understand how common and life-threatening it could be, especially in children. Sebastian did nothing wrong; one day, something was simply not right with my baby. The world seemed to fall silent as the cancer diagnosis overshadowed all other concerns, reminding me of the preciousness of my children. When Sebastian's life was threatened, so was mine, and that realisation has changed me forever.

*"Someday when the pages of my life end,
I know that you will be one of its most beautiful chapers."*
-Unknown-

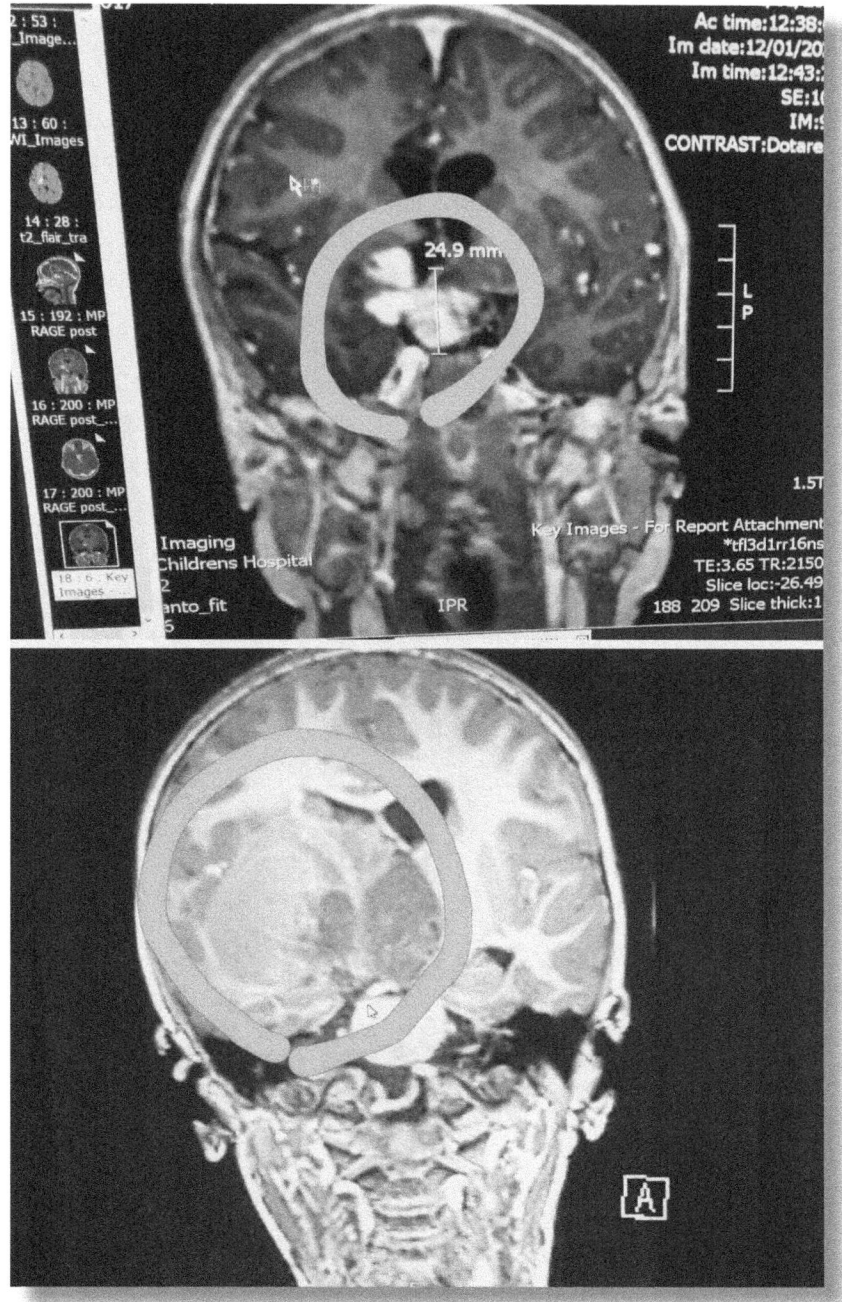

A picture of progress. The top MRI is from January 2021, 1 year after the very first haunting MRI from 8 January 2020

ACKNOWLEDGEMENTS

I'd like to express my deepest thanks and gratitude to the medical staff who treated Sebastian throughout 2020 and beyond. Dr Gert Tollesson and Dr Rick Walker lead teams of highly capable, professional and compassionate specialists who guided Sebastian's body through life-saving surgery and treatment. QLD Children's Hospital embraced our family and honoured our son with world-class care and support. I feel so very privileged and humbled that my son has access to such an extraordinary medical facility, in our home state of QLD.

To all the charitable organisations that extended their hand to us in our darkest moments, thank you. For everything you do for children with serious illness and their families, we appreciate you, for all the unnoticed generosity, we appreciate you, and for the loving hugs, the extra mile and your compassion, we thank you. Your kindness will remain close to my heart forever.

My completion of this project could not have been accomplished without the guidance of several proofreaders, editors and mentors. I am extremely grateful to my cousin, Georgia who was the first to read an excerpt of the first draft. Georgia, you provided me with invaluable advice and gave me the courage to tell my story and focus on my purpose and motivation to help other families in a similar situation. To my dear friends Yvette, Angelica and Chantal, I give special thanks to you for always being my spiritual support and guiding light when I need clarity, grounding and a reminder of just how powerful I can be.

Finally, to my loving and supportive family, my deepest gratitude. Your courage and resilience when times get tough inspire me to be better every day. I feel blessed to be part of such an honest, nurturing, close-knit family who have always made me feel loved. To my husband, Sam, my toughest critic but my staunch pillar of strength, I love you. You inspire me to work hard, have fun and enjoy the simple pleasures in life. Together, we can do anything.

SEBASTIAN'S MEDICAL TEAM

Dr Tim Hassall	Senior Paediatric Oncologist, QLD Children's Hospital Director, Centre for Children & Adolescent Brain Cancer
Dr Gert Tollesson	Adult & Paediatric Spine & Brain Surgeon, QLD Children's Hospital
Jason	Neurological Nurse, QLD Children's Hospital
Dr Peter Wilson (Happy)	Oncologist & Palliative Care Specialist, QLD Children's Hospital
Dr Rick Walker	Oncologist & Palliative Care Specialist, QLD Children's Hospital
Brooke Spencer	Paediatric Oncology Liaison Nurse, QLD Children's Hospital
Dr Ahmad	Neurosurgeon, QLD Children's Hospital
Dr Sarah Mills	Neurosurgeon, QLD Children's Hospital
Dr Sherie	Neurosurgeon, QLD Children's Hospital
Dr Jordan Staunton	Oncology Registrar, QLD Children's Hospital
Denise Peterson	Paediatric Oncology Liaison Nurse, Cairns Hospital
Dr Tim Warnock	Paediatrician, Flecker House, Cairns
Dr Gary Litherland	GP, Cairns Travel Clinic, Cairns
Dr Anandakumarasamy Murugesampillai	GP, Mountain View Medical Centre, Mossman
Dr Dyanne Wilson	Paediatric Endocrinologist, Cairns Hospital
Dr Louise Conwell	Paediatric Endocrinology & Diabetes Specialist, QLD Children's Hospital
Chrissy	Paediatric Endocrinologist, QLD Children's Hospital
Emma	Paediatric Endocrinologist, QLD Children's Hospital

Jessica Tibbs	Paediatric Occupational Therapist, Cairns Hospital
Anshu Sharma	Paediatric Occupational Therapist, QLD Children's Hospital
Anne-Maree King	Paediatric Physiotherapist, QLD Children's Hospital
Joanne Backer	Paediatric Physiotherapist, Cairns
Donna Fallon	Paediatric Physiotherapist, Cairns Hospital
Hannah	Orthotic Solutions, Brisbane
Rebecca Petre	SSS Prosthetics & Orthotics, Cairns
Claire Radford	Senior Speech Pathologist, Oncology & Palliative Care, QLD Children's Hospital
Evyenia (Nia) Michellis	Speech Therapist, Cairns Hospital
Laura Nelson	Speech Therapist, Tablelands Speech Pathology
Cathryn (Cat) Grubb	Speech Therapist, Chatter Cat Speech Pathology, Cairns
Eimear Mahon	Dietician, QLD Children's Hospital
Aria Kerz	Dietician, QLD Children's Hospital
Katie Lindeberg	Senior Social Worker, QLD Children's Hospital
Diane Hoy	Guidance Officer, Far North QLD
Rachel Cartwright	Welfare Officer, QLD Children's Hospital
Maria Atkinson	Administration Officer, Patient Travel, Mossman Hospital
Beris Walsh	Administration Officer, Patient Travel, Mossman Hospital

CHARITIES & VOLUNTEERS

Brainchild Foundation Australia

Camp Quality Cancer Charity Australia

Cancer Council QLD

Cuddle Carers – QLD Children's Hospital

Cure Brain Cancer Foundation Australia

Kerrie Gillis – Resource Centre Level 2, QLD Children's Hospital

Kids In Need of Donations Inc. (KIND) – Mossman, QLD

Kirran & Savid Gurr - Porty Shirt Crusade

Missy's Donors - Atherton, QLD

Redkite – A lifeline for families facing childhood cancer

Ronald McDonald House Charities Australia

Starlight Foundation – QLD Children's Hospital

Therapy Dogs – QLD Children's Hospital

This Strong Mum Foundation - Atherton, QLD

Welfare – Level 6f, QLD Children's Hospital

GLOSSARY

Adrenal Gland Disorder/ Failure	Adrenal gland disorders occur when the adrenal glands make too much or too little hormone.
Bactrim	Bactrim is a prescription antibiotic used to treat and prevent certain bacterial infections. It is a combination of sulfamethoxazole and trimethoprim.
Bilaterally	Affecting both sides.
Cerebral Arteries	The cerebral arteries describe three main pairs of arteries and their branches, which perfuse the brain's cerebrum. The three main arteries are the: -The Anterior Cerebral Artery (ACA) supplies blood to the medial portion of the brain, including the superior parts of the frontal and anterior lobes. -The Middle Cerebral Artery (MCA) supplies blood to the majority of the lateral portion of the brain, including the temporal and lateral-parietal lobes. It is the largest of the cerebral arteries and is often affected by stroke. -The Posterior Cerebral Artery (PCA) supplies blood to the posterior portion of the brain, including the occipital lobe, thalamus, and mid-brain.
Cerebral Edema	Excess accumulation of fluid (edema) in the intracellular or extracellular spaces of the brain.
Cerebral Palsy (CP)	A group of movement disorders that appear in early childhood. It is caused by abnormal development or damage to the parts of the brain that control movement, balance, and posture.
Cerebrospinal Fluid (CSF)	Clear, colourless bodily fluid found in the brain and spine.
Chemotherapy	A type of cancer treatment that uses one or more anti-cancer drugs (chemotherapeutic agents or alkylating agents) in a standard regimen.
Computed Tomography (CT) Scan	Medical imaging technique used to obtain detailed internal body images.
Coronavirus Disease 2019 (COVID-19)	A contagious disease caused by the coronavirus SARS-CoV-2. The first known case was identified in Wuhan, China, in December 2019.
Craniocaudal	Extending from the cranium to the posterior (back) part of the body. The cranium is part of the skull that protects the brain and allows passage of the cranial nerves.

Craniocervical Junction	A critical Osseo-ligamentous anatomic structure that serves vital motor and sensory functions.
Craniopharyngioma	A rare type of brain tumour derived from pituitary gland embryonic tissue that occurs most commonly in children but also affects adults.
Cystic Mass (Cyst)	A cyst is a sac that may be filled with air, fluid or other material. A cyst can form in any body part, including bones, organs and soft tissues. Most cysts are noncancerous (benign), but sometimes cancer can cause a cyst.
Debulk	The reduction of as much of a tumour's bulk (volume) without the intention of a complete eradication.
External Ventricular Drain (EVD)	Also known as a ventriculostomy or extra ventricular drain, is a device used in neurosurgery to treat hydrocephalus and relieve elevated intracranial pressure when the normal flow of cerebrospinal fluid (CSF) inside the brain is obstructed. An EVD is a flexible plastic catheter placed by a neurosurgeon or neurointensivist and managed by intensive care unit (ICU) physicians and nurses. The purpose of external ventricular drainage is to divert fluid from the brain's ventricles and allow for intracranial pressure monitoring.
Frontal Lobe	The largest of the four major lobes of the brain in mammals, located at the front of each cerebral hemisphere.
Hemiplegia	The complete paralysis or weakness of one entire side of the body.
Haemorrhage	Excessive bleeding, which can occur internally or externally, often due to injury, surgery, or medical conditions.
Hydrocephalus	A condition characterised by cerebrospinal fluid (CSF) accumulation in the brain's ventricles, leading to increased pressure inside the skull.
Intravenous (IV) Fluids	Fluids administered directly into a patient's bloodstream via a vein, often used for hydration, medication delivery, or nutritional support.
Joint Hypermobility	A condition where joints have an increased range of motion, which can sometimes lead to pain or injury.
Juvenile Polycytic Astrocytoma (JPA)	A type of brain tumour that typically occurs in children and is usually slow-growing, originating from astrocytes (star-shaped brain cells).

Meningitis	Inflammation of the protective membranes covering the brain and spinal cord, often caused by infection. It leads to symptoms like fever, headache, and neck stiffness.
Magnetic Resonance Imaging (MRI)	A medical imaging technique that uses magnetic fields and radio waves to create detailed images of organs and tissues within the body.
Nasal Gastric (NG) Tube	A thin tube inserted through the nose into the stomach, used for feeding, medication administration, or draining stomach contents.
Neuro-Oncologist	A medical doctor who specialises in diagnosing and treating brain and spinal cord tumours, as well as other neurological conditions related to cancer.
Neurosurgeon	A surgeon specialising in the surgical treatment of disorders of the brain, spine, and nervous system.
Occlusion	The blockage or closing of a blood vessel or hollow organ, often leading to impaired function or reduced blood flow.
Occupational Therapist (OT)	A healthcare professional who helps individuals improve their ability to perform daily activities and work-related tasks through therapeutic interventions.
Oncology	The branch of medicine deals with diagnosing, treating, and studying cancer.
Ophthalmology	The branch of medicine and surgery that deals with diagnosing and treating eye disorders and diseases.
Optic Nerve Gliomas	Tumours that develop on the optic nerve, which can affect vision and are often associated with conditions like neurofibromatosis type 1.
Paediatric Intensive Care Unit (PICU)	A specialised Hospital unit that provides intensive care for critically ill infants, children, and adolescents.
Paediatric Oncology	The branch of medicine that deals with diagnosing and treating cancer in children.
Physiotherapist	A healthcare professional who helps patients improve movement and function through physical methods, including exercise and manual therapy.
PICC Line (Peripherally Inserted Central Catheter)	A long, thin catheter inserted into a peripheral vein and advanced to a central vein, used for long-term intravenous access.
Pituitary Gland	A small gland located at the base of the brain that regulates various hormonal functions, including growth, metabolism, and reproductive processes.

Port-a-cath	A small medical device implanted under the skin, allowing for easy access to the bloodstream for administering medications or drawing blood.
Radiation	The emission of energy as electromagnetic waves or particles, often used in medical treatments, especially for cancer, to destroy or damage cancer cells.
Stenosis	The abnormal narrowing of a passage or opening in the body, such as blood vessels or the spinal canal, which can cause various health issues.
Suprasellar	Referring to a location above the sella turcica, a bony structure at the base of the skull where the pituitary gland is located, often associated with tumours.
Triage	A department of the Hospital system that determines the priority of patients' treatments based on the severity of their condition prior to admission.
Tumour	Any abnormal mass of tissue or swelling. Like a cyst, a tumour can form in any part of the body. A tumour can be benign or cancerous (malignant).
Ventricles	Fluid-filled cavities within the brain that produce and contain cerebrospinal fluid, which cushions and protects the brain and spinal cord.
World Health Organisation (WHO)	A specialised agency of the United Nations responsible for international public health, coordinating responses to health crises and setting health standards globally.

MedlinePlus - U.S. National Library of Medicine. (https://medlineplus.gov/)
Mayo Clinic - (https://www.mayoclinic.org/)
WebMD - (https://www.webmd.com/)
Merck Manual - (https://www.merckmanuals.com/)
Dorland's Illustrated Medical Dictionary: Dorland, W. A. Newman. Dorland's Illustrated Medical Dictionary. 32nd ed. Philadelphia: Saunders, 2011.
Stedman's Medical Dictionary: Stedman, Thomas Lathrop. Stedman's Medical Dictionary. 28th ed. Baltimore: Lippincott Williams & Wilkins, 2006.

BO2OK

An Unexpected Privilege
- Celebrating 5 Years -

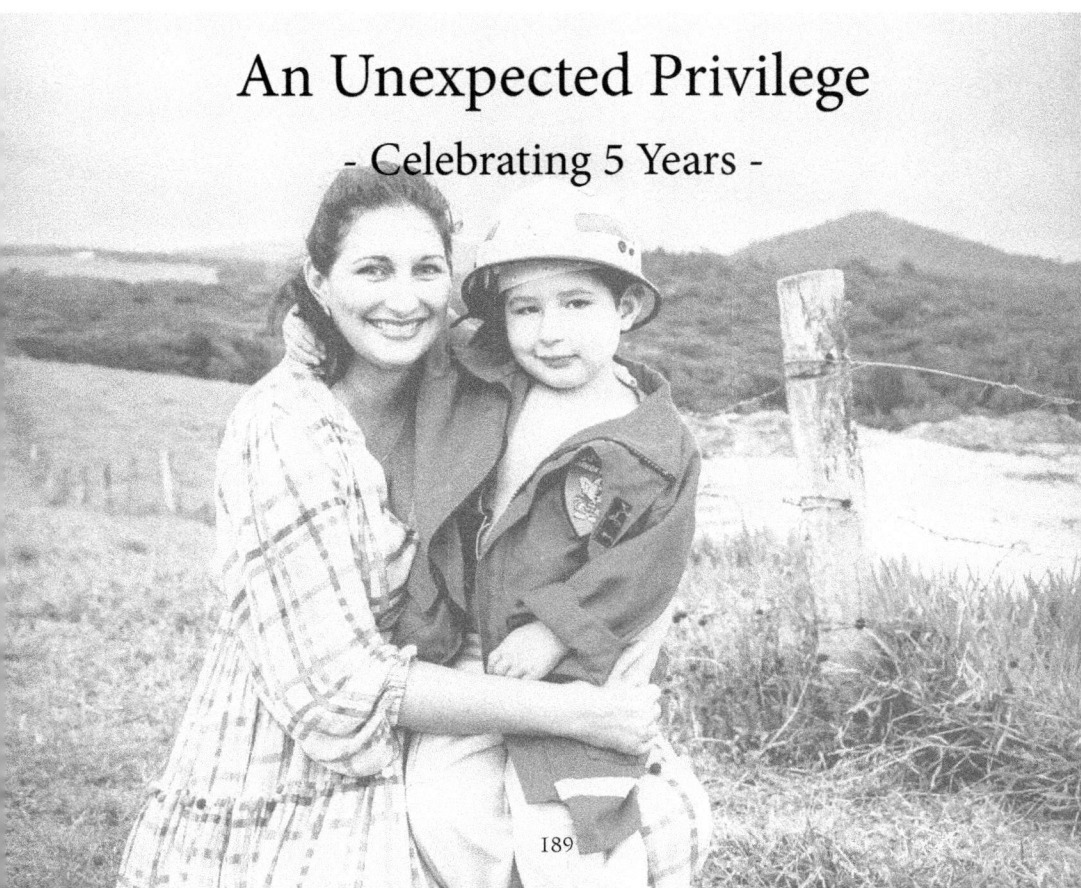

To my husband, Sam,
whose unwavering support has accompanied me
on this journey of recovery.

Though our paths to peace have been different,
we walk united, hand in hand. I love you.

Disclaimer: This book addresses sensitive topics, including cancer, mental health, and death. The content may evoke strong emotional responses and is only intended for informational and educational purposes. It is not a substitute for professional medical advice, diagnosis, or treatment. Readers are encouraged to seek guidance from qualified health professionals for personal concerns or issues related to these topics. The stories and experiences shared in this book are not exhaustive and may not reflect every individual's experience.

CONTENTS

	Foreword by Justine Christenson	Page 192
	Introduction	Page 194
1	Living in Limbo	Page 197
2	Pain into Power	Page 199
3	Little Fish, Big Cancer Pond	Page 201
4	Living Life Again	Page 202
5	Something's Gotta Give	Page 204
6	Giving In Vs Giving Up	Page 206
7	The Future is Right Outside Your Window	Page 208
	Timeline of Events 2022	Page 210
	Author's Note	Page 212
8	Freedom of Choice	Page 214
9	Tiffany – The Perfect Storm	Page 217
10	Unpacking Baggage	Page 219
11	It Is Written	Page 221
12	Just a Man	Page 223
13	It's Love	Page 226
14	No Time To Celebrate	Page 228
15	Room Twenty-Four	Page 230
16	Casualties of Cancer	Page 233
17	Chasing Dragonflies	Page 237
18	Waiting is the Worst	Page 239
19	The Chemo Rollercoaster	Page 240
20	Reflections	Page 243
	Timeline of Events 2023-24	Page 245
	Acknowledgements	Page 250

FOREWORD

Written by Justine Christerson
Founder of Breaking Down the Barriers for Rural Patients in City Hospitals - Brisbane

Imagine this sudden shift: one moment, you're in the comfort of your own home, and the next, you're confined to a sterile Hospital room, cut off from loved ones and support networks. Now, add the chaos of a global pandemic—masks, lockdowns, social isolation, and the constant fear of illness. This unimaginable reality became Crystal's when her son was diagnosed with brain cancer in 2020.

In Clarity, Book 2 of Crystal Leonardi's next chapter, you'll find the ongoing challenges faced by a family seeking specialised medical care that wasn't available in their local Hospital—care that required them to travel hundreds, even thousands, of kilometres from home. Crystal's narrative captures the emotional rollercoaster of a mother forced to leave behind the comfort and familiarity of life as a farmer's wife, traveling 1,800 kilometres to ensure her child receives life-saving treatment.

Crystal's story is a testament to the strength of the human spirit. With raw honesty, she paints a vivid picture of a mother's love and the unwavering determination to survive the unthinkable.

In November 2012, I founded 'Breaking Down the Barriers for Rural Patients in City Hospitals – Brisbane' to address the needs of rural patients and their families who must travel to Brisbane for medical care. From cancer diagnoses to traumatic injuries, appointments, surgeries and scans, these individuals often face a daunting journey, marked by isolation, financial strain, and the emotional toll of uprooting their lives due to ill-health. I am committed to providing a free and essential support service to help alleviate burdens and ensure that rural patients and their families have the resources they need to focus on healing. Families much like the Leonardi's.

Over the years, my role has evolved beyond providing basic services. I've become a lifeline for countless rural families, offering not only practical assistance but also compassionate support during their most difficult times. I've been there to listen, advise, and guide them through the complexities of navigating urban healthcare systems.

In 2020, my own family faced a devastating diagnosis. My niece was tragically diagnosed with an aggressive form of brain cancer. Despite the best efforts of medical professionals, she passed away just five days later, at the tender age of four. During this time, my sister and her husband, both from rural Victoria, found themselves not only caring for their terminally ill daughter but also navigating the challenges of a city Hospital and the isolation of a global pandemic. This heart-wrenching experience deepened my commitment to supporting rural patients and their families.

How do you find clarity when every day feels uncertain? In Clarity, Book 2, you'll witness Crystal's courageous journey after Boy of Steel, as she moves through life's in-between moments, toward a sense of clarity.

e: ruralpatient@gmail.com
fb: Breaking Down the Barriers for Rural Patients in City Hospitals
ig: ruralpatientsupport

INTRODUCTION

Publishing 'Boy of Steel' was the greatest gift I didn't know I needed. Now, in its third year since publication, I feel ready to reflect and share how such an experience has shaped me. It is no secret that Sebastian's diagnosis changed us forever, but what has been the most unexpected outcome is how much the experience has nurtured immense personal growth in me.

Writing 'Boy of Steel' kept me busy for a good 6-12 months, so once it was published, I realised that my time needed to be spent on something worthwhile. By writing and publishing, I was, for the first time in my life as a parent, doing something solely for me and for pure enjoyment. I yearned for substance, impact and inspiration to feed my grateful soul. My heart was open, and my mind was ready to embrace life's opportunities fearlessly.

If I've done my job well as a writer and you loved this book, you won't be surprised to hear that 'Boy of Steel' was the catalyst for me wanting more from and for my life. It is now 2025, and my 6th book is about to be published.

For certain, Sebastian's diagnosis was both the best and worst thing to happen to us. I will be forever grateful for the journey it has taken us on and for the way it has enriched our lives. I'm always in search of the silver lining, and I don't make light of the fact that we are living with a devastatingly cruel diagnosis, but I know more than ever that every day is a blessing and our lives are meant to be lived.

Now, as a published author and founder of Bowerbird Publishing, I share my experiences through keynote speaking, editorial writing and blogging. Sometimes I write poetry, other times, I use the space for pure reflection. Here, I'd like to share some of my writings as a way of allowing you, my greatest supporters, an insight into how life has been since publishing 'Boy of Steel.'

The following chapters are dedicated to my writing during these times of reflection. In the good and bad times, I continued to turn to journaling as a way of processing reality, our new normal, and the unknown. I read back on these pieces now and see a traumatized and lost soul, a mother helpless. However, I also see a journey of growth and how I got to a place of peace. I learned to live with Sebastian's diagnosis and how to turn the experience into something bigger than me. Through the struggles, the pain, and the small victories, writing became my sanctuary. It became the tool through which I navigated the darkest days and celebrated the brightest moments.

In Part Two, I share with you not just the words, but the emotions and insights that have defined my path. These writings are a testament to resilience, love, and the unyielding hope that carries us forward. As you read them, I hope you find inspiration and perhaps a bit of your own story within mine. Thank you for being a part of this journey with me.

1

LIVING IN LIMBO

22 July 2021

Limbo.

It's a horrible place to live, and just like that, we're back there again.

Last week we didn't get the news we'd hoped for from Sebastian's MRI—the remaining tumor has increased in size. We don't know what it means or why it's happened so quickly, but it aligns with the unpredictable nature of Sebastian's diagnosis. Our parental power to 'kiss it better' has been snatched away once again, and I'm left feeling trapped between hope and hopelessness. A fresh reminder of just how unfair the big 'C' can be.

Living with the unknown is difficult, but the reality is we do it every day without even realising it. No one can tell us what our destiny is, and no one has a crystal ball to guide us through the many ups and downs life throws at us. So how do we survive? I'm yet to figure out the perfect answer, but I know that resilience has a lot to do with it.

It's funny, I don't consider myself to be a resilient person; I loathe change, I love control and routine, and I crumble under pressure, yet I somehow got through a year where resilience was mandatory.

It makes me wonder, do we underestimate our resilience and how much our 'fight or flight' instinct contributes to our survival?

I know we all have our strengths and weaknesses, but when you become a parent, I believe our 'fight' instinct and the resilience we didn't know we had will get us through the toughest of times.

When you least expect it, survival happens.

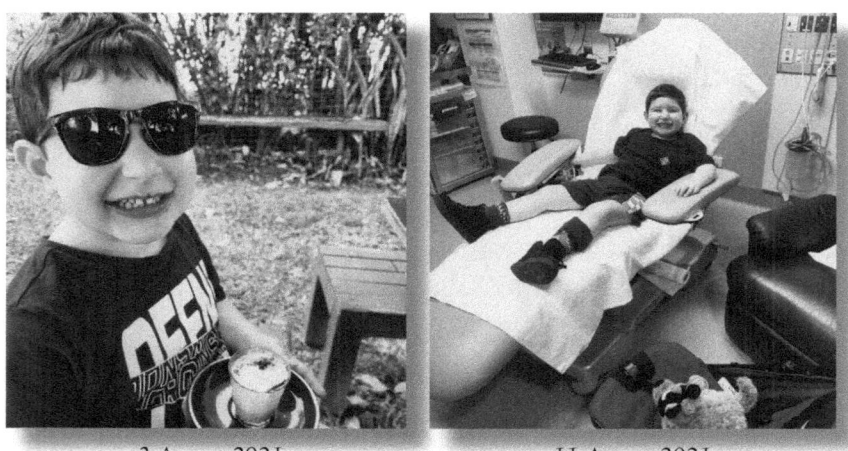

3 August 2021   11 August 2021

27 August 2021

An Unexpected Privilege: Celebrating 5 Years

2

PAIN INTO POWER

3 August 2021

In Sebastian today, the pain of 2020 is almost invisible, and the power of his strength is visible in unquantifiable amounts.

What happens when suddenly, you find yourself working on a 'passion project'? Like so many parents who turn their pain into power by writing about their experiences through a childhood cancer diagnosis, I find myself on the verge of publishing a very personal story about our battles through what was, quite frankly, an absolute hell of a year.

The saying 'everything happens for a reason' awakens a level of irritability in me and has me asking, "Why?... Why was my baby born with a brain tumour?... Why are there so many children confined to Hospitals, who've had their carefree, healthy lives snatched away...?" For me, that doesn't need to happen for a reason, but sadly, it just does.

In Oprah's book 'The Path Made Clear,' I found peace. "Passion whispers to you through your feelings, beckoning you toward your highest good." So rather than Sebastian's diagnosis being for a reason, it happened, we survived, and now I have the experience to help others. The experience has provided me with so much sadness but also endless amounts of growth. It has broken me but also helped put me back together, not as the same person, but as a better person. A more courageous person, a more compassionate human, and a more generous spirit.

My dream is that 'Boy of Steel' lands in the hands of parents enduring the same hell we went through in 2020, and that its message helps other families survive and continue raising awareness for childhood cancer research, so that no more children will suffer like Sebastian has.

Happy times at Camp Quality, 28 August 2021

3

LITTLE FISH, BIG CANCER POND

31 August 2021

Two days after hearing of yet another little boy whose life was taken too soon, I'm thrust back into the front seat of the emotional rollercoaster that came with my own son's cancer diagnosis. Earlier this year, it was Nate. Earlier this week, it was Slater. Two young Queensland boys with terminal brain cancer whose lives are now legacies and examples of bravery for the families left behind.

When I hear the news of yet another loss, I feel so scared. I go from carefree and confident about Sebastian's current medical status to completely overwhelmed with the reminder that there are very few survivors of brain cancer. That Sebastian, although not yet in remission, is one of the lucky few. One of the very few survivors. So far.

4

LIVING LIFE AGAIN

14 September 2021

What happens when you've been through the worst of it, the dust settles, and you're living life again? When you've returned to the mundane but necessary tasks that you missed so much when life was far less complicated? When you're back to doing things for yourself again— for me, that's playing sports and the occasional cuppa with friends. When life is pretty much 'normal' again.

Why, then, does it all feel so different?

It's no surprise to me that life hasn't felt the same since Sebastian's diagnosis, but it's nothing like I imagined either. During the hardest day of my life—January 12, 2020 (surgery day)—I felt like the world was spinning around me, but I was standing still, frozen in time by fear. The problem is, although that was 20 months ago, I am still waiting to thaw out properly. I'm about 50% there most days. Physically, I'm there. Mentally, I'm there. Emotionally, though, I'm still far away and unsure if I'll ever fully return.

It's innocence stolen, hearts broken and mended again, and it's so much about emotional recovery. Some days, the emotions are easy to digest, but on others, it's a struggle. On the harder days, I feel blessed to have Sebastian with us but overwhelmed by his future and jaded by what we've already had to endure to get this far.

An Unexpected Privilege: Celebrating 5 Years

I am yearning to overcome the trauma of 2020, and despite being confronted by formidable obstacles along the way, I was raised knowing the value of a good day's work. I have a vision for what 'Boy of Steel' will be—a story that inspires courage but also a wonderful way to heal.

> *"A vision that grows inside of you, a vision that wakes with you, sleeps with you, moves with you, a vision that you can tap into on your worst days —that vision will pull you forward."*
>
> -Iyanla Vanzant-

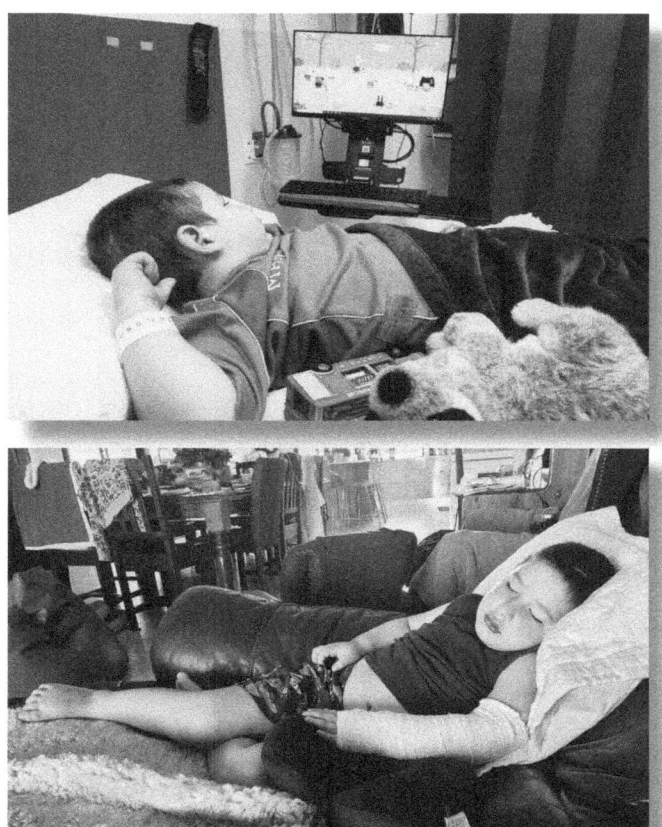

In Hospital and at home, 13 September 2021

5

SOMETHING'S GOTTA GIVE

5 October 2021

When I'm feeling overwhelmed with the many 'hats' I wear—mother, carer, writer, cook, cleaner, gardener, farmer's wife—I try to remind myself that no one can be everything to everyone, and that ultimately, something's gotta give.

For example, on days when I'm nailing the cook and cleaner roles, I'm often too exhausted to play handball or hopscotch with my children after school. Or when I get to the end of the day and feel really good about how much one-on-one time I spent with each of my children, I can't help but notice the piles of neglected dishes in the sink or mountains of dirty clothes all over the bathroom floor.

So how do we find balance in our crazy busy lives? Maybe the answer is simple… we don't. Battling to achieve 'balance' each day is exhausting, and truthfully, we all need different amounts of balance to maintain a satisfactory level of sanity.

I know I write from a place of fulfillment and gratitude after publishing 'Boy of Steel' and living through an earth-shattering reality check, but the over-achieving, structured mother that existed inside of me pre-childhood cancer diagnosis yearns to return some days. What's changed for me, though, is the realisation that life isn't perfect and neither are we. 'Perfectly imperfect' is my new mantra, and remembering that almost always, something's gotta give frees me from the shackles of my own perception of perfect.

Balance within is what we ought to strive for. Just doing one or two little things for myself each day helps keep me afloat. After all, motherhood really is one big game of survival, and if you're lucky, self-preservation.

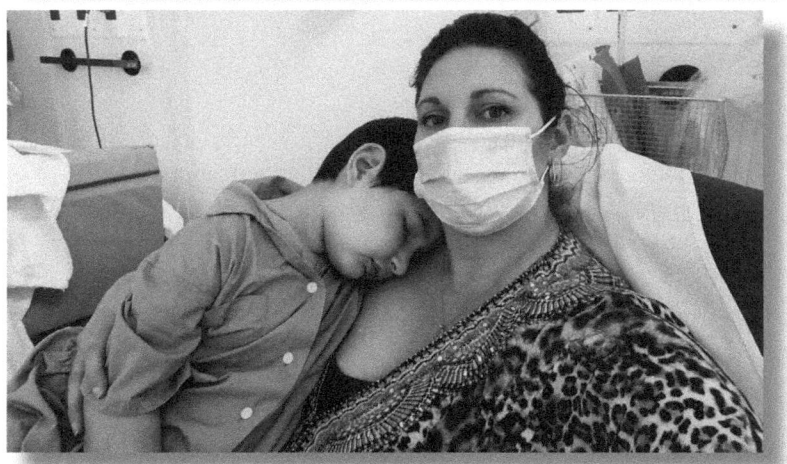

At Medical Imaging at QLD Children's Hospital, 12 October 2021

6

GIVING IN VS GIVING UP

21 October 2021

As we continue on this path of unknowns with Sebastian and his brain tumour, I've realised that at some stage, a parent in my situation gets to a point where they have no choice but to give in or give up.

It's terrifying to think that so many parents are left with no choice but to give in to the cancer. I don't ever want to contemplate being in that situation. When every treatment option has been tried, every drug, every home remedy, every natural alternative, but still, the cancer wins, how do you get to a place where you accept defeat and surrender? How do you stop the fight?

So far on our journey with Sebastian's brain cancer, I've only experienced an overwhelming 'never give up' attitude. I've sadly met so many mums, however, who have felt the same but then suddenly realise it's all been in vain.

My heart aches for those families. For the mums and dads who realise one day that no matter how hard they try, it will never be enough. When they finally realise that their only option left is taking their child home and making them as comfortable as possible until they fade away.

I also find myself contemplating whether or not giving up is something a parent will never do, especially when it comes to their child. I know I won't ever give up, but will I be forced to give in one day? It must be a completely broken spirit that leads to a parent's submission to their child's cancer or illness.

This is a heavy subject but something I sadly contemplate from time to time. So many of these mums who've been broken have redirected their hurt and heartbreak to the greater good. I feel honoured to have had conversations with mums who've lost their child to a cancer diagnosis, fought a courageous, admirable fight, and then devoted their lives to helping other children and their families. What a phenomenal response to adversity.

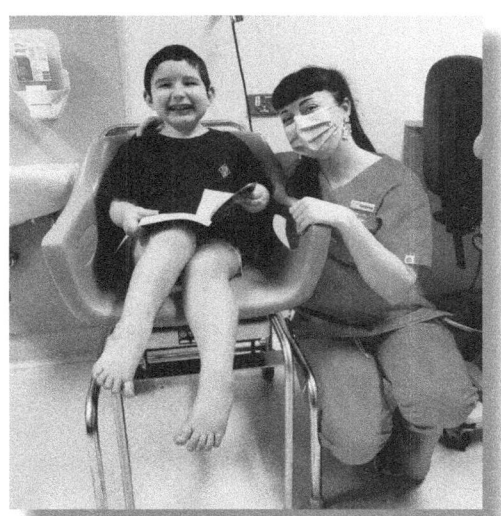

Sebastian with one of his amazing Chemotherapy nurses, Gemma at QLD Children's Hospital, 13 October 2021

Playing peek-a-boo with 'Old Baba' in Mossman, 20 October 2021

7

THE FUTURE IS RIGHT OUTSIDE YOUR WINDOW

24 November 2021

When I look outside my window, I see the staunch green mountains of the Great Dividing Range, nestled amongst the hills and farmland of ever-green Julatten. The landscape is lush and enchanting, perfectly matching the spirit of the local community. The air is fresh and the birdlife abundant. I've heard Julatten described as 'idealistic,' but I prefer to use the word 'paradise'.

Looking outside my window, I see my past, my present, and my future. Like a compass, I follow the magnetic pull to remain in this physical space as often as possible, allowing me to navigate through obstacles, unhindered by the stresses brought on by myself and the common ailment of 'stretching myself too thin'.

This is the place I choose to call 'home'. It's where my heart is full and where creativity and writing flow without inhibition. It is my 'happy place,' and I wouldn't change it for the world.

Recently, I attended a writer's workshop where I had the opportunity to write a piece using a topic prompt—something I rarely get the chance to do. The topic was 'When I look outside my window, I see...'

Although it's easy to take the literal approach to this topic, it got me thinking about how we sometimes need to look outside ourselves and take a moment to appreciate all the good in the world to remain grounded and focused on what's really important. This might sound pie-in-the-sky, but they say happiness comes from within, and while I agree, happiness also comes from what's outside our 'window.'

Inside my window, I have a very busy home. An office desk piled up with school notes, writing notes, inspirational pieces, books, diaries, photos, authors' journals, etc. This little corner of busy chaos can sometimes trap me in an 'I'm so busy' frame of mind and weigh me down with unachievable to-do list stress. However, this topic prompt made me stop and realise the beauty in my world. Outside my window is a world of possibilities and a future that I am looking forward to exploring.

So, if you're feeling overwhelmed in your small corner of chaos, just stop and look out the window. Find the beauty in what's outside yourself and acknowledge the smells, sights, feelings, and sounds of the future, right outside.

Timeline of Events: 2022

27.01.2022	Neurosurgery review via telehealth.
06.02.2022	Sebastian starts Kindergarten at Julatten Sunbird Centre. 6-weekly physiotherapy appointments continue with Joanne Backer in Cairns.
08.02.2022	Port-a-cath insertion surgery at QCH. Accessed and flushed, bloods taken. Day 1 of chemotherapy, Round 2. Weekly chemotherapy (Vinblastine) in Cairns Hospital to follow.
09.02.2022	Return home.
17.02.2022	Travel to Brisbane after port access failed at Cairns Hospital during chemotherapy.
18.02.2022	Port-a-cath correction surgery at QCH. Accessed and flushed, bloods taken. Returned home with weekly chemotherapy to resume the following week at Cairns Hospital.
08.03.2022	Return to QCH for chemotherapy, Cycle 2.
22.03.2022	Bloods from previous week show neutrophiles low. Port accessed and bloods taken. Asked to return tomorrow for chemotherapy infusion, if bloods are ok.
23.03.2022	Chemotherapy completed at Cairns Hospital.
25.03.2022	A weekend away in Townsville for the whole family, thanks to Camp Quality.
12.04.2022	Scheduled 12-weekly MRI, Oncology review & chemotherapy infusion continue at QCH.
22.05.2022	A day out at Cairns Aquarium for the whole family with Camp Quality.
31.05.2022	Sebastian fitted for wheelchair after fatigue levels remain high. This could be due to the ongoing treatment, or his left-sided hemiplegia.
26.07.2022	MRI at QCH shows 1-2mm growth since May. However, there is an area of around 8mm of what looks like dead cells within the tumour. Growth has slowed so treatment continues.
27.07.2022	Sebastian films with the QLD Children's Hospital Foundation at QCH for the 2023 Calendar.

12.08.2022	Sebastian fitted for new orthotic boot to assist with hemiplegia related difficulty.
06.09.2022	Kids film with Juiced TV on Cairns Esplanade.
18.10.2022	MRI at QCH.
02.11.2022	Sebastian completes first chemotherapy infusion without sedatives.
01.11.2022	Sebastian diagnosed with Precocious Puberty by Dr Dyanne Wilson at Cairns Hospital during a scheduled Endocronology check up. This is treated with 6-monthly injections to delay the onset of puberty.
08.12.2022	Sebastian graduates Kindergarten.
20.12.2022	Sebastian is announced as a Night Owl/Children's Hospital Foundation Ambassador and features on publicity and promotional material in Night Owl stores throughout QLD.
Total COVID-19 confirmed cases in QLD as at 30.12.22 = 1,743,616	

AUTHOR'S NOTE

In January 2022, during Sebastian's scheduled MRI, oncology, and neurology review, we received the news that his tumour had grown approximately 1cm over the past 12 months. This development prompted the medical team to recommend further treatment. Although a specific treatment plan was not confirmed at that time, the team unanimously decided it was time to implant a new Port-a-cath into Sebastian's chest in preparation for a second round of chemotherapy. We agreed to this, although we were prepared to begin researching treatment options once again.

After a new Port-a-cath was successfully implanted, Sebastian and I returned home, awaiting further instructions. Within a week, we received a call from Rick, who confirmed that the team had agreed on a proposed second round of treatment involving 68 weeks of Vinblastine chemotherapy infusions. We were assured that the pediatric oncology team at Cairns Hospital could administer these treatments, which was a great relief as it meant less travel than in 2020. If we agreed to this new plan, treatment was scheduled to begin in February 2022 and conclude in May 2023.

Sam and I felt helpless once again at the thought of Sebastian needing further chemotherapy treatment. After researching the Vinblastine drug and investigating case studies in younger cancer patients, we found that this was a tried and tested option and had great success as a secondary treatment to the Carboplatin/Vincristine combination Sebastian had already had. Reluctantly, whilst holding high hopes, Sam and I agreed to the team's plan for Sebastian's second round of treatment.

The change in chemotherapy drugs during Sebastian's second treatment resulted in a different set of side effects. During our research, we learned that Vinblastine was a plant-based drug, so it often had a milder effect on cancer patients. Sebastian lost five teeth in quick succession, experienced tender bones and fatigue, and suffered from nausea and vomiting two to three times a week. He also had red and hot ears, occasional rashes, and pain in his joints and muscles. While he did not lose hair from his scalp this time, he did lose all remaining hair on his body, including his arms, legs, back, and eyebrows. Reflecting on the side effects now, it does sound horrific, but in comparison to our experience with Carboplatin/Vincristine in 2020, it was a relief to have a 'gentler' drug infused into our son each week.

8

FREEDOM OF CHOICE

1 January 2022

At a time when decision-making is part of our daily existence, it is difficult to process conflicting feelings of loss of control and maintain the right to have a choice. When the COVID-19 pandemic hit, the world was left with no choice but to decide: do we vaccinate or not?

I've been sitting on this one for a few days now, unsure whether to publish or not... It's an opinion from my perspective on a topic that has gone from a global pandemic to a political taboo. I respect everyone for the decisions they've made, and are making, and believe we should all have the freedom of choice...

Is it just me or is everyone else's insides in knots about the COVID-19 vaccine? I'll admit, I am double vaccinated, but my opinion on whether or not to vaccinate may surprise you.

I felt sick getting my two needles, and not from Trypanophobia (needle phobia), but from that strong gut feeling you get when you're doing something you wish you didn't have to.

I stood my ground against getting vaccinated for as long as possible but sadly, our situation with Sebastian made the decision for us. We have a very sick little boy who needs his parents to ensure that every medical option is made available to him. My decision to get vaccinated was made with a heavy heart and overwhelming levels of anxiety. The end goal, however, was to eliminate any barrier my choices may create for Sebastian's medical journey. If the Hospital had told me to get a barcode tattooed on my forehead, I would have done that too. In my current world, anything other than Sebastian's medical needs comes secondary to my own health and well-being—saying it now sounds so short-sighted—because if I'm not in good health, then how can I nurture and nurse my child to better health?

Sadly though, the truth is that I haven't been well since receiving the two Pfizer COVID-19 vaccines. I won't go into details, but I'm just not alright. And to add to not feeling physically well, I'm also feeling completely overwhelmed with anxiety about COVID-19... what happens if I don't fully recover from the vaccine? What happens if I don't get the booster? What about the children—how will life change if/when the Government makes it mandatory to vaccinate our kids, but we choose not to? Technically, we do still have the freedom to choose, but if we choose to NOT vaccinate, then we find ourselves limited to basic human connection. The ability to freely go about life without being stopped and asked to prove that you've been vaccinated. The freedom to make plans to socialise with loved ones or travel around our own country. Since when, Australia? Since when are my personal health decisions and medical records anybody else's business? This isn't what freedom feels like. I'm vaccinated, yet I feel like I have absolutely no choice when it comes to COVID-19.

COVID-19 is a serious global pandemic. It is taking the scientific and medical worlds for a ride like no other. It is leaving the most brilliant minds scratching their heads in bewilderment and dispelling the usually reasonable minds to simply 'do what is recommended because it is mostly safe.' But—it isn't 100% safe, is it?

It's a topic that can be spoken about for hours on end and never come to a conclusion or sensible outcome. It has families separated by opinion and friendships lost because of fear. If Australia truly wanted its people to maintain their freedom of choice, it would, but I don't think it does. It's a realisation that's unsettling and confusing. As a proud Australian, I am now more in fear of choosing not to get a booster shot than I am of getting COVID-19. Perhaps that's been the plan all along.

We head to Brisbane again soon for Sebastian's medical appointments, into a Hospital that has active COVID-19 patients. It's our reality now, but if it wasn't COVID-19, I have no doubt that it'd be something else. I look forward to the day when we are living with just another endemic, rather than a pandemic, and a time when we once again have the 'choice' to vaccinate or not. Kudos to those who have been in an ideal situation to have the choice to not vaccinate, and hats off to those who've consciously made the brave decision to trust in the science and get vaccinated free of fear, unlike me.

My ass is firmly placed on the fence on this topic.

Stay safe and make the right choices for you and your family. I still pinch myself at times, reflecting on Sebastian's journey with brain cancer, in amongst a global pandemic. The timing is impeccable.

12 January 2022

9

TIFFANY: THE PERFECT STORM

11 January 2022

They say 'timing is everything,' and this week, we demonstrated a lack of perfect timing to perfection. It was the perfect storm... Tropical Cyclone Tiffany, COVID-19 outbreaks, and a trip to Brisbane.

Sebastian and I returned to QLD Children's Hospital this week for his scheduled MRI, blood tests and oncology review. For the first time in a year, we're staying at Ronald McDonald House (RMH) in an effort to have as little contact with the general public as possible. Staying here means no Hospital transfers, no eating out, and basically no physical contact with anyone other than Hospital staff.

It's been really nostalgic being back here at RMH and surprisingly comforting. The last time we stayed here, Sebastian was just a baby and reduced to a somewhat vegetative state after undergoing brain surgery, followed by meningitis and the commencement of intensive chemotherapy. He really didn't understand much of what was going on at the time, so RMH acted as a sanctuary for Sam and me. A place to call home for many months while Sebastian was still so unstable.

When we arrived yesterday, the familiarity of the place only brought back fond memories for me and a new adventure for Sebastian. He was excited by every 'magic door' (card-activated automatic doors), lift buttons, and all the bright colours of this amazing place.

I was also reminded of the generosity of the human spirit and the overwhelming support we continue to receive as a family of a sick child. I finally met the wonderful Justine Christerson, who volunteers her time transporting families to and from the airport to their accommodation and/or Hospital, as well as gifting families with care packages. She began the program 'Breaking Down the Barriers for Rural Patients in City Hospitals - Brisbane' in 2012 when a friend from rural QLD had a son who was diagnosed with a brain tumour and was required to relocate to Brisbane to receive treatment.

At the time, the Hospital did not fund or organise airport and Hospital transfers. It was quite a stressful situation that Justine wanted to improve for her friend and families like mine. Justine is one of the many outstanding Queenslanders who have made every step of the way just that little easier for us, taking away the burden and stresses of the mundane that suddenly become super overwhelming when you're delivered a devastating diagnosis like Sebastian's.

12 January 2022

10

UNPACKING BAGGAGE

20 January 2022

We returned home 8 days ago, which is also about the time I started feeling unwell. Yes, it finally happened; we've all had COVID-19 here in the Leonardi house. It's been an added worry on top of an already anxious and, honestly, cruel week.

Since returning home, I haven't been able to 'unpack.' Not my suitcase, nor my emotions. Overwhelmed with feeling frozen in time—a familiar feeling—not wanting to commit to our return home just yet. We didn't receive much good news in Brisbane and were left with the all-too-common 'we'll be in touch' outcome. After confirming that the tumour is continuing to grow, it was agreed that action needed to be taken, but what and when needed to be planned and considered with great care and precision—which would take T.I.M.E.

Totally appreciate this. Trouble is, whilst the medical team discusses options and investigates alternatives, we are left waiting. Wondering whether or not we'll receive a call to get back on the plane and return to QCH for immediate treatment or not hear anything at all. I figured, my suitcase is packed, I might as well leave it that way so I can take off in a hurry if needed. So, in the physical sense, I've been walking past my suitcase on our dining room table for the last week, trying to ignore it and not make eye contact. Its inconvenient and bulky presence has also weighed heavily on my emotional stillness, neither sad nor happy, just still.

I'm so grateful for our gold-standard medical team and medical resources in this wonderful country, but it's just hard. I feel like this sort of news will never be easy to hear, nor will I ever get used to it. Emotional baggage is normal to carry; it's how we manage it that determines how it manifests in each of us.

In an effort to process the ups and downs, I've recently begun writing again and am excited to share that I've written a children's book. Titled 'My Brother Sebastian,' and told from the perspective of a girl whose brother is diagnosed with cancer, the book focuses on helping siblings of sick kids deal with the emotions and fears that come with a childhood cancer diagnosis. I'm excited to continue to help those affected by childhood cancer, especially the children.

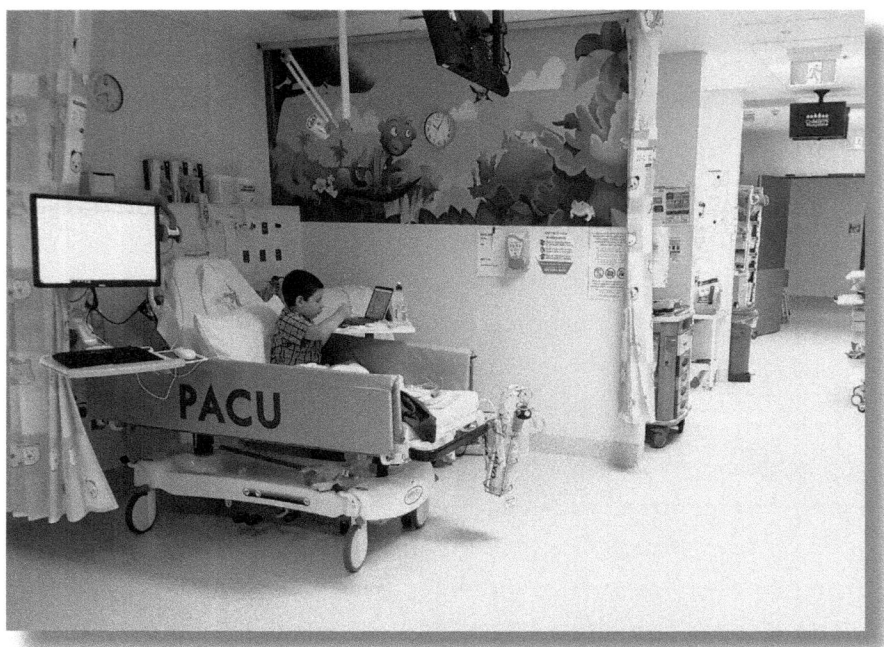

QLD Children's Hospital, 13 January 2022

11

IT IS WRITTEN

16 February 2022

Sitting in Sebby's darkened recovery room at QCH the week of February 7, 2022, I once again faced familiar emotions and a new sense of appreciation for how far we have come. I wrote this piece during the night as I watched over Sebastian's heavily medicated and sedated body, bruised from surgery. I willed him to wake and look up at me with his charming smile once again, unable to sleep in case he woke and fearfully realised where he was.

It is written in the lines on my face. It is written in the way my eyes feel sad. In the way my body is relaxed but tortured on the inside. In the way my heart has been broken but still so full of love.

I am a mum of a child with cancer.
The diagnosis shattered my soul.
The trauma broke my spirit.
His strength glued me back together.
His recovery restored my faith.

As I watch over my baby in his Hospital bed, the familiarity of our surroundings ignites each of my senses. My body is confused and my emotions are conflicted. I feel *safe but scared. I am grateful but downcast. I am trusting, but hesitant. The way the door clicks when it shuts, the pungent smell of alcohol wipes, and the heavy heart I carry when encountered by sick children at every turn, bring a familiar flood of emotions, remnants of 2020.*

As we embark on a new wave of treatment, I feel prepared to stand up and fight but also ready to lay down and begin to dream. The build-up to this moment has been months in the making and now that we're here, the emotional weight has me falling on my sword, barely able to maintain my strength. I feel tired, I feel trapped and I feel sad, once again. The sudden reminder of this ongoing health battle was delivered like a brutal blow to my stomach, winding me, leaving me gasping for air. Like pressing pause on the healing my heart has worked so hard to accomplish.

I'm anxious about when he wakes and is confronted by his surroundings. Wondering whether his mind will remember, certain that his intuition will. Realising that this new setting is far from paradise, bringing trepidation and fear to his body, I have no doubt.

It is written in the fear in his eyes. It is written in the scars on his torso. In the tremble of his body. In the brave face that breaks my heart and fills it back up again.

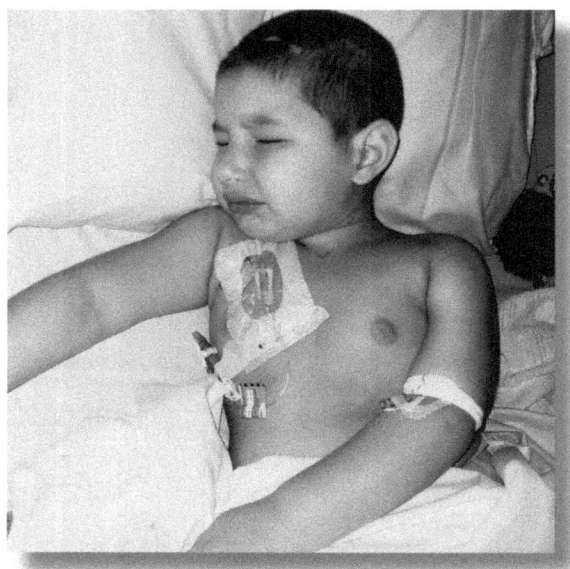

Every single time.

It is written.

7 February 2022

12

JUST A MAN

17 February 2022

After a tremendously difficult day in the Hospital yesterday with Sebastian, I found myself turning to writing to process all of the emotions of the day. Below is a poem I wrote last night, titled 'Just a Man.'

Sebastian was due to start his first day of chemotherapy at Cairns Hospital yesterday, but unfortunately, there were complications. After two failed attempts to access his port, an x-ray was ordered on suspicion that it had flipped or moved since being de-accessed last Wednesday at QCH. The x-ray was inconclusive, but it was agreed that it had definitely turned at least 90 degrees and should be accessed from the side rather than from the top. After sedation (which didn't really help) and a third failed attempt, the port was deemed faulty, and we were sent home.

It was a day of many tears (from us all), pain, fear, and unfortunately, trauma for Sebastian. We left the Hospital after seven hours, no chemotherapy, no port accessed, and no idea what was going to happen next. Now, we await a call from Dr. Walker (QCH Oncology) after further discussions with the surgical team.

Let me go! Daddy, don't leave me alone!
Let me go! Daddy, please take me home!

A man broad and strong,
No longer stoic like King-Kong.
Brought down like a feather,
Grasping for courage, a waning endeavour.

The pleading screams of his son,
Accumulated trauma unable to be undone.
Sheer desperation fills the air,
A small boy confined to a chemo chair.

A lonely tear rolls down his cheek,
No match for his son's soul-crushing peak.
His heartbroken, red eyes and quivering voice,
Evidence of helplessness and loss of choice.

The years of watching his son suffer,
Never having witnessed anything tougher.
Pain and anguish prolonged, engrained, unfading,
Brought to the surface like an intruder invading.

Once unafraid and filled with certainty,
His heart now bruised and battered for eternity.

An Unexpected Privilege: Celebrating 5 Years

A man left completely shattered on the inside,

A dad forever frightened but full of loving pride.

Time stands still like a concrete statue,

Tears fall, emotions stall, my love will always catch you.

Sebastian's first day of
Kindergarten,
6 February 2022

Nurse administering
chemotherapy to a sleeping
and recovering Sebastian at
QLD Children's Hospital,
7 February 2022

13

IT'S LOVE

25 February 2022

When away with Sebastian on these medical trips, I suddenly find myself free to feel. I realise that my headspace is so full in my everyday life as a mother, wife, farmer, and writer, and as I near closer to Brisbane, my mind space slowly clears. Like sun rays striking the earth from a bed of clouds, a feeling of hope and clarity suddenly appears after a day of heavy rain.

I once approached Brisbane with such trepidation and anxiety, fearing an unexpected encounter with adversity just around the next corner. However, with time passing us by and our growing confidence as Sebastian's carers, I have learned that the more I live, the more I find life mystifying.

So much of life just doesn't make sense. Sometimes, life just is. And when the blows seem to come in thick and fast with little time to recover, life itself can be overwhelming. Dwelling on the negative is so easy to do. Rising above, getting up every day, and shining bright, just like those sun rays, is what keeps you from drowning in sorrow and self-pity.

I try my best to approach life with grace and gratitude. To take a win as a win and a loss as a loss and accept that both are a part of what makes life worth living. Every loss is often a lesson and an unexpected twist in our destiny. With every win, we are reminded of how glorious life is.

If there's anything I've learned from Sebastian's recent loss of health, it's that you will regain your strength. You will laugh again; you will forget the pain and love wholeheartedly again. Like the sun shines every day, so will you. Especially, if you have one or two good people in your corner. It's love. Love makes anything possible.

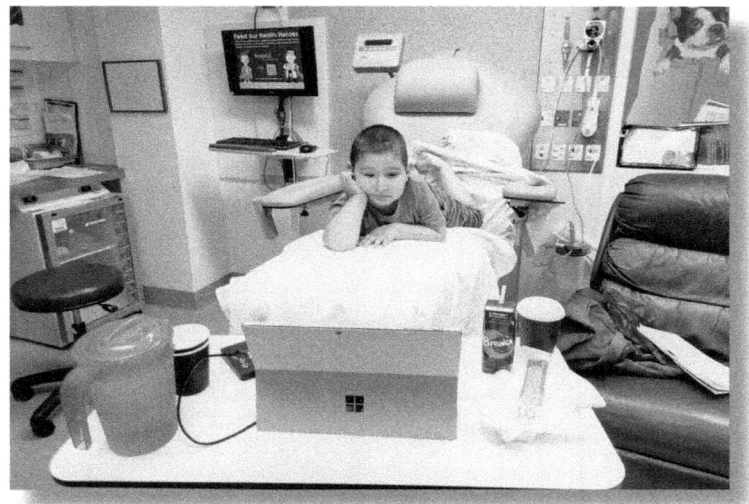

At a scheduled check-up at Cairns Hospital, 15 February 2022

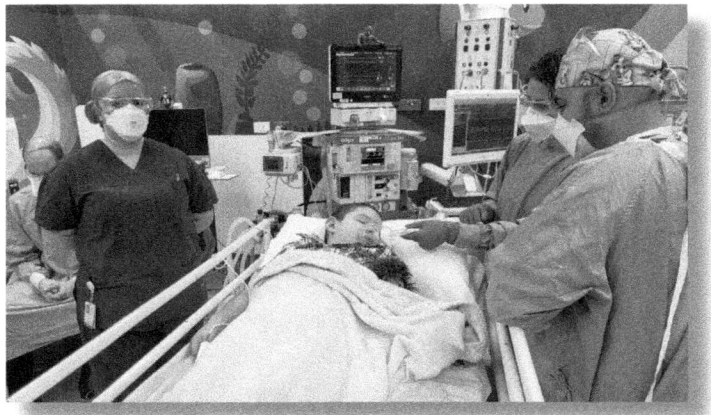

MRI at QLD Children's Hospital, 18 February 2022

14

NO TIME TO CELEBRATE

4 May 2022

Tears, sorrow, trauma, devastation, and still more bad news,
So far from the celebration, much closer to the blues.

I find myself longing for months filled with joy and the absence of tragedy,
Hopeful that a visit to Emergency doesn't end in a travesty.

My family endured the ultimate devastation,
Losing innocence to cancer, a wellness defloration.

Celebration is now something that happens more often than regularly,
Small wins along the way, the reason for quiet gratitude, yes, absolutely!

Birthdays and Christmas occasions are now so much more precious,
Feeling like time is limited and so cruelly measured.

When Christmas ham, balloons, pavlova, and streamers return in the future,
The happiness will once again find its place like a surgical suture.

An Unexpected Privilege: Celebrating 5 Years

In the meantime, fear lingers, trauma haunts me and time remains still,
My boy clasps his teddy bear, sure it will shield him from being ill.

My son is a champion who I vow to always celebrate,
Win, lose, fail or defeat cancer, my love will always dominate.

Maybe all I need right now is to celebrate more,
make memories and look for the rainbow,
Focusing on the bright colours and beauty around me,
keeping out of that dark cancer shadow.

I hope and pray for a brighter, carefree future ahead,
Realistic that surprise is something I'll now always dread.

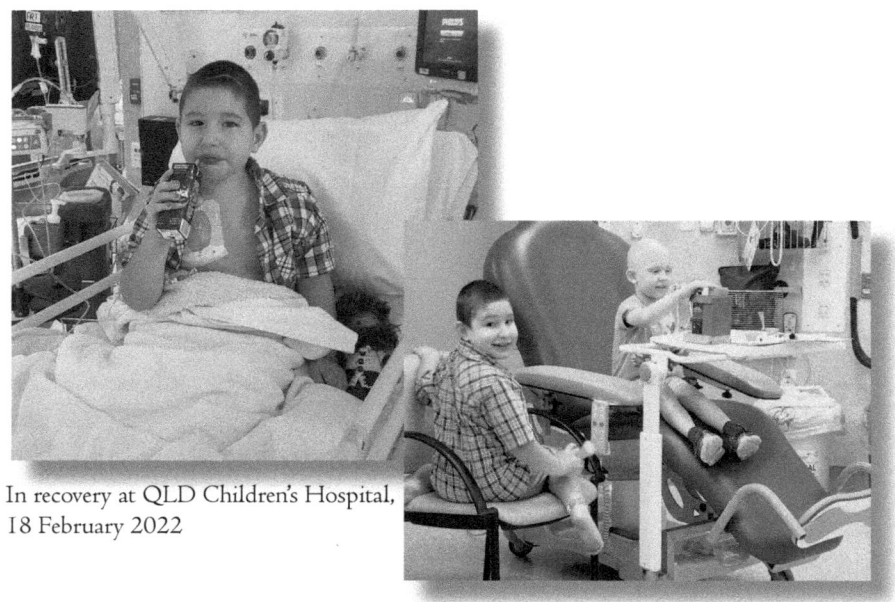

In recovery at QLD Children's Hospital, 18 February 2022

Sebastian making friends during chemotherapy at QLD Children's Hospital, 23 February 2022

15

ROOM 24

15 June 2022

Something I love about making new friends who are also writers is their pertinent feedback on my work. Recently, I had a chance meeting with talented author Maxine Turner. She had recently finished reading 'Boy of Steel' and was eager to discuss my experience. Something interesting she pointed out was that I rarely wrote about the physical environment inside the Hospital. She wanted to know what the Hospital wards looked like, where I sat, whether I slept in a bed or chair, what I could see outside the Hospital windows, etc. It was something I suppose didn't really matter to me at the time as I was so focused on Sebastian; however, it is an important detail when setting the scene. So, this one's for you, Maxine...

Cold, freezing cold, is the memory of our time at QCH that is at the forefront of my mind.

Sound proof walls, busy halls and devastating numbers of children calling level eleven home.

The walls of the hallways were filled with interactive murals, photographs and children's artwork, in an effort to dull the doom and gloom of their new reality, and their new 'home away from home'. A parade of clowns, musicians, starlight entertainers, therapy dogs & their handlers, cuddle carers, volunteers with book trolleys, Hospital school staff clutching prepared learning resources. Teams of doctors and surgeons moving through, stopping at each room on their daily rounds. Paediatricians accompanied by social workers, physios, OTs, speech therapists, wheeling their computers around, huddling outside each room before entering, discussing the patient inside. The clunking and clacking of the Phlebotomist's trolley, speeding through the halls to their next appointment, several times a day.

Inside Room 24 was just cold, freezing cold.

There wasn't really a smell but there was a sterility about it that can only be described as a 'Hospital smell'. 24 was huge. Equipped perfectly for long stays. Sebastian had his own bathroom & shower, kitchenette, wardrobe, desk, and a single bed below a huge bay window. There were only 2 basic chairs, not recliners like we had in ICU, we assume to discourage parents from sleeping bedside. Thankfully, we figured out how to get around that; Sam or I would get into bed with Sebastian or wheel his bed over next to the single bed during the night. There was something about being able to touch him during the night that comforted us all. Our fatigue was so intense that the constant drip of the IV never disturbed our sleep. I can't say the same for the bedside stand filled with medications, all on timers, that beeped at intervals, around the clock. It seemed particularly too often when trying to get some rest. 24 was painted in bright colours, but the lighting was dim in an effort to keep Sebastian's recovering brain under-stimulated. Latex balloons and flowers are not permitted at QCH so 24 was filled with teddies, at least 20, sent from all over Australia. One even made its way from old work colleagues now calling the US home. Lovingly donated handmade quilts were always draped over Sebastian's bed and regularly changed to keep the room more 'homely'.

A floor light under Sebastian's Hospital bed provided enough light for me to write at night. There's no surprise when I reminisce on this memory that on my return home, my eyesight had declined dramatically.

The nurses that monitored Sebastian around the clock were suitably adorned in brightly coloured scrubs and fun name badges. I was surprised at how young the team of nurses were at QCH. As many male as female nurses, another surprise. All well-schooled and experienced at creating a calm environment for the children. What they lacked in age, didn't equate to their experience and ability. Sebastian particularly took a liking to several nurses, despite being severely traumatized from very early on. A true testament to the quality of the staff chosen to care for the children at QCH.

Sunshine. I don't remember many rainy days. Just lots of sunshine. Despite the brightly coloured rooms, and the sunny QLD days outside the window, it always felt 'grey' and cold, freezing cold, inside Room 24.

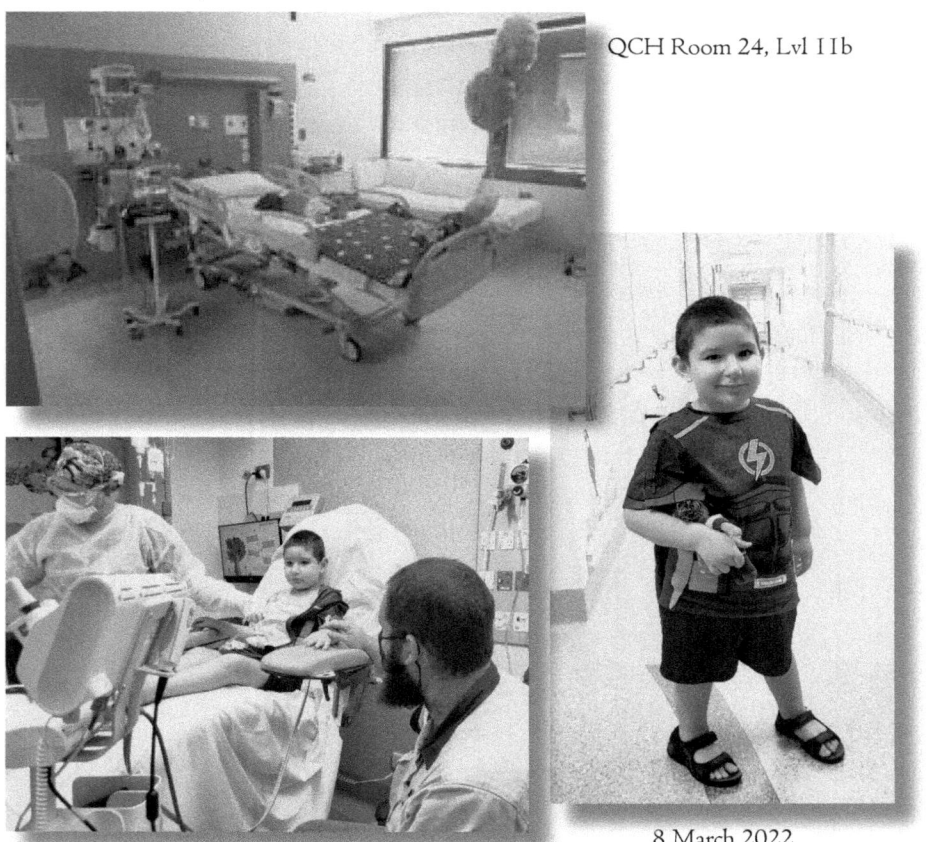

QCH Room 24, Lvl 11b

8 March 2022

Nurse Caz administering chemotherapy at Cairns Hospital, 2 March 2022

16

CASUALTIES OF CANCER

29 June 2022

Babies. They are my kryptonite (along with all things that sparkle). I love babies. I am, honest to goodness, a mascot for all the clucky people out there who just cannot get enough of life's little cherubs. Especially my own, but also any chubby-cheeked, chunky-legged bundle of squishiness, I just cannot get enough. My heart flutters when I see a cute baby, and it seems the more I have of my own, the cluckier I get. God help my future grandchildren!

I found a photo last night by accident. It's Sebastian and me when he was just 4 weeks old. I was feeding my baby with my body and enjoying the sudden absence of my well-ripened 9-month-old 'baby bump.'

Immediately, my focus was on how adorable Sebby was as a baby and how I'd forgotten how squishy and healthy he was for a newborn. After a couple of minutes, though, my eyes moved over to me. The youthful, glowing, oblivious me. Still in that beautifully blissful bubble us mothers are in after having a baby. When so much time is spent staring at the miracle we created, adoringly watching on as every sound and movement they make generates heart explosions of love, over and over again.

Sadly, though, it was like stumbling across a photo of someone I used to know. A young mum and her son, who'd since lost their lives. For the first time in a long time, I unwillingly found myself feeling really sorry for myself. The floodgates opened and I sobbed. The grief was overwhelming and I cried, and cried, and cried. I was abruptly reminded by the youthful, innocent face in the photo that cancer has aged me both physically and emotionally. I feel it every day, but I don't 'see' it ever. Cancer has also matured me, which, for the most part, I can live with and see as a positive, rather than one of cancer's casualties.

I avoid looking at baby photos of Sebastian usually because I just feel sad. It's like I've grieved for that child, and instead of remembering, I shift my focus to the little boy in front of me today. Because sometimes, life's ups and downs leave us feeling really let down and betrayed. No matter how 'up' I'm feeling today, the times I've been 'down' still cripple my spirit.

I have written before about grief in 'Boy of Steel,' and how cancer forced me to grieve Sebastian, the Sebastian that you saw in that photo. But I suddenly realised last night, that I haven't grieved for myself. Not even begun to grieve me. I think about it a lot, how my life has changed, and the optimist in me only ever sees growth. I'd almost forgotten about the other side of me that is lost forever. The innocence in that photo is cripplingly tragic. Both Sebastian and I are completely oblivious to the true definition of trauma and that our lives would change forever over the next 20 months.

In those days, back in 2018, I spent my days enjoying my children and genuinely loving being a mum and all the mundane tasks that came with it. Now I spend my days driven by a need to make every day count. To relentlessly make sure that not a day is wasted. I literally force-feed my emotions, to keep them from bubbling out. Willingly pushing myself so far out of my comfort zone, in an effort to better myself professionally and distract myself from what's really going on with me. I rarely look in the mirror these days, fearful of realising that my reflection is unacceptable and so far from the high standard I used to live by. Terrified that I'll notice the extra 30 kgs that my body now carries around. I call it my trauma weight and I just can't seem to shake it.

An Unexpected Privilege: Celebrating 5 Years

I disguise myself in bright colours and fun clothing, trying to distract any onlookers from just how sad my soul is, and how truly exhausted I am. My work is a welcomed distraction for sure, but the absence of self-care and time spent on my own health is taking its toll. I guess I was choosing not to see it until it slapped me in the face with the photo last night. The 'slap' burns my cheek and haunts me like a guilty plea to a crime I didn't realise I was committing.

I've been successfully nourishing my mind, to distract from my neglected heart and body. Overwhelmed with the enormous task of repairing a grieving heart and a broken body. Mostly because every 12 weeks, my heart is broken all over again when Sebastian's MRI reveals a healthy tumour, nestled in and feeding off his brain and healthy cells. It's a revolving door that keeps hitting me on the way out. An unsubtle reminder that trauma is still present, an end is not near, and that I need to remain on guard.

It seems I have let cancer win. Unbeknownst to me, Sebby's cancer is desperately trying to take my life now too, and slowly breaking me down.

If anyone knows how to help, let me know. And no thanks, Jenny Craig, Lite 'n' Easy, or radical weight loss surgery, as some have suggested, can't fix my broken heart.

I get it. Science tells us that healthy eating and good choices can increase the levels of serotonin in our body, which in turn, regulates our anxiety and mood. On top of that, exercise helps the body release endorphins, which make us happier and help us to feel more 'alive.' But what happens when you don't feel like you have the strength to focus more on balancing your time between nourishing your heart, mind, and body in equal amounts? This is where I'm at. I just feel like I don't have the energy to face what has become of me in mearly 3 short years.

Maybe it's just not my time. That my life is about getting Sebastian better. Mending his broken brain is Priority 1. My time will come. I truly hope we both get the time we need to mend. But how much breakage can a soul and spirit take before they too is a casualty of cancer?

Me and baby Sebastian, 2018

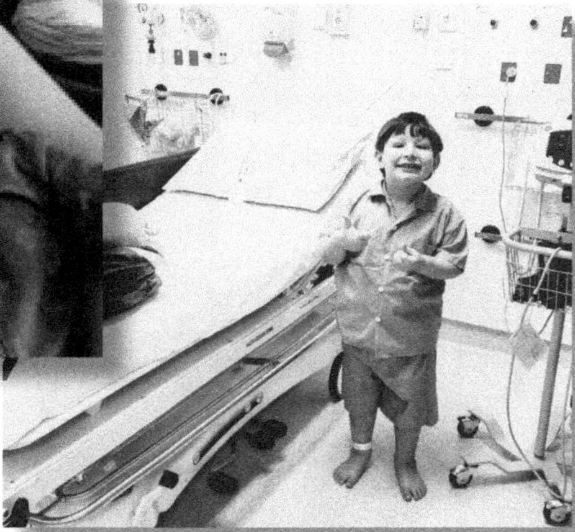

18 October 2022

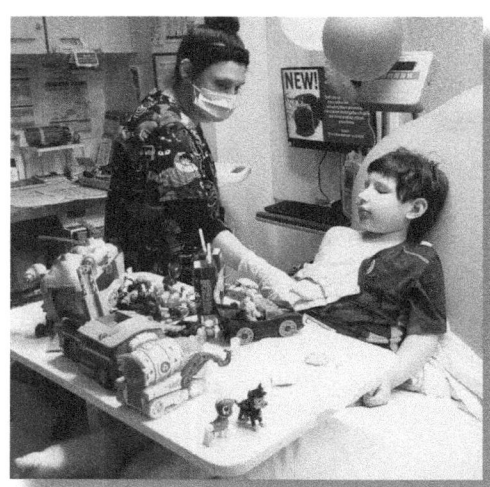

Nurse Rachel administering chemotherapy at
Cairns Hospital, 23 October 2022

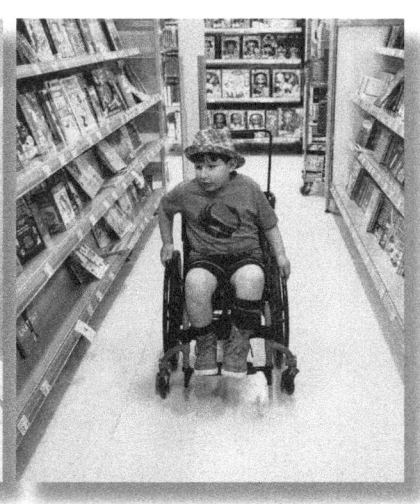

18 November 2022

An Unexpected Privilege: Celebrating 5 Years

17

CHASING DRAGONFLIES

January 2023

Have you ever wondered what happens when someone dies?
I like to believe they become dragonflies.

When you feel sad, lost, or hurt,
find peace in the garden, watching a dragonfly flirt.
The energy of the dragonfly will transform your worries,
from overwhelming to loving fairy heart flurries.

Their long slender body and mystical transparent wings will gracefully hover,
kissing your spirit with love, sprinkling joy,
and encouraging your heart to recover.

Dancing through the air,
their beauty and acrobatics will catch your attention,
conquering life's storms with elegant strength and little to no apprehension.

Watching them flutter their long busy wings,

dainty darting, swooping and circling,

A guardian angel and reminder that someone truly special is watching.

When a dragonfly is near,

catch its divine energy with open arms,

and be reminded that the light and love inside of you will bring calm.

Be brave and radiate light in the atmosphere.

Watch the blue, green, silver, red, and yellow colours of the dragonfly that flew around your aura, into your heart, and out of your garden.

A symbolic creature as powerful and divine as you.

18

WAITING IS THE WORST

14 January 2023

I feel like I could write about this forever, even though the words struggle to flow onto the page. The exhaustion, overwhelming. During days like this, the wait is the worst.

So much anxiety, too many thoughts, unequivocal expectations. The care of my boy taken away, scheduled on the calendar, a notion still unnatural, however somewhat normal to us now.

A mother-in-waiting holds a different meaning for an oncology mummy. A mother waiting for news, a mother waiting for relief, a mother needing to take a breath.

During days like this, my entire being battles with the fight and the surrender. Too much in love to stop, too tired to continue. Feeling totally drained by the situation but completely motivated by my little one.

I wish so hard that this wasn't our reality, living on a knife's edge. Constantly reminded that we are living proof that miracles happen. That something magical keeps our spirits and our boy alive.

19

THE CHEMO ROLLERCOASTER

14 April 2023

We are officially on the countdown to the end of treatment; only six weeks to go, making the 23rd of May a day of celebration.

My heart really only settled on this realisation today, a whole week and a half after Sebby's last MRI and oncology review in Brisbane. For a welcome change, we had a good scan, good results, and a high-five from the team in Brisbane - awesome, yes? Or no?

My mind said yes, but my heart said no. A predicament that's become all too common for me. Conflicting emotions, regardless of the news, wash over me as I try to understand it. I'm sure many oncology families and individuals go through this, reminded of their mortality and the fragility of life, a nudge back to some of the darkest moments already endured.

I know I'm not alone because others share their struggles through Facebook support groups. In my way of helping others, I share my experiences through my blog. Here's an entry from my journal last week, illustrating how lost and confused I feel every 12 weeks, when Sebby's fate is reviewed.

Why do I struggle to process good news? When shit hits the fan, I feel in control, calm, level-headed, and shielded from the blues. Focused on finding a solution, there's no room for emotional confusion or alarm. So why, then, do I feel numb to positive results? A search for peace, unachievable for this tortured soul. I should be popping the bubbly, anticipating the inevitable dizzy assault that my body can't handle, but desperate to forget our fate.

The anxiety leading up to our quarterly oncology review is the same every time. The week before is full of sleepless nights, restless days, and a lack of focus. I just don't get it. I should feel relieved and exhilarated about dodging a bullet this time. But no. Nothing. I feel nothing.

Almost like I'm in disbelief; I don't feel like celebrating in case the turn of good fortune is short-lived. I've almost become conditioned to expect the worst to happen still, building up to disappointment in hope that it'll shield me from the power of the blow, even though today's results suggest we're almost out of those woods.

Struggling to feel happiness like it never existed. I guess this is all part of the grief. The harsh reality is that this shitty situation is the best we can hope for. Despite promising results this time, we're still dealing with a monster every day who is trying persistently to take our child. It's a battle we can't win, and the trouble is, we don't know how long the fight will last. We have the strength to never give up, but what toll will that take? It's not just grey hairs and weight gain; it's heartbreak and soul destruction, breaking away tiny fractions with each new day.

Here's the thing – today, I feel great. After time to process the emotions and realise once again that all we can do is take life one day at a time, I feel relieved that we can now look forward to ending treatment this time around on a high. Sebby couldn't 'ring the bell' after his 1st chemotherapy treatment as it was cut short due to anaphylaxis (technically, he didn't complete treatment). However, our little superstar has almost completed 68 rounds of chemo, and we all look forward to seeing him finish on a high.

For those of you who have or are fighting cancer, I take my hat off to you. It's hard, it's brutal, and it is just so emotionally exhausting. I know I don't have cancer, but I sometimes feel like I do. Just like I said in 'Boy of Steel,' 'when someone in the family has cancer, so do we.'

Keep fighting, warriors, you are my inspiration. xo

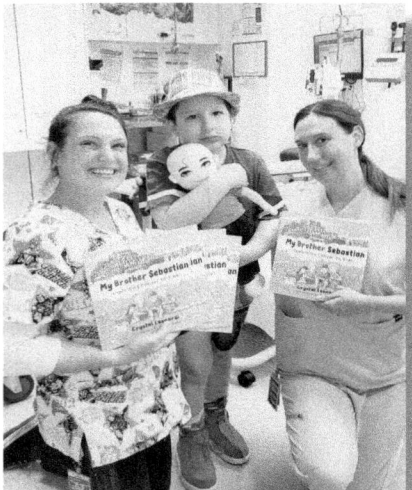

With nurses Rachel & Jessie at Cairns Hospital, 14 March 2023

With nurse Caz, 16 April 2023

Sebastian ringing the end-of-treatment bell at Cairns Hospital, 23 May 2023

20

REFLECTIONS

26 September 2023

This poem came to me this morning as I reflected on a special book, I started reading last night. 'FEARLESS' by Jelena Dokic is offering me an opportunity for self-reflection and a reminder that life is what we make it. I cannot wait to review this book once completed, another stellar publication by one of my true inspirations and hero to many, Jelena Dokic.

When you look in the mirror, what do you see?
A reflection of you or who others want you to be?

It can be hard to see past the wrinkles, age spots and fatigue,
But if our mindset could shift, beauty, wisdom, and life is what we'd see.

Society encourages us to be perpetually critical of ourselves,
Rarely allowing positive thoughts, leaving self-love on the shelves.

The freedom to change our appearance weighs greatly on our self-worth,
Social media the new benchmark we rate from as young as birth.

In a world where AI is becoming the norm,
it's sad we feel the need to aesthetically reform.

To live with inadequacy and never feel satisfied,
placing ourselves on a platform, a very slippery slide.

To feel love for ourselves like we do for others,
Could be life's greatest achievement, a lesson from our mothers.

I have to admit, I still catch myself often,
Feeling doubtful of my worth, my confidence prepared to soften.

Because of one person's opinion of who I should be,
Forgetting who I am and the direction I want my life to see.

Listening to negative feedback, doubters and critics has made me realise,
That self-loathing behaviour could be the perfect recipe for our demise.

So, the question we need to ask ourselves,
Is who do we want to see,
A reflection of ourselves,
Or who others want us to be?

The many faces of 'me.' The good, the bored, and the sad. Life isn't always roses. Enjoy life for what it is, which is not perfect. Celebrate the little wins and learn from the adversity that inevitably comes. We are what we manifest, and life is what we make it.

Timeline of Events: 2023

08.01.2023	Scheduled 12-weekly MRI, Oncology review & chemotherapy infusion continue at QCH. Findings: enlarged ventricle indicating brain unable to drain fluid satisfactorily. Recommendation from team to insert a Shunt. Preparations begin for surgery at QCH with Dr Gert Tollesson.
11.01.2023	Bloods taken from 08.01.2023 show low neutrophils so team don't want to operate until bloods are back in the morning.
12.01.2023	Shunt insertion surgery at QCH. Sebastian suffers from excessive pain after surgery. CT scan reveals failure in shunt. Further surgery planned to correct.
13.01.2023	2nd shunt surgery completed. Chemotherapy paused for 1 week to allow him to recover.
16.01.2023	CT scan confirms shunt in good order.
19.01.2023	Sebastian meets and plays cricket with the QLD Heat men's cricket team. This scores him a feature in the Courier Mail and on the nightly news. Sebastian and I also feature in an article for That's Life Magazine this month, telling his story of survival and resilience.
20.01.2023	Return home.
24.01.2023	Chemotherapy resumes at Cairns Hospital.
25.01.2023	Sebastian starts Prep at Julatten State School.
07.02.2023	Endocrine review at Cairns Hospital with Dyanne Wilson. All ok.
23.02.2023	Neurosurgery review via telehealth.
05.03.2023	Further investigation with Endocrine in Cairns reveals Sebastian's cortisol levels are normal and his hormone axis is working well. This is an indication that his injection to treat precocious puberty is working.
06.03.2023	Camp Quality and the Puppets visit Julatten State School to educate the students on cancer and what it means when a child is diagnosed.

04.04.2023	MRI at QCH. Ventricles have shrunk to normal size. No tumour growth. Chemotherapy completed at QCH.
23.05.2023	Bell ringing at Cairns Hospital after final chemotherapy infusion - 68 long weeks.
03.07.2023	MRI at QCH. Report shows tumour is stable (less than 20% growth).
08.09.2023	MRI at QCH. Sebby completes first MRI without any sedatives (General Anesthetic).
13.09.2023	Discharged from QCH and return home after MRI is stable.
29.11.2023	Endocrine requests full blood count during Port flush at Cairns Hospital after I raised concerns about his increased appetite and inability to lose weight.
07.12.2023	Blood results show thyroid function normal, cortisol levels normal and his male/puberty hormones suppressed. No need for further investigation for now.
Total COVID-19 confirmed cases in QLD as at 31.12.2023 = 1,759,225	

Timeline of Events: 2024

04.01.2024	Neurosurgery review via telehealth.
20.01.2024	Sebby discharged from Mossman Hospital after collapsing in pain at home. No cause known but pain free now and clinically stable.
22.01.2024	Sebastian starts Grade 1 at Julatten State School.
31.01.2024	MRI at QCH reveals evidence of stroke within tumour. This confirms the source of pain Sebastian experienced earlier in the month.
01.02.2024	Return home.
13.02.2024	CT scan at Cairns Hospital after Sebby complains of headaches and has increased fatigue.
13.05.2024	MRI at QCH. Further evidence of 'upset' tumour as further darkening appears at centre of tumour. Cyst appears to be attached to tumour. This is a new finding. As Sebastian is clinically stable, the team decide to watch & wait.

23.05.2024	Neurosurgery review via telehealth.
03.06.2024	Port-a-cath removal surgery at QCH.
19.11.2024	MRI at QCH reveals evidence of another stroke, this time within the cyst. This explains Sebastian's increased fatigue, headaches and dizziness over the past two months. The cyst has also increased in size substantially. It looks as though the bleed from the cystic stroke is leaking into the tumour. The shunt is working well to keep the CSF flowing through the ventricles without clotting. Due to the increased size of the cyst, the ventricles are showing evidence of a small collapse, which is being monitored closely. The team have booked Sebastian in for surgery on Wednesday, 27th November, at QLD Children's Hospital. The procedure will include a burr hole to lance the cyst. It is hoped that the cyst's contents will be absorbed by the ventricles. This procedure is called a Burr Hole Fenestration. The surgeon will then watch to see if the cyst ceases to bleed. If not, a craniotomy will be conducted, and a Cystoperitoneal Shunt will be inserted. The ophthalmology report confirmed that Sebastian has total tunnel vision, meaning he does not have peripheral vision on either side. The ophthalmologist also reported that Sebby's optic disc is pale which would reflect increased pressure created by the cyst. 6 on 6 is normal eyesight (the old 20/20). Sebby is 6 on 30, so will need text increased by 5 times to be able legible for him. While in QCH, Sebastian will be undergoing cortisol, hypothalamus and thyroid stress tests as the team believes these may also be newly compromised.
26.11.2024	Sebastian is admitted into QCH for observations before surgery.
27.11.2024	Sebastian undergoes brain surgery and enters the PICU. Once back with Sebastian in PICU, Sam & I learned that a RIKM was inserted into Sebastian's brain. This will allow the team to drain the cyst again if needed, without major surgery. Concern for return of Diabetes Insipidus when Sebastian begins to dump excessive urine after surgery. After 12 hours of monitoring, his urine input and output stabilise, and DI is ruled out.

28.11.2024	Follow-up MRI shows successful operation. The RIKM is placed well, and the cyst appears to be completely drained.
29.11.2024	Sebastian has been moved from the PICU to the Acute Ward on Level 12, QCH. Sam and I believe we are already seeing improvement in Sebastian's speech. Sam flies home to be with the girls and relieve my mum from the farm.
30.11.2024	Neuro, Oncology, and Endocrine have cleared Sebastian for discharge later today. He is unable to fly until Saturday, December 7th, so he is ordered to stay close to QCH. We will stay at East Brisbane with Aunty Julie and Uncle Brendon. Sebastian is being treated for pain with Panadol only, and other than increased fatigue due to the surgery, he is recovering very well. The wound also looks good.
02.12.2024	Sam returns to Brisbane.
03.12.2024	I return home to be with the girls for end-of-year school celebrations.
05.12.2024	Sebastian has blood tests at QCH to keep an eye on levels post-surgery. OT Lauren Fitzpatrick from QCH assists with managing Sebastian's fear of needles.
07.12.2024	Sam and Sebastian return home from Brisbane.
Total COVID-19 confirmed cases in QLD as at 31.07.2024 = 1,808,403	

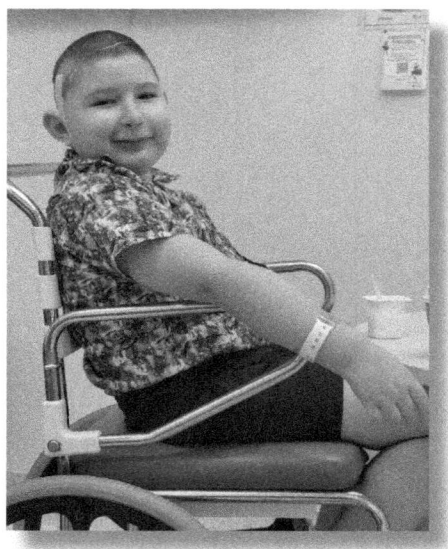

Recovering well after surgery on 27.11.2024

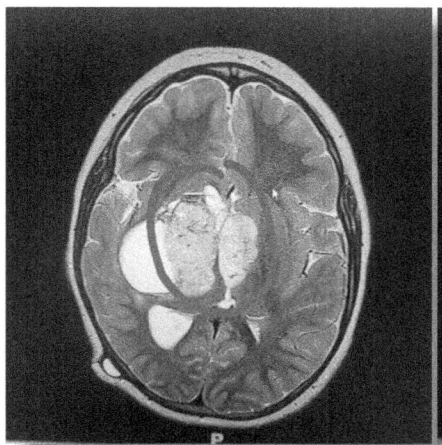
Before surgery MRI - tumour circled

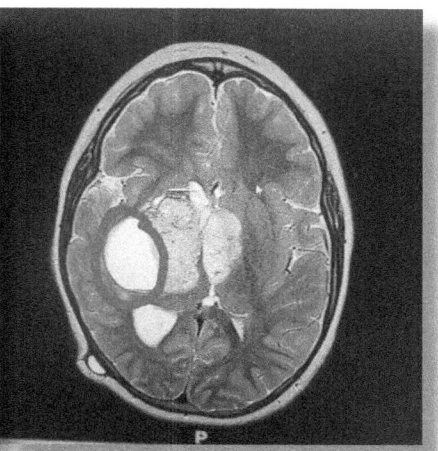
Before surgery MRI - cyst circled

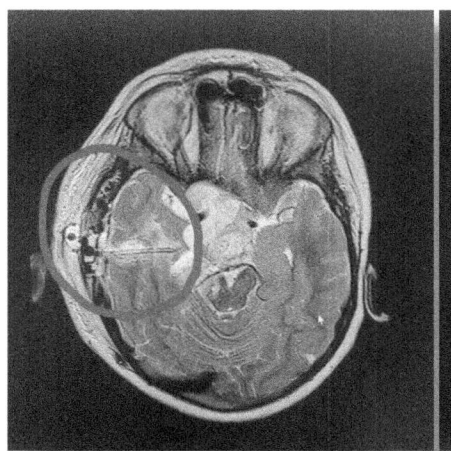
Post-surgery MRI - RIKM circled

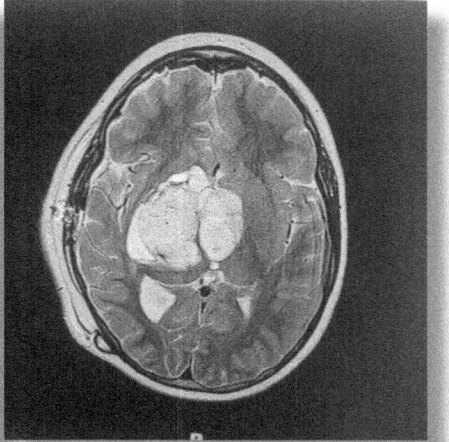
Post-surgery MRI - tumour remains

ACKNOWLEDGEMENTS

When I started writing, I had no idea it would become a foundation for my personal transformation and, ultimately, a lifeline for our family.

Each word written in 'The Unexpected Privilege' felt like an act of resilience; knowing that my words resonated with so many of you brought a profound sense of purpose to my life.

To my beloved family, who walked this path by my side: Sebastian, you are the heart and soul of this story, and your strength has inspired every page. To Antonia, Josephine and Alyssa, thank you for your understanding and love and for sharing your brother's story with me in a way only siblings can. I am endlessly grateful for the depth of compassion and care you show towards Sebastian every day.

To my friends and readers who have embraced us through thick and thin, and to those who followed our journey on my blog, thank you for giving me a space to be vulnerable. Your encouragement reminded me that I wasn't alone in this journey, and your support has helped me find light even in the darkest moments.

To my team of editors and proofreaders, thank you for helping me bring this story into the world with sensitivity. Your belief in this book has allowed it to reach readers in ways I could have only dreamed of.

Finally, to you, the reader, my hope is that within these pages, you find not only our story but pieces of your own. May you be uplifted by the strength that comes from facing life's challenges and feel empowered to find hope, even when the path seems uncertain.

BOOK 3

Daring to Dream
- From Farm to Fergie -

To my sisterhood.

Stronger together, always.

Disclaimer: This book addresses sensitive topics, including cancer, mental health, and death. The content may evoke strong emotional responses and is only intended for informational and educational purposes. It is not a substitute for professional medical advice, diagnosis, or treatment. Readers are encouraged to seek guidance from qualified health professionals for personal concerns or issues related to these topics. The stories and experiences shared in this book are not exhaustive and may not reflect every individual's experience.

CONTENTS

	Forewords by Peace Mitchell & Andrew Griffiths	Page 254
	Introduction	Page 257
1	Knowledge is Power	Page 259
2	Wearing All the Hats	Page 262
3	Paying it Forward	Page 266
4	Becoming My Own Champion	Page 268
5	Small Budget, Big Dream	Page 270
6	Jed	Page 275
7	Small Business, Big Deal	Page 277
8	Becoming an Ausmumpreneur	Page 279
9	The Imposter	Page 282
10	The Fame Monster	Page 285
11	Being the Advocate	Page 287
12	The Role of Survival & Resilience	Page 290
13	The Ripple Effect	Page 292
14	From Farm to Fergie	Page 295
15	London	Page 299
16	A Story Still Unfolding	Page 301
	Photo Gallery	Page 303
	Acknowledgements	Page 310
	About the Author	Page 311
	Other Titles by the Author	Page 312
	Book Club Questions	Page 313

FOREWORD

Written by Peace Mitchell

Global Community Leader, TEDx Speaker, Publisher, Author & Investor

Crystal Leonardi is one of the strongest people I know. She has faced every hard experience, devastating setback, and seemingly impossible challenge with grace, continuing to stand strong and believe in the possibility of a positive outcome. Clarity is the story of how she not only transformed her pain into power but led the way for others, inspiring and uplifting them every step of the way.

Crystal does everything she does with love, a positive spirit and confidence, whether working with her authors, writing her own books, connecting with her local community or caring for her family. Her love and positivity shine through. This love and optimism have helped her weather the hardest storms and find the strength to be resilient, determined and persistent in finding her way through every challenge and creating new opportunities for growth, hope and connection.

Crystal is the epitome of conscious leadership. Her huge, generous heart and positive spirit are combined with a fierce, passionate voice that tells it how it is. Her advocacy, whether for her own son, for her authors, for other families caring for a child with serious illness, or for herself and what she believes is right, is powerful.

The ripple effect of Crystal's work is felt far beyond her farm in Far North Queensland. Through her advocacy work for sick children, her work publishing authors, her writing, and more, the impact of her voice and her generous heart create change and empower and inspire people everywhere to believe in the possibilities available to them.

w: https://ausmumpreneur.com
e: hello@ausmumpreneur.com
fb: AusMumpreneur
ig: ausmumpreneur

FOREWORD

Written by Andrew Griffiths
International Bestselling Author & Global Speaker

Every once in a while, a book comes along that doesn't just share a story, it leaves a mark on your soul. Part 3, 'Daring to Dream: From the Farm to Fergie' is one of those books. In it, the author, with raw honesty and boundless courage, takes us on a journey of resilience, creativity, and an unyielding belief in the power of dreams.

Crystal's journey is both deeply personal and universally inspiring. She brings us into her world, from the quiet fields of her family farm to the bustling streets of the city, where her dreams began to take shape. This book is not just a memoir; it's a roadmap for anyone who has faced overwhelming challenges and dared to keep moving forward.

The heart of this book lies in its humanity. Crystal's candid reflections on watching her son, Sebastian, battle cancer during the dark days of 2020 remind us of the fragility of life and the extraordinary strength we find within ourselves when we least expect it. Her writing became her refuge, her journal a lifeline, and through her words, we see the profound transformation of grief into growth, fear into determination, and survival into triumph.

Crystal's experiences are a testament to the universal truths of resilience and hope. Whether she's standing as an advocate for her son, navigating the complexities of small business ownership, or celebrating her journey as an AusMumpreneur, she embodies what it means to turn adversity into opportunity.

This book is more than a celebration of survival. It is a call to action, a reminder that we all have an inner warrior ready to rise when life's storms threaten to pull us under. From lessons on empowerment and self-belief to the intricacies of building a business and embracing our unique paths, Daring to Dream speaks to anyone yearning for something more, something extraordinary.

Crystal's story isn't finished, it's still unfolding, page by page, dream by dream. As you read this remarkable book, you'll find yourself inspired to face your own challenges, embrace your own dreams, and step into a future filled with possibility.

This isn't just a book to read; it's a journey to experience. I invite you to turn the page and join Crystal as she dares to dream and dares us all to do the same.

w: www.andrewgriffiths.com.au
e: info@andrewgriffiths.com.au
fb: Andrew Griffiths
in: Andrew Griffiths

INTRODUCTION

In a world where dreams often feel distant, I embarked on a journey that took me from the quiet expanse of our family farm to the world stage. 'Daring to Dream: From Farm to Fergie' is not just the next chapter in my memoir; it's the story of how I turned my new-found resilience into a business that has fulfilled my dreams in so many ways.

Writing has been my survival. During the trappings of 2020, it became my haven, a place where I could unload the overwhelming emotions that came with watching my son's body being slowly taken by cancer. It was a time filled with anxiety, fear, and post-traumatic stress disorder. Often in the middle of the night, woken by nightmares, I would pour my thoughts onto paper—sometimes on napkins during plane rides, on the backs of medical paperwork in emergency rooms, but mostly in my journal.

What happened to my son was a wake-up call—a call to pay attention to the strength I didn't know I had. When I least expected it, I survived the unthinkable. My inner warrior, forever dormant, had awakened. Years of building resilience beneath the surface manifested in the strength I would need to endure a year of hell.

For many of you, survival may have started in childhood, during a first marriage, or after a life-altering tragedy, as it did for me. But I've learned, especially from Sebastian, that survival is instinctive. Children know only survival, while adults choose to sink or swim, fight or fly.

'Daring to Dream' is a testament to survival, resilience, and determination. As a mother, writer, and now publisher, my journey has been shaped by both challenges and triumphs. From our quiet family farm to the bustling streets of the city—and now, the prospect of reaching London—each chapter reflects on the profound lessons I've learned.

In this, Book 3 of 'Clarity,' I hope to provide you with insights into navigating your own challenges while inspiring you to embrace your dreams, no matter how distant they may seem. This book is a celebration of resilience, a guide to personal growth, and a tribute to the power of daring to dream.

Where it all began... at the typewriter in the early 1990s

1

KNOWLEDGE IS POWER

A clash of opportunity and perfect timing saw the birth of Bowerbird Publishing in 2021. Starting as a self-published author, I quickly fell in love with the quirks and politics of the publishing industry in Australia. The whirlwind of self-publishing 'Boy of Steel' forced me to reflect on the enormity of the task, filled with challenges and countless lessons learned. Navigating the ins and outs of self-publishing made me acutely aware of a significant market gap that left many aspiring authors feeling lost and unsupported. I felt that real-life experiences and practical solutions were often missing from the self-publishing conversation.

Determined to bridge this gap, I documented my experiences and insights, leading to the creation of '6 Steps to Self-Publishing with Crystal Leonardi.' This guide condensed my journey into actionable advice. This process allowed me to reflect on what had worked, what hadn't, and what I would do differently in future projects. Ironically, I self-published this, my second book, a book about self-publishing.

Creating '6 Steps' was more than just an exercise in reflection; it was somewhat of a surprise. Once published, I was overwhelmed by its popularity. Suddenly, I found myself at the centre of eager writers seeking guidance. Libraries reached out, asking me to lead workshops on self-publishing, and I embraced these opportunities without hesitation. Helping others tell their stories felt amazing. I revelled in empowering authors to take control of their publishing journeys, especially those struggling to secure traditional publishing contracts. In those moments, I experienced a sense of purpose that transcended the challenges of Hospital visits and parenting.

This newfound trust in me catalysed something even greater: the foundations of Bowerbird Publishing. Sharing my knowledge ignited a spark within me, revealing the need for a supportive platform dedicated to helping authors navigate the fiercely competitive and sometimes overwhelming publishing landscape. It spoke deeply to my Aries traits of being an innovative leader and brought me immense feelings of worth. What began as an extension of '6 Steps' quickly evolved into a full-fledged publishing company, originally established to assist writers in self-publishing.

Creating an inclusive environment where writers felt valued and supported was paramount to me. I wanted Bowerbird Publishing to be the publisher I wished I had access to when I first embarked on my publishing journey. Each interaction—whether through workshops or one-on-one consultations—further fuelled my passion for empowering others. I knew firsthand the challenges of self-publishing and was determined to make the process more accessible and less intimidating for aspiring authors. Moreover, it would lay an excellent path for myself and my future publications.

Reflecting on my journey from author to publisher, I realise how far I have come. The initial steps of sharing my story blossomed into a mission to uplift and empower a community of writers. Knowledge truly is power, and I am honoured to pass it on to others, helping them carve their paths as published authors.

Ultimately, what started as a personal journey of healing and storytelling evolved into a vibrant community of creators, all daring to dream and share their voices with the world. In this community, I am reminded that when we lift others, we rise together.

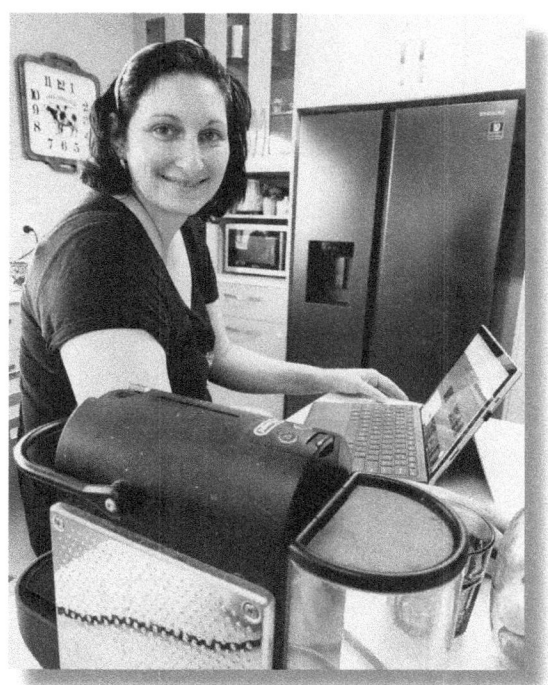

The extremely humble beginnings of Bowerbird Publishing.
Working from my tablet on the kitchen bench, 28 July 2021

At my official launch of Boy of Steel in September 2021 at Whileaway Cafe & Bookshop in Port Douglas, Queensland. And with friends who surprised me by popping in; Casey, Deb & Ally

2

WEARING ALL THE HATS

The birth of my babies and my business were moments of clarity and resolve. Their growth has been woven into my life as a mother and businesswoman. Each day, I navigate a world where my family's needs intersect with the demands of running a business and where the complexities of Sebastian's care remind me of the importance of resilience, adaptability and flexibility.

Truthfully, Sebastian is both my joy and my greatest challenge. His smile can brighten even the most exhausting days, but his medical and developmental needs require a level of attention and planning that shapes every aspect of our lives. As his primary carer, I continuously shift between mother, advocate, and caregiver roles.

A typical day begins long before the sun rises. I cherish those quiet pre-dawn hours, settling into my home office to respond to emails and plan the day ahead. This early start (sometimes as early as 4:00 am) ensures I have time to dedicate to my business while meeting my family's unique lifestyle and needs.

Importantly, I prioritise Sebastian's care over my business. This is a non-negotiable component of my business model and a big reason why working for myself perfectly complements my life with Sebastian. I cannot be reliable to an employer nor offer them my undivided loyalty when I have a child whom I need to be 'on call' for during school hours. Due to Sebastian's frequent and unpredictable fatigue, he is only a part-time student. His days start at 8:00 am and finish at 12:30 pm. He has a one-on-one carer when at school to ensure his needs are met, and he can tackle challenges with confidence.

Each day is a logistical puzzle and each day is different. During my early morning planning, I look ahead at what is scheduled for Sebastian (appointments, schooling, therapy sessions) and weave my business tasks and responsibilities amongst them. Sometimes, it means doing only one hour of work in the office before dawn, prioritising sending out invoices, responding to publishing enquiries and checking on progress and deadlines for upcoming releases. Of course, some days are better than others.

This is how my day looks when Sebastian is at school until 12:30pm:

4 – 5 am	Sam (hubby) and I wake up, make a coffee, and head into the office. For Sam, that's a 1.5-hour drive Monday through Friday.
6 am	Wake Antonia (eldest child).
6:30 am	Make lunches and help Antonia with getting ready for her 7:00 am bus.
7 am	Antonia leaves for the high school bus. I wake the other three children and get breakfast started.
7 – 7:45 am	Clean up kitchen and assist younger children with packing bags, dressing, hair, shoes, etc.
7:45 – 8 am	Drive three children to bus stop for 8:00 am bus.
8 – 8:15 am	Load washing machine, tidy house, tend to dogs and water garden.
8:15 – 12:15 pm	Bowerbird Publishing time in the home office.
12:30 pm	Pick up Sebastian from school.
1 pm – 2:30 pm	Lunch and quiet time with Sebastian.
2:30 pm	Prepare afternoon tea.
3:15pm	Collect Josephine & Alyssa from the bus stop.
4 pm	Antonia arrives home from high school.
3:15 – 6 pm	Spend time with children/afternoon activities.
6 pm	Sam arrives home. Dinner, showers & quiet time.
8 pm	Children in bed, closely followed by Sam & I.

The children do approximately 9 hours of after-school activities between Monday and Friday each week during the term. On the days we have sporting commitments, Sebastian and I collect Josephine and Alyssa from school in Julatten at 3:00 p.m. and meet Antonia in Mossman (around 20km from home), where we stay until everyone is finished training/practice.

When Sebastian's medical appointments and therapy sessions are due, I try my best to schedule them during school hours so that I can be back in time for 3:00 p.m. school pick-up and after-school commitments with the girls.

I know it seems like a lot to fit into a day, but in reflection during 2020, when I didn't have a choice but to stop, I realised how important balance is. Not just for adults but also for children. For me, allowing the children to dance, play basketball or go to theatre group isn't about over-committing and complicating our lives; it's about stepping outside of our comfort zone, meeting people from outside of the schooling community and our small rural town, setting goals and enjoying the freedom to learn a new skill. It's up to the children how much or how little they commit to each term (budget permitting) and I always encourage them to try something new when an activity ceases to exciting or challenge them.

It has a lot to do with decompartmentalising each activity in my day, being 100% present in the moment, and letting go of feeling like I've not achieved or completed enough. After all, if no one dies or ends up in the Hospital and the children and Sam know they are loved, my 'job' is done.

The demands of motherhood are always multifaceted and never without sacrifices. There are days when the weight of responsibility feels overwhelming, when the demands of motherhood clash with the immediacy of running a small business. But there are also moments of profound clarity—watching Sebastian thrive at school, hearing the excitement in an author's voice when they hold their published book for the first time. These moments remind me why I do what I do.

Sebastian's journey has taught me to celebrate progress, no matter how small, and to find joy in the process of overcoming obstacles. These lessons have made me a better mother and carer and given me the tools to wear all the hats, and lead with empathy and authenticity in my business. Together, my family and my work remind me daily that resilience is not just about surviving difficult times—it's about thriving in spite of them.

… 3

PAYING IT FORWARD

At the beginning of 2022, I found myself more motivated than ever to support families of children with cancer. This motivation grew from the depths of my own experiences and the desire to make a meaningful impact. Helping others navigate the labyrinthine world of childhood cancer became a calling—one that aligned with my passion for storytelling and my hope to make a difference in the lives of others.

In the shadow of grief, I discovered an unexpected light—the power of storytelling. When Sebastian was diagnosed with cancer, our lives turned upside down, and the weight of that reality felt almost unbearable. Yet, amid the soul-crushing uncertainty, I found solace in writing. It became my lifeline, a way to navigate unfamiliar emotions while offering hope and understanding to others walking a similar path.

One of my most cherished projects was creating my first children's book, 'My Brother Sebastian: Explaining Cancer to Kids.' Lovingly written with the help of my daughters, this book focused on the profound impact a cancer diagnosis can have on young siblings. It explains each stage of diagnosis and treatment through a lens children can understand, easing the burden of tough conversations for families.

Writing 'My Brother Sebastian' allowed me to honour our journey while empowering others to voice theirs. I wanted families to know they were not alone, that it was okay to feel the burden of their circumstances, and that hope could shine through even in the darkest times. It wasn't just for Sebastian but for my daughters, who navigated their brother's illness with resilience and grace. This book became a way to support both the sibling and the sick child, a dream fulfilled in my mission to create empathy and understanding in a world where people are quick to judge others.

In addition to My Brother Sebastian, I have published two more children's books; 'My Friend Alice, Explaining Disability to Kids' and 'My Mate Jed, Explaining Stroke to Kids'; all inspired by my own family's struggles. These stories aim to ensure that children understand our differences are what make us special. With suggestions on inclusive play and celebrating diversity, these books foster compassion and understanding in young readers, offering a sense of belonging to children facing their own challenges.

Looking back, these projects reflect a balance of humility and confidence that has guided my path into business. They are testaments to the strength that comes from vulnerability. By paying it forward—whether through words, actions or simply being present for others—I've found healing for myself. My pain has transformed into a force for good, creating a ripple effect that touches the lives of others, turning grief into a lasting legacy of hope. Through storytelling, I continue to honour our journey while helping others find light in their darkest moments.

BECOMING MY OWN CHAMPION

My journey into the publishing world began long before I even realised it. In high school, I fell in love with Shakespeare and literature, which led me to study English at university. However, it wasn't until Sebastian was diagnosed with brain cancer that I realised my true purpose and passion in life.

The experience of self-publishing was immensely enjoyable and eye-opening. I instantly fell in love with every aspect of writing and publishing, from the initial spark of inspiration to the final product in readers' hands. As I shared my experiences with fellow writers, a lightbulb moment occurred. Some writers attending my workshops expressed that while they now understood self-publishing, they preferred the convenience of hiring someone to guide them through the entire process. This demand triggered an ambitious thought: What if I expanded my role from mentor to independent publisher?

Starting a business based solely on my limited experience as a self-published author was daunting. I had no budget, no funding, and no formal training in running a business. Yet, fuelled by passion and a desire to make a difference, I wanted to step up to the challenge. There were moments of self-doubt when I questioned whether I had what it took. Could I meet the demands of aspiring authors? Could I maintain the confidence I'd just begun to build?

Determined to equip myself for this new venture, I researched. I took publishing courses, sought insight from professional editors and graphic designers, and dived into the industry's business side. My experiences—whether from university studies nearly twenty years ago, corporate roles before starting a family, or simply being a naturally hardworking and creative person—all began to come together. These experiences laid a foundation for Bowerbird Publishing, giving me the tools to approach this new venture confidently.

In January 2022, I took a leap of faith and engaged my first paying client. I initiated a manuscript call-out through local media, and the response was overwhelming. Manuscripts flooded in—each one brimming with potential. Seeing so many eager writers looking to me for professional guidance was extraordinary. It was a moment that marked a significant shift in my journey. I was no longer a self-published author or workshop facilitator; I was becoming a champion for other writers.

Building Bowerbird Publishing from the ground up was no small feat. Further to my industry research, as mentioned earlier, I also attended workshops and conferences and connected with other published authors and industry professionals. I also set about building a brand that authors could depend on, ensuring that Bowerbird Publishing would be known for its exceptional services, integrity, and dedication to helping writers succeed. Developing a professional website, social media presence, and logo were all part of this early process.

Naming my business Bowerbird Publishing was symbolic. The bowerbird, a creature native to my region, represents creativity, flair, and individuality—qualities I hoped my business would embody. Just as the bowerbird collects and arranges items to create a beautiful space, I wanted to gather knowledge and tools to help authors flourish in their creative journeys.

Becoming an independent business owner taught me that becoming my own champion wasn't just about believing in myself—it was about believing in the stories of others and nurturing their journeys. With each new client, I was carving out a place for myself in the publishing world—one rooted in community, empowerment, and shared dreams. In helping authors bring their stories to life, I also find my story growing richer.

SMALL BUDGET, BIG DREAM

Starting a business is an exciting venture, but it can feel daunting when funds are tight. For many, the fear of financial risk overshadows the dream. I know that feeling all too well. When I started Bowerbird Publishing, I didn't have deep pockets or a safety net; what I had was a fresh perspective and a big dream.

Initially, I used the profits from 'Boy of Steel' to fund the self-publishing of '6-Steps to Self-Publishing.' That single investment became a catalyst for an entirely new income stream. Workshops, presentations, and appearances followed, building my brand and business. However, I quickly realised that while making money was important, spending it wisely was even more crucial.

The fundamentals of starting a business—education, publicity, and growth—cost money. But they don't have to cost a fortune. What I've learned in my experience and other business owners is that sustainability is often the missing piece in the entrepreneurial puzzle. Many businesses, especially those that seem to have it all—large marketing budgets, company cars, and corporate partnerships—are often drowning in debt. The pressure of unpaid bills and looming deadlines can create stress and reactive decision-making.

While some may argue that debt is a necessary investment in growth, I've chosen a different path. My business is self-funded and sustainable. Yes, my profit margins might be slimmer, and my growth more organic, but I'm not beholden to financial institutions, investors, or partners. That independence allows me to make decisions based on what's best for my business and lifestyle, rather than what's necessary to meet a financial obligation.

This approach hasn't just benefited my bank account—it's given me peace of mind. Running a debt-free business removes a significant layer of stress and allows for greater creativity and flexibility. It also builds resilience. I've had to be resourceful, learning to stretch every dollar and find innovative ways to achieve my goals without overspending.

In the early days, here's how I made it work:

Leverage Free and Low-Cost Resources

One of my biggest assets in the early days was my willingness to learn. I took advantage of free courses and workshops, many of which were available online. Platforms like YouTube, Skillshare, and Canva provided invaluable tutorials on everything from graphic design to social media marketing.

I also found free online resources tailored to writers and publishers, including blog posts, podcasts, and forums. These tools gave me the foundational knowledge I needed without spending a cent.

Join Professional Associations

Investing in memberships with organisations like the Australian Society of Authors (ASA), Queensland Writers Centre, and Writer's Digest paid off in spades. These groups offered access to discounts on courses, exclusive information on industry trends, and valuable networking opportunities. The ASA, in particular, provided direct access to trusted service providers like editors and mentors, which saved me time and money.

Use Cost-Effective Service Providers

When I needed professional help, I turned to platforms like Fiverr where I could hire talented freelancers at a fraction of the cost of traditional agencies.

Whether designing a book cover or typesetting a manuscript, these services helped me produce high-quality work affordably.

Tap into Social Media Communities

Particularly in the publishing industry, I have found trusted peers few and far between. Most keep their cards close to their chest and aren't interested in mentoring someone new to the industry. I combatted this through social media, joining both author and publisher platforms and gaining insight into both sides of the industry.

Social media communities were a goldmine of advice, encouragement, and resources. Connecting with like-minded individuals provided practical tips and helped me feel less isolated as I navigated the challenges of running a business.

Network Beyond Your Industry

On a whim, I joined the Cairns Business Women's Club and attended my first trade table and one-minute elevator pitch event without knowing what to expect. Nervous and feeling like a fish out of water, I almost convinced myself to turn around and go home. But once I arrived, I was immediately struck by the supportive and encouraging atmosphere. This is when I first learned the importance of networking beyond the publishing industry. I gained fresh perspectives and uncovered unexpected opportunities by connecting with professionals from diverse fields. Organisations like the Cairns Business Women's Club and events like AusMumpreneur introduced me to inspiring entrepreneurs whose experiences and advice broadened my horizons. These connections often led to collaborations, book sales, and exciting new partnerships that I wouldn't have found otherwise.

Give First, Receive Later

One of the most valuable lessons I learned from Michelle Bridges in 2022 is that working for free is okay. Whether speaking at an event, providing advice to a fellow writer, or offering a free workshop, these experiences can often pay off in other ways. For example, I have assisted authors with grant applications free of charge so that they can fund their publishing dreams, hopefully with Bowerbird Publishing. I have also offered writers free manuscript appraisals in the early stages of their writing journey to build a foundation for a mentor or publisher relationship. What I have learned, most of all, is that people love people. The relationships we build with others are invaluable to sustainability in business. And if working for free means getting your foot in the door where you wouldn't have otherwise, then it's worth it anyway. A healthy balance between working for free and knowing your worth is key.

Start with What's Established

Don't try to reinvent the wheel. I used platforms like Amazon for distribution, Instagram for printing, and social media for marketing. These established systems gave me the tools to reach a wider audience without building everything from scratch. Over time, I gained confidence and access to resources that helped me develop my own procedures and strategies with that worked for me.

As my business started generating income, I reinvested in areas that directly drove growth, such as improving my website and expanding my marketing reach. Running a lean and adaptable business meant I could pivot quickly when needed and avoid unnecessary expenses.

One of the key lessons I learned was the value of starting small and testing strategies before making larger commitments. For example, I experimented with using SEO and metadata on social media to enhance my online visibility. By analysing the results of these small investments, I could see what worked and adjust my future efforts accordingly. If a campaign performed well, I'd tweak the length, budget, or target audience to maximise the value of my investment.

This approach also extended to traditional media. I began with small, 1/8th-page advertisements in local print publications to test their impact. When referrals and inquiries started coming in as a direct result of these ads, I knew they were effective. From there, I could scale up—opting for more frequent ads or even a yearly advertising contract, which often provided better value for money.

Being adaptable also meant knowing when to use established systems and platforms to save time and money. I relied on tools like Amazon for distribution and Instagram for printing until I had enough experience and resources to develop my own procedures. This allowed me to focus on growing my business without reinventing the wheel prematurely.

Reinvesting wisely and staying adaptable enabled me to make thoughtful decisions that balanced immediate needs with long-term goals. By starting small, measuring success, and scaling up when the time was right, I created a sustainable path for growth without the stress of overcommitting.

Dream big, even on a budget. If you are considering starting a business on a budget, know this: limitations often force creativity. When you don't have the luxury of throwing money at a problem, you find smarter, more efficient ways to solve it. You can achieve more than you ever thought possible with a little resourcefulness and determination. And when in doubt – sleep on it!

6

JED

Publishing my first client as an independent publisher was a pivotal moment that solidified my purpose and passion in this new role. In 2022, I was introduced to Nicola Baker, a remarkable woman whose story resonated deeply. Nicola's son, Jed, had a stroke at just 11 months old. Some years later, he was diagnosed with Moyamoya disease, a rare brain condition. In her manuscript, 'The Thing About Jed,' she chronicled their journey. It was written with courage and determination and spoke directly to my heart.

The personal nature of Nicola's narrative echoed my own experiences with Sebastian's illness. As I read through her manuscript, I felt an undeniable connection—not just to her words but to the shared emotions of fear, love, and resilience that we both knew too well as mothers navigating the terrifying world of childhood illness. I immediately knew this story needed to be shared, and I believed I was the only publisher who could bring it to life.

Nicola had spent nearly twenty years on her journey with Jed, and her experience brought me profound comfort and inspiration. We instantly connected personally, and our shared experiences created a bond of mutual respect and empathy. Nicola placed her complete confidence in me, trusting me to help her share her story with the world. I was both excited and humbled by the opportunity of publishing 'The Thing About Jed.'

The process was not without its challenges, but those challenges were incredibly rewarding. Professionally, this project taught me valuable lessons, especially about managing client expectations. I realised the delicate balance required between offering my guidance and allowing Nicola to maintain her creative control. I have continued to fine-tune these skills in my business, and I've learned to stand firm when necessary, helping authors see the bigger picture while honouring their voices.

Nicola and I didn't stop at just one book. She approached me with another idea in early 2023: to co-author a children's book aimed at helping families affected by stroke. We poured our hearts into creating 'My Mate Jed, Explaining Stroke to Kids,' a resource designed to provide both education and comfort to children and their families. This project, like the first, was deeply personal and profoundly rewarding.

Working with Nicola on these two projects has been one of the most fulfilling experiences of my publishing career. The success of 'The Thing About Jed' and 'My Mate Jed' reinforced my belief in the power of storytelling to heal and educate.

This collaboration with Nicola has reminded me of the incredible impact that sharing our stories can have on the world. Together, we've created a ripple effect, transforming our struggles into stories of hope and inspiration for readers everywhere.

Nicola and I at the launch of My Mate Jed in May 2024

7

SMALL BUSINESS, BIG DEAL

Launching a small business is an exhilarating experience. However, when I started out, I quickly realised that no amount of preparation could fully shield me from the growing pains of running a new business. Some of the steepest lessons I learnt were through trial and error, and some skills could only be fine-tuned through time, experience, and sheer persistence.

By 2023, I had already completed several graphic design and editing courses, giving me a professional services foundation to build upon. While I had the ambition, the reality of balancing multiple roles in a growing business began to weigh on me. I knew that if I wanted to elevate my projects and maintain the quality I envisioned for Bowerbird, I needed to take a step back and reassess my approach.

This was when I made the pivotal decision to enlist the help of a professional editor and graphic designer to support me. It was time to further fine-tune the delicate balance between financial and artistic control.

The phrase 'work in progress' perfectly describes the constant evolution of my business and myself as a publisher. As mentioned in the following chapter, developing the skills necessary to lead a business takes time, patience, and resilience. There were days when I wanted to be the best at everything right away, but sometimes, the best way to become truly great is to let experience shape you. Time became my greatest teacher, and with it came confidence in the choices I made for my business.

Ultimately, starting a small business isn't about perfection from the outset but growth. It's also about having the patience to learn and that each difficulty is an opportunity to improve. Building Bowerbird Publishing wasn't just about publishing books; it was about crafting a sustainable and thriving business that could serve me and my family for years to come. With one step at a time, I was ready to constantly adapt, evolve, and improve. Running a small business has presented big challenges, but the rewards have been just as significant.

At the 2024 Ausmumpreneur awards with my SILVER trophy for Professional Services Business

BECOMING AN AUSMUMPRENEUR

Being an AusMumpreneur represents more than just a business achievement—it symbolises a community of women breaking boundaries, lifting each other, and striving to turn their dreams into reality. Founders and sisters Peace Mitchell and Katy Garner created this incredible space where entrepreneurial women and mothers like myself can connect, grow, and inspire each other. It's more than an awards platform—it's a sisterhood of resilient, powerful women supporting each other as they reach new heights personally and professionally. Ausmumpreneur was integral to my business early on. It reminded me that I am not alone in typical small business struggles and that juggling motherhood and business is an ongoing but achievable task.

From the beginning, Peace and Katy cultivated an environment where success is celebrated, and setbacks remind us that challenging times are opportunities for growth. Being part of this community has transformed me as a businesswoman, encouraging me to face personal and professional challenges head-on.

My journey with AusMumpreneur began in 2022 when I serendipitously met Sam Oraya, who encouraged me to enter the upcoming awards. After nominating myself later that year, I was honoured with a bronze award in the Author of the Year category. Being recognised among such talented finalists was both humbling and validating. It boosted my confidence, reaffirming that I was where I was supposed to be.

For some business owners, awards may be embellishments, but they are strategic tools for me. Just like paid advertising, awards help raise awareness, build trust, and signal to potential clients that my work meets exceptional standards. I see each recognition since my first is a testament to my hard work, resilience, and dedication to my business.

The 2022 AusMumpreneur award, along with others I have received since have significantly elevated Bowerbird Publishing's profile. It has attracted more clients and collaborators, expanded my network, and connected me with like-minded industry professionals who have become mentors and friends to me. These accolades have opened doors to opportunities I hadn't imagined, pushing me to strive even harder for excellence.

In the competitive world of publishing, every accolade counts. It sets me apart, builds my reputation, and reinforces my commitment to excellence. But as I celebrate my achievements, I stay focused on the big picture—creating meaningful stories, supporting authors in realising their dreams, and continuing to grow.

Bowerbird Publishing's journey is one of growth and celebration. Each award is a milestone marking my progress and propelling me forward. With each achievement, I honour the spirit of resilience and the power of storytelling, and together with my authors, we're creating a legacy that will endure for years to come.

A very proud moment to receive a 2024 Telly Award for my work in book trailer production

Awards and recognition for Bowerbird Publishing to-date:

Winner (Bronze) – Author of the Year, Ausmumpreneur, 2022

Finalist – Sole Entrepreneur of the Year, Cairns Business Women's Club, 2023

Finalist – Woman of the Year, Beam Awards, 2023

Finalist – Author of the Year, Ausmumpreneur, 2023

Winner (Bronze) – Book Trailer Series, Media & Entertainment, 45th Telly Awards, 2024

Winner (Bronze) – Woman in Literature, Women Changing the World Awards, 2024

Finalist – Business Services, Australian Small Business Champion Awards, 2024

Finalist – Regional/Rural/Remote Business of the Year, Beam Awards, 2024

Finalist – Excellence in Diversity & Inclusion, Beam Awards, 2024

Finalist – Woman of the Year, Beam Awards, 2024

Finalist – Author of the Year, Ausmumpreneur, 2024

Finalist – Rural & Remote Business, Ausmumpreneur, 2024

Finalist – Professional Services Business, Ausmumpreneur, 2024

Finalist – Sustainability, Ausmumpreneur, 2024

Finalist – Making a Difference – Environmental Impact, Ausmumpreneur, 2024

9

THE IMPOSTER

In today's competitive publishing market, being a good author is not enough. Publishing success hinges on creating an emotional connection with readers—often before they've even opened your book. Establishing an author brand that clearly articulates your vision or the purpose behind your work is essential. In my opinion, whether you're actively building your brand or not, it's happening. So why not be deliberate in shaping the direction it takes? Consider this (As of 2023):

- Approximately 1 in 5 published authors in Australia are self-published.

- An estimated 6,000 books are published monthly in Australia, not including self-published titles.

- Book sales in Australia have increased by 7.2%, making the industry valued at around $1.3 billion.[9]

Despite these encouraging statistics and the immense effort I've put into building my brand and professional profile, I still, at times, feel like an imposter. This unsettling feeling, imposter syndrome, affects many high achievers. It's the sense that you're not as capable as others perceive you to be and that it's only a matter of time before you're exposed as a fraud.

Authorship is, in many ways, an ego game. It requires vulnerability—putting yourself out there and opening your work to both criticism and praise. Imposter syndrome is inevitable in this profession. It constantly challenges your

---

[9] Australian Publishers Association (APA) and other industry reports.

self-perception and forces you to confront your deepest insecurities—the very insecurities that often drive us to write in the first place.

For me, imposter syndrome manifested as self-doubt and a constant fear of being 'found out.' For me, I thought it was easy for others to attribute my success to luck or external factors rather than my abilities and hard work. I sometimes question whether I truly belonged in the world of publishing.

Over time however, I've learned to embrace these feelings rather than let them hold me back. Living fearlessly has become my new mantra, a perspective strengthened by my experiences with Sebastian's health struggles. The challenges we've faced together have given me more strength and courage than I ever realised I possessed. I've learned that life balances wins and losses, each having value. Authorship is no different—celebrating every milestone, no matter how small, while learning from every setback. The key is to acknowledge our fears without letting them define us.

As Donna Ashworth perfectly articulates in her book 'Words to Live by'...

To the woman who looks around and wonders why everyone else is so much more capable, stronger, and more ambitious than her.

To the woman who thinks everyone else is blazing a fiery path through this thing we call life while she limps behind, barely getting through the days. Somewhere, another woman is looking at you, thinking the same.

You see, we all look like we're kinda nailing it from the outside in. We all look 'together' sometimes. Catch us on the right day; we look like we have it all. Because, guess what? We learned to look that way a long time ago. We learned to hide our struggles behind a smile and whack on the mask every day. And actually, we are doing each other a favour when we show up, just as we are, warts and all, late, flustered, human.

What we need to see is that we are all the same. We all struggle. We all fall apart. Some days, we nail it, and other days, we get nailed. By hiding our own weaknesses, fears, and worries, we give them more power. If you let it out, shine a light on it all, it becomes so much less scary, funny even... and goodness knows we need to laugh.

So, to the woman who wonders if she is good enough... if this is you. Yes, you are. You always were. You don't have to live up to everyone's expectations of how you should be coping. You are human, flawed, wonderful, miraculous, loveable, and loved. I see you; now do me a favour and go see all the others, too. Spread the word that we are good enough, just as we are.[10]

The confident and fearless side of me, captured in Melbourne 2023

---

10 Ashworth, D. (2020). Words to Live By. Wombat Books.

10

THE FAME MONSTER

There's a strange, almost surreal moment when you realise that people start recognising you in public. It's not something that happens overnight, and it's certainly not something I ever prepared for, but the moment it hits, you can't ignore it. Suddenly, you're no longer just a small business owner or a mother on the school run. You're a public figure—a face people associate with your work, brand, and story. And whether I like it or not, with the growth of my business, awards, and events on a global stage, this new reality has become part of my life.

At first, the recognition was surprising and a little uncomfortable. There's something deeply unsettling about strangers knowing you when you have no idea who they are. When you build a platform for yourself, as I have through Bowerbird Publishing and my achievements, there has to be a level of acceptance that notoriety follows.

With accolades comes recognition, and with recognition comes the potential for the ego to rear its head. I've learned that the trick is to stay grounded—and no one does that better than my family. After winning an award, I could be on top of the world, feeling proud of my business and accomplishments, but then come home to find my husband and children utterly oblivious to any of it. To them, I'm just Mum. To Sam, I'm just Crystal. I'm the one who makes dinner, helps with homework, and manages our busy household. There's no room for ego in the everyday hum of family life. My role as a mother humbles me in a way that nothing else can. It reminds me that no matter how many accolades I achieve, the most important part of my identity is being there for my family, not the public persona I present to the world.

It's a delicate balance, accepting the public recognition without letting it take over. A part of me appreciates the acknowledgment and sees it as a testament to my hard work and the brand I have built, but I also remind myself daily that fame is fleeting. It's not the reason I do what I do. The valid reward comes from the joy of creating something meaningful, helping others, and seeing my work's impact on people's lives.

The Fame Monster, as I like to call it, is real. Coming from a small farming community, it's a part of the journey I never anticipated but one I've learned to live with. The key is not to fear or fight it but to manage it. I choose to stay focused on my purpose, surround myself with people who keep me grounded and never lose sight of the fact that the titles and accolades are only part of the story. The real story is in the work, the relationships, and the impact I make along the way—both in business and in my most important role; as a mother.

Feeling grateful and grounded in moments like this with my children.

BEING THE ADVOCATE

Speaking of grounding, while navigating small business and my ego, I have experienced some extremely humbling situations where my role as advocate took on an even greater challenge—getting Sebastian started at school.

For Sebastian, transitioning from a long-term Hospital patient to a school student was a monumental shift. After spending so much of his life in Hospitals, surrounded by medical care, entering a school environment brought both excitement and anxiety to me as his mother. I had been longing for the independence that came with my baby becoming a student, but the impending freedom also meant confronting the fear of the unknown—the unpredictable challenges that lay ahead.

Sebastian's life as a student meant navigating a world different from his peers. He faced challenges that many of the other children couldn't understand: managing his health, coping with the side effects of his treatments, and sometimes missing school due to Hospital appointments or illness. These realities set him apart, making his journey unique.

As his mum, I had to step into a role I never expected—that of his advocate, ensuring Sebastian received the education he deserved. Advocacy went beyond making academic accommodations; it was about creating an environment where he could thrive. It meant fighting for understanding, flexibility, and empathy in a system that wasn't always equipped to meet his needs.

I worked closely with his teachers and school administrators to develop individualised education plans that catered to Sebastian's unique challenges. This involved constant communication, ensuring his absences didn't put him at a disadvantage, and pushing for accommodations like an in-classroom rest area when fatigue took over. It also required us to educate the broader school community about his condition, fostering a culture of empathy and support among his peers and their families. Organisations like Camp Quality provided resources and educational tools to help Sebastian's classmates understand his journey.

Through this process, I learned that advocacy is not a one-time effort—it's an ongoing commitment. Sometimes, it felt like an uphill battle, constantly pushing for the resources Sebastian needed to succeed. But the victories, however small, made it all worthwhile. Seeing him engage with his classmates, build meaningful friendships, and progress academically filled me with immense pride.

This journey has also taught me the power of persistence and the importance of standing up for what is right, not just for my child but for all children who face challenges. Regardless of their circumstances, every child deserves a chance to learn, grow, feel safe and be part of their community. Being Sebastian's advocate has strengthened our bond with the school and the families around us, creating a supportive network for which we are deeply grateful.

Furthermore, the lessons I learned advocating for Sebastian have seamlessly transferred into my professional life. Just as I fought for him to have every opportunity to succeed, I now apply that same resilience and dedication to my work with authors. I advocate for their stories, helping them overcome self-doubt, guiding them through the publishing process, and ensuring they can grow and make an impact. Like Sebastian, my authors deserve to have their voices heard and their stories shared.

Advocacy has become a defining part of who I am as a mother and professional. It's about believing in the potential for greatness, even when the path is filled with obstacles. It's about fostering a sense of belonging and ensuring that everyone has the opportunity to thrive. Most importantly, it's about turning challenges into opportunities, not just for Sebastian but for everyone whose story needs to be told.

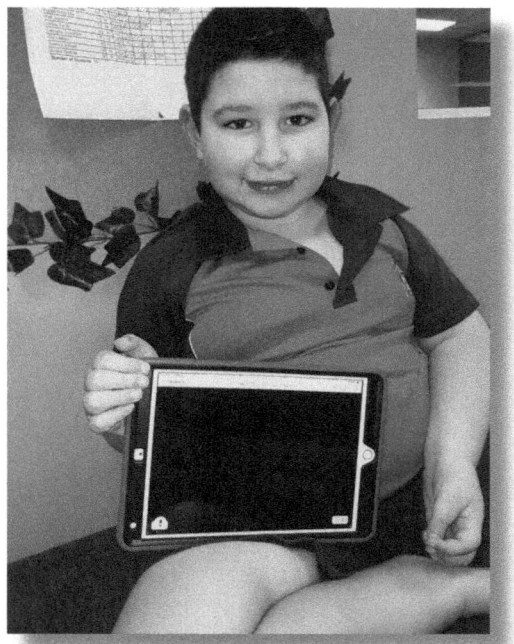

Sebastian at school in 2024

12

THE ROLE OF SURVIVAL & RESILIENCE

On January 8, 2020, my understanding of survival and resilience was forever changed. That day, when Sebastian was diagnosed with brain cancer, my world turned upside down. In an instant, I was forced to tap into a strength I didn't know I had. The experience wasn't just about surviving for myself—it was about surviving for him.

Survival became a conscious choice that required me to push beyond the heartbreak and devastation to harness the power of resilience in ways I'd never imagined. The trials of 2020 awakened something within me, revealing an inner warrior I didn't know existed. Then, I realised how profound the connection between survival and resilience truly is.

In Books 1 & 2 of 'Clarity,' survival isn't just about enduring hard times—it's about embracing them and transforming them into something greater. It peers into every crevice of my heartbreak but balances that pain with a message of hope. The power of a mother's love made survival possible, turning the darkest moments into a testament to perseverance. There's a quote in chapter 15 of 'Boy of Steel' by Bob Riley that resonates deeply with me: "Hard times don't create heroes. It is during the hard times when the hero within us is revealed."

That quote embodies what 2020 taught me—resilience is built, layer by layer, in the most difficult moments. It's not just about enduring pain but finding strength within it. As Oprah Winfrey once said, "Turn your wounds into wisdom and let your challenges serve as stepping stones to becoming a better version of yourself." These words have become my muse, reminding me that every challenge can be an opportunity for growth.

Survival and resilience are not confined to my personal life; they are also the foundation of my business. Starting Bowerbird Publishing brought its trials—financial strain, creative burnout, and learning every aspect of the industry from scratch. But the lessons I learned from Sebastian's battle—how to adapt, persevere, and face uncertainty—were the same skills that helped me grow my business. Resilience became my most valuable asset, allowing me to thrive amid adversity.

I encourage you, reader, to reflect on your moments of survival. Whether it was an illness, the loss of a loved one, an accident, or facing an unrelenting test of courage, these moments of survival are more than just trauma—they are opportunities for growth and wisdom. With that wisdom, we help and empower others to find strength in their own stories.

Ultimately, it's not about avoiding challenges but facing them head-on and finding a way through. Every challenge you overcome reveals more of who you are and your capabilities. My trauma has allowed me to survive, thrive, and continue to grow, no matter what life throws my way.

13

THE RIPPLE EFFECT

Publishing creates an amazing ripple effect. It's more than just a business in books; it's shared experiences that bring immense satisfaction to the authors and me as their publisher. Watching an author's journey, from the tentative first draft to holding their finished book in their hands, is like seeing a chick take flight for the first time. There's a sense of pride and awe as they soar, full of newfound confidence and ready to take on the world, with book in hand. That moment when they realise their dream has come to life is unforgettable and never gets old for me.

But the ripple doesn't stop there. The impact of a published work extends beyond the author. It reaches their readers—whether it's a tell-all memoir that lays bare the truths of someone's life, a thrilling page-turner that keeps readers on edge, or a romance that makes hearts race. These books stir emotions, create communities, and spark conversations. Readers see pieces of themselves in these stories, connect with characters, and sometimes even find solace or joy within the pages.

The ripple effect also brings deep personal fulfilment. Knowing that I've played a part in helping an author's vision come to life and seeing their work's impact on others is a source of profound happiness. It's a reminder that my work goes far beyond the business of publishing; it's about connection.

In many ways, publishing is about sharing a vision, a voice, and a passion. Its impact reminds me daily that one dream can manifest into so much more. This is the ripple effect, one of the most beautiful parts of what I do.

My very first paying client, Nicola Baker (left) and my FGM (Fairy Godmother), Chantal Munro, who pushed me to publish 'Boy of Steel'

Always looking for ways to shine a light on local talent, here I am photographed with authors Colleen Taylor, Alan Isherwood, Sandy Davies, Chantal Munro and Nicola Baker in Mareeba 2022

With Bowerbird authors Mary Pearson, Chantal Munro & Alan Isherwood (left). With Bec Wright (below right) and Rob the Poet (below left) in 2024

Celebrating local talent at the 2023 Yungaburra Book Fair with authors Sandy Davies, Regina Meyer, Debra Gavranich & Megan Formanek

14

FROM FARM TO FERGIE

When opportunity meets vision, magic unfolds.

As the new financial year ticked over in July 2024, I created an ambitious vision board in my office, capturing my wildest dreams—personal and professional. It wasn't about mundane goals like buying a new car or planning a holiday; it was about dreams as grand as meeting Sarah Ferguson, attending the Women Changing the World Summit in London and Paris, and witnessing the Southern Lights from Antarctica.

Admittedly, these dreams seemed distant. Yet, I displayed them as a daily reminder to stay motivated and manifest whatever my heart desired. And manifest they did. Although a trip to London felt daunting, especially with my roles as a wife and mother of four, I held onto hope. Then, two weeks ago, a Sunday afternoon scroll through social media changed everything—Fergie was coming to Perth! I assumed tickets would be sold out, but I contacted my friend and fellow publisher Karen Weaver, who lives in Perth, to ask if she knew much about Sarah's Australian plans. To my surprise, Karen responded, saying she was the event organiser for the event in Perth on 1st November! Without hesitation and after a flurry of messages and rapid flight and accommodation arrangements, I secured the opportunity to meet Sarah Ferguson, Duchess of York on home soil.

Reality set in with the classic, "What will I wear?" Fast forward 10 days, and I found myself at Joondalup Resort in Perth, surrounded by 700 elegantly dressed women, waiting for Sarah Ferguson to be interviewed by acclaimed author Tess Woods. I managed a seat in the second row, just behind Karen. Sarah's hour-long talk was captivating and filled with humour, honesty, and warmth. When it was time to meet her, I felt profoundly grateful to Karen for this once-in-a-lifetime chance.

It is extraordinary to think that Sarah now holds my books, possibly sharing them with children and families in need. This moment was particularly poignant as Sarah had already encountered Bowerbird Publishing this year through various opportunities—a testament to the incredible and serendipitous connections that have shaped my journey.

Meeting Sarah Ferguson was more than a personal milestone; it affirmed that the sky truly is the limit. Success isn't defined by how we measure up against others but by pursuing our passions and contributing to the world. Even Fergie, a successful author and duchess, exemplifies this by continually pushing her boundaries. She openly shared her ambition of adapting her novel The Intriguing Woman into a mini-series and winning an Emmy, then an Oscar. I was surprised—she is already a New York Times #1 best-selling author, a duchess, and a champion of literature. Yet, she still dreams big. This inspired me to embrace my own aspirations unapologetically.

Success is subjective. To outsiders, my meeting with Fergie might signify 'success,' but true success, for me, is loving what I do each day and helping writers share their stories. It's about the journey, not an endless chase for recognition.

Sarah shared lessons on living fully and nurturing self-love. Her wit, warmth, and candid nature charmed the audience, as did her dedication to helping children navigate life's challenges through fiction writing. Her work has my deepest respect and admiration.

Sarah's bond with Australia is strong. Her sister has lived in Perth for 50 years, and she mentioned connections to the parents of her grandchildren's nanny and her publisher, Karen. She's collaborated with Australian authors and illustrators, cementing her literary ties here.

Her memories of Princess Diana and Queen Elizabeth were touching. Sarah spoke fondly of their unwavering support, recounting light-hearted anecdotes, like how the Queen would offer treats to her corgis during meals—gestures Sarah has continued, bringing daily comfort and a sense of connection to the Queen.

Reflecting on her life, Sarah described her wedding to Prince Andrew as her happiest day and proudly claimed she had married the best-looking royal. Before her marriage, she worked for a London publishing house, showcasing her literary talents long before her 80 published books. This full-circle moment resonated with my career path deeply and reminded me always to acknowledge how far we have come.

At 65, Sarah exudes pride and resilience. A breast cancer survivor with a double mastectomy, she humorously refers to her reconstructed breasts as 'Derrick' and 'Eric.' She spoke proudly of her daughters' health journeys—Beatrice's battle with severe dyslexia and Eugenie's with scoliosis—and their choice to display their scars as symbols of strength.

One insight that stayed with me was her advice to treat ourselves as we would our six-year-old selves, offering the kindness and reassurance often needed in moments of doubt.

Meeting Sarah Ferguson reinforced my role as a storytelling advocate. She belongs to a community of like-minded individuals, including Karen Weaver, Justine Martin, Peace Mitchell, and Katy Garner, who all champion creativity and community. Together, we inspire and support each other, standing out by embracing our unique paths.

With Sarah 'Fergie' Ferguson, Duchess of York in Perth 2024

15

LONDON

As I look ahead to 2025, the possibility of travelling to London and Paris with Ausmumpreneur fills me with both excitement and a sense of achievement. While offered to me in 2024, this opportunity didn't feel right then—it felt premature for my business. But now, as my business grows and evolves, I feel ready to take this next bold step. London represents so much more than just another destination on the map. It's a milestone in my personal and professional journey—a leap toward furthering global recognition for Bowerbird Publishing.

Travelling with Peace Mitchell, Katy Garner, and the incredible Ausmumpreneur community isn't just about expanding my brand. It's about being surrounded by women who are just as driven, passionate, and daring as I am. Their support, along with Peace and Katy's guidance, would make this leap more than a solo endeavour—it's a collective journey, where I can draw strength from the sisterhood around me.

But, of course, it's not without its challenges. I have a life rooted in responsibility—a farm, a husband, and four children who need me. The logistics of stepping away from that for a while are daunting. It's a balancing act: managing a thriving business and being present in the lives of those I love most. Yet, I can't help but feel that London is firmly in my future.

This opportunity represents a crucial step toward growing my business and brand on a global stage. I can't ignore the chance to network, learn, and expand my vision for Bowerbird Publishing internationally. While it's not easy to juggle these dreams with the demands of family life, they're on my vision board—clear and tangible.

I've learned that dreams don't happen overnight, but they do happen if you keep daring, keep striving, and keep evolving. I don't know if 2025 will be the year I make it to London, but I know it's coming. And when it does, it will be another step in my journey to becoming the woman and business leader I've always aspired to be.

Founders and hosts of The Women Changing the World Awards, (left to right) Peace Mitchell, Dr. Terari Trent, Sarah Ferguson, Katy Garner

16

A STORY STILL UNFOLDING

Reflecting on my journey, it's clear that no chapter of my life could have unfolded without the resilience, passion, and love that have guided me. From my beginnings as an unsure, traumatised self-published author to becoming the founder of Bowerbird Publishing, the story has been one of personal and professional survival and growth. Each step, from Hospital rooms to school classrooms and my first award as an AusMumpreneur winner to the bustling publishing world, has been a page in my book, etched with lessons and triumphs.

Publishing has become more than just a business to me; it's a way of sharing joy and building a community. It's a ripple effect that touches not only my life but the lives of the authors I work with, the readers who are moved by their stories, and the industry that recognises the importance of giving these voices a platform. Watching those I mentor and publish spread their wings is one of the most significant rewards I could have imagined. It's a reminder of the power of words to tell a story and inspire, connect, and change lives.

This ripple effect doesn't stop at publishing—it flows into the ways I've had to become an advocate for Sebastian, and how the lessons of resilience and survival have shaped both my motherhood and my business. The parallels between these two parts of my life are impossible to ignore. In both arenas, I've learned that success is more than skill or knowledge—it's about persistence, humility, and the courage to repeatedly step outside my comfort zone.

That's why I'm so excited about the future. The opportunity to take my business global and bring the stories I've helped shape to the world stage is a dream I never thought possible. Now, as I look toward 2025 and the chance to represent my business in London and beyond, I see it not just as a milestone but as the next step in a life driven by growth and possibility.

Through all the recognition, from my first award to the accolades that continue to come, I've realised that success is not about standing in the spotlight—it's about using that light to illuminate the paths of others. It's about creating spaces for authors to thrive, for stories to be heard, and for dreams to be realised.

The power of the written word, the joy of publishing, and the strength of community have all led me here. As this chapter closes, I look forward to the stories yet to be written—the new adventures, the inevitable risks, and the dreams I have yet to chase.

For me, it's not just about turning pages; it's about living a life full of purpose, passion, and possibility.

The special little boy who started it all, Sebastian

Some extraordinary moments captured since Bowerbird Publishing began…

My very first professional keynote speaker appearance in Cairns where I met Michelle Bridges in 2022

Meeting Dr. Karl Kruszelnicki in 2023 & with 2023 Australian of the Year Taryn Brumfitt

Collaborating with some of my favourite local authors in 2022, LJ Kidd, Debra Gavranich, Chantal Munro, Rob the Poet and Sandy Davies

Sam & I at the Cairns Business Women's Club awards night where I was a finalist in the Sole Entrepreneur category in 2023 (middle left) and keynote speaker moments in 2023

Reading to children at Cairns City Library in 2024

Reading to students at Kirai State School in 2023

Meeting Layne Beachley and Kate Toon in Melbourne 2024

With Karen Weaver of KMD Publishers (top left) and Kristina Karlsson (top right) in 2024

With Justine Martin of Morpheus Publishing (above) and author Kate Fisher in 2024 (right)

The Far North Queensland crew at Ausmumpreneur in Melbourne 2024

Meeting author Kirsten Pilz (above left) and Lisa Wilkinson (above right) in Cairns 2024.

Sharing a laugh with Nicola Baker in Melbourne 2024 (left)

Feeling like a Queen after winning at the Ausmumpreneur awards in 2024 - my first in the professional business category

My heart and soul in one photograph; my family.

Featured on the back cover of Connect in Harmony, 2024 edition (top) & on the front cover of What's on Tablelands, December 2024 edition (bottom)

ACKNOWLEDGEMENTS

To my mum, mums-in-law, grandmothers, grandmothers-in-law, aunties, aunties-in-law, sisters, daughters and nieces, thank you for grounding me and being a source of love and trust in my life. You were my first sisterhood, a love that spans a lifetime.

To Justine Martin, Letizia De Rosa, and Karen Weaver, for being fellow publishers who share my passion for lifting others up. I look up to you and will never forget your generosity and kindness. You have all helped make Bowerbird Publishing the success it is today.

To my Fairy Godmother, Chantal Munro, for always being someone I can turn to in good times and bad, for honesty, compassion, and a swift kick up the pants if self-doubt overwhelms me. You are why I was brave enough to become an author; I will always be grateful to you for believing in me.

Peace Mitchell and Katy Pearce, thank you for being the most important mentors to me as a businesswoman and mother. You have shone a light on my business and directed me into greatness. Thank you for your ever-generous space at your table, on your stage, and in your hearts. You are queens to me.

Nakia Morrison, you are a true visionary, and I cannot thank you enough for perfectly capturing my vision of 'Clarity' through photography. The images you have produced over the years have served my business and brand well, and I look forward to capturing many more moments with you behind the lens.

To the women who have contributed to Clarity, from advisors to editors, writers of forewords, and proofreaders, thank you for helping me see this project through to the end. It wouldn't be the book it is without you.

Rob the Poet, thank you for granting me permission to use your poem 'Clarity' in this publication. It can be found in his anthology, 'It's All Good' (poem #52).

To the world's authors, writers, and storytellers, your gift is profound and worthy, and it creates history. Keep writing; you are my heroes.

ABOUT THE AUTHOR

In a world where dreams can feel just out of reach, Crystal Leonardi is proof that determination can turn even the most challenging paths into stories of transformation. Now an accomplished author and founder of Bowerbird Publishing, she has dedicated her life to sharing stories and championing the next generation of readers and writers.

With an unwavering belief in the power of manifestation, Crystal has faced obstacles many would find overwhelming. Yet, her journey has also been rich with moments of celebration—none more powerful than winning the Author of the Year award for her inspiring memoir, Boy of Steel. This pivotal moment cemented her role as both advocate and storyteller, expanding her mission to uplift voices and inspire resilience, particularly among oncology families.

Join Crystal in 'Clarity' as she reflects on the ripple effects of living fearlessly. Exploring a journey that began with a cancer diagnosis and continues to inspire far beyond. In the pages of 'Clarity,' she hopes to encourage others to dare to dream and manifest success no matter how distant fulfilment may seem.

To connect with Crystal Leonardi visit her website: www.crystalleonardi.com

Or on Social Media:

TikTok - bowerbirdpublishing

Instagram - bowerbird_publishing

Facebook - Bowerbird Publishing

LinkedIn - Crystal Leonardi

YouTube - Bowerbird Publishing

OTHER TITLES BY CRYSTAL LEONARDI

Boy of Steel: Little Sebastian's Big Miracle - 2021

6 Steps to Self-publishing with Crystal Leonardi - 2022

My Brother Sebastian: Explaining Cancer to Kids - 2022

My Friend Alice: Explaining Disability to Kids - 2023

My Mate Jed: Explaining Stroke to Kids - 2024

Clarity: When Everything Suddenly Becomes Crystal Clear - 2025

- Upcoming Releases -

Pages to Published: 6 Steps to Self-publishing - 2025

- My dream is to continue adding to the 'Explaining to Kids' series with these titles -

My Bestie MacKenzie: Explaining Type 1 Diabetes to Kids - 2025

My Neighbour Danny: Explaining Downs Syndrome to Kids - 2026

My Cousin Clover: Explaining Autism to Kids - 2027

BOOK CLUB QUESTIONS

1. If you faced a sudden medical crisis with a loved one, how do you think you'd respond? Did the author's journey affect your perspective on resilience?

2. How does the author's journey reflect the power of storytelling in overcoming trauma?

3. How do you handle stress in times of crisis? Does the author's approach inspire any new ways of coping?

4. Have you ever turned to a creative outlet during difficult times?

5. Has there been a time when you had to pay it forward?

6. How do you feel about balancing career and family? Do you relate to the author's journey, and does it inspire changes in your life?

7. Have you ever had a time when you felt like a survivor?

8. If you were in a similar position, would you choose to share your struggles publicly or keep them private? How has the author's openness about her mental health influenced your perspective?

9. Have you ever felt imposter syndrome in your own life?

10. Have you ever had to choose between following your dreams and family responsibilities?

11. How does the author's pursuit of dreams inspire you to embrace your own?

12. How does the author's story inspire you to reflect on your own life and the legacy you wish to leave? What role do you think storytelling plays in creating a lasting legacy?

www.ingramcontent.com/pod-product-compliance
Lightning Source LLC
Chambersburg PA
CBHW061733070526
44585CB00024B/2649